MW00564961

CAMBRIDGE IGCSE® ENVIRONMENTAL MANAGEMENT

David Weatherly and Nicholas Sheehan

William Collins' dream of knowledge for all began with the publication of his first book in 1819. A self-educated mill worker, he not only enriched millions of lives, but also founded a flourishing publishing house. Today, staying true to this spirit, Collins books are packed with inspiration, innovation and practical expertise. They place you at the centre of a world of possibility and give you exactly what you need to explore it.

Collins. Freedom to teach.

Published by Collins
An imprint of HarperCollins*Publishers*
1 London Bridge Street
London
SE1 9GF

**Browse the complete Collins catalogue at
www.collins.co.uk**

© HarperCollins*Publishers* Limited 2017

10 9 8 7 6 5 4 3 2 1

ISBN 978-0-00-819045-3

British Library Cataloguing in Publication Data
A Catalogue record for this publication is available from the British Library.

Commissioned by **Anne Mahon**
Project managed by **Rachel Allegro**
Copy-edited by **Donna Cole**
Proofread by **Louise Robb**
Typesetting and illustrations by **Jouve India Private Limited**
Indexed by **Lisa Footitt**
Cover design by **Gordon MacGilp**
Printed in Italy by **Grafica Veneta S.p.A**

IGCSE® is the registered trademark of Cambridge International Examinations.

Contents

Introduction

Welcome to your new textbook which has been carefully designed and written to help you understand all of the requirements needed to succeed in the *Cambridge IGCSE®️ Environmental Management* course.

By the end of this century, world population will reach eleven billion. The desire of all humankind to improve their standard of living and quality of life and that of their children is both instinctive and timeless. Exploiting the natural resources of the ecosystems of the surroundings in which people live in order to help achieve this has been part of human life since the evolution of ancient humans up to two million years ago. Today the life of everyone on Earth is highly globalised. This means that our exploitation of the environment ranges far beyond our immediate area and impacts on places we will never visit and people we will never meet. Advances in technology and communications allow us today to identify and utilise natural resources at a rate of consumption that would have been considered impossible fifty years ago.

All human life is dependent for its very existence upon the healthy functioning of the myriad of ecosystems which make up the Earth's biosphere. However, in many parts of the world these life-sustaining natural systems are being depleted at a scale which threatens their integrity and continuing existence. The implications of this unregulated and short term approach to resource consumption for the continuing existence of humankind are very serious. The future of everyone depends upon utilising the natural resources of the environment in a manner which enables people to improve the quality of their lives on the one hand, whilst conserving and enhancing the ecosystems which provide those resources on the other. This approach is referred to as sustainable development, and throughout this book, you will be encouraged to reflect upon different ways in which sustainability might be achieved alongside exploiting the natural environment.

Environmental management draws upon a range of disciplines including geography, science, philosophy, design and technology and mathematics in order to assist in identifying sustainable practices when it comes to balancing human development and environmental conservation. Above all, environmental management is about identifying holistic solutions to environmental challenges, which recognise the interconnectedness of people and the natural world and of finding ways of balancing the needs of one with the other.

Exploiting the environment has been a feature of human life for two million years.

About this book

This Student Book covers all of the content for the *Cambridge IGCSE Environmental Management* syllabus. It is divided into nine sections – one for each of the areas of the syllabus. Each section is split into topics which cover the essential knowledge and skills you need as specified by the syllabus. Each of the nine sections is organised in the same way and has the following features:

- A brief **introduction** to give you the context and overview of the content covered.
- The **section contents** which shows the separate topics to be studied matching the syllabus order.
- A list of **learning objectives** which covers all of the key things you need to learn.
- All of the **topics** clearly identified with the **key terms and vocabulary** you need to know highlighted.
- A range of maps, graphs, illustrations and numerical data carefully selected to support your understanding of the key content and concepts.
- **Case studies** which focus on different areas of the world and help to provide a real life context for applying many of the ideas which you have investigated in each section.
- An **end of section checklist** which includes the key terms and important vocabulary covered, as well as the most important things you will have learned through your study.

This book also includes two other sections which are there to support your knowledge and understanding of the syllabus content:

- **Questions** on the content of each section which allow you to apply what you have learned and to demonstrate your knowledge and understanding of the facts, key terms, concepts and case studies included in the book. These questions can also be used to assess your own progress in achieving the learning objectives of each section before moving on to the next.
- A **glossary** in which the key terms and vocabulary highlighted in the text – which are important for you to know – are defined and explained. Words in bold throughout the book can be found in the glossary.

Although each section and the topics within it appear separately, they are always interconnected in the real world. For example the world's population is growing by eighty million a year. This fact has enormous implications for agriculture and the environment, water and its management, the consumption of energy, access to improved water and sanitation, deforestation, and atmospheric pollution. So when you are working through each section, try to think holistically by considering what the connections might be between what you are learning now and the topics you have covered elsewhere in the book. This is what environmental management is all about.

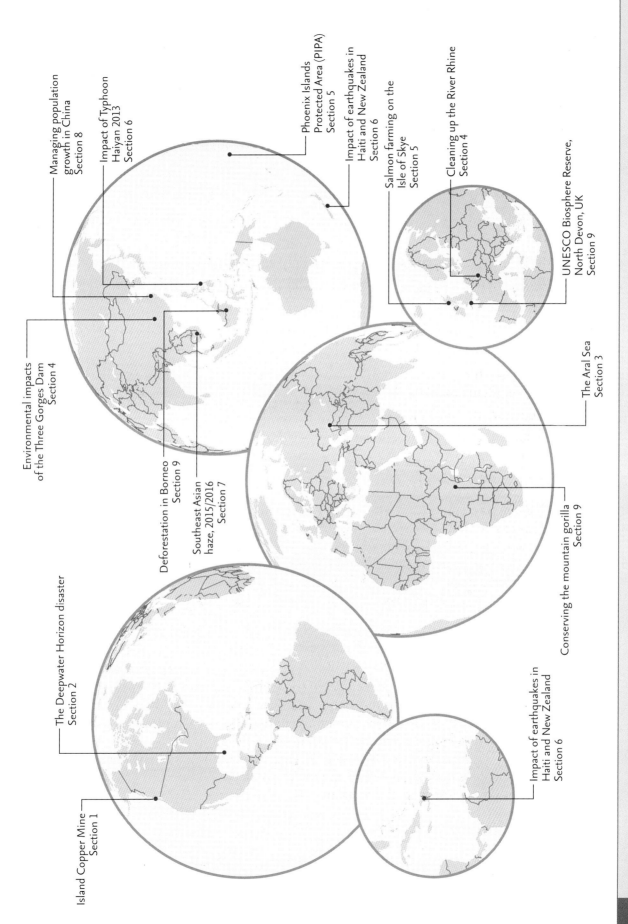

Managing population growth in China
Section 8

Impact of Typhoon Haiyan 2013
Section 6

Phoenix Islands Protected Area (PIPA)
Section 5

Impact of earthquakes in Haiti and New Zealand
Section 6

Salmon farming on the Isle of Skye
Section 5

Cleaning up the River Rhine
Section 4

Environmental impacts of the Three Gorges Dam
Section 4

Deforestation in Borneo
Section 9

Southeast Asian haze, 2015/2016
Section 7

UNESCO Biosphere Reserve, North Devon, UK
Section 9

The Aral Sea
Section 3

The Deepwater Horizon disaster
Section 2

Island Copper Mine
Section 1

Conserving the mountain gorilla
Section 9

Impact of earthquakes in Haiti and New Zealand
Section 6

7 LOCATIONS OF CASE STUDIES USED IN THIS BOOK

Rocks and the minerals they contain are of immense economic value – the 165 000 tonnes of gold already in circulation alone has a value of over eight trillion US dollars. Gold is just one of seventy mineral commodities mined globally; all are vital necessities for modern ways of life.

Deciding on whether or not to exploit mineral reserves is a very complex process. Many economic, social and environmental factors must be evaluated. Once operational, a mine can bring many benefits nationally and globally, but if not carefully regulated there can be serious social and environmental costs.

Mineral reserves are non-renewable and rising consumption is presenting huge management challenges. Plans for the future of mineral use are being based on the principles of sustainable development with the long-term objective of balancing economic growth with the conservation of resources and the ecosystems on which humanity depends.

CONTENTS

a) Formation of rocks

b) Extraction of rocks and minerals from the Earth

c) Impact of rock and mineral extraction

d) Managing the impact of rock and mineral extraction

e) Sustainable use of rocks and minerals

f) Case study: Island Copper Mine

LEARNING OBJECTIVES

Describe and interpret the rock cycle.

State and explain the formation and characteristics of named igneous, sedimentary and metamorphic rocks.

Describe surface and subsurface mining methods of extracting rocks and minerals from the Earth.

Describe and explain the environmental, economic and social impacts of rock and mineral extraction.

Describe and evaluate strategies for restoring landscapes damaged by rock and mineral extraction.

Define *sustainable resource* and *sustainable development*.

Describe and evaluate strategies for the sustainable use of rocks and minerals.

Study the development, impact and management of a mine including land restoration after the mine has closed.

1
Rocks and minerals and their exploitation

FORMATION OF ROCKS

Rock is the solid and naturally occurring material that forms the Earth's hard outer layer or **crust**. Although rocks come in an incredible variety of shape, size, colour, texture, weight, consistency, **permeability** and hardness, they are almost all composed of an aggregate of grains of different chemical elements called **minerals**. Rocks are classified according to how they are formed.

Igneous rocks

These rocks are created from the solidification of **magma** (molten rock found in the **mantle** below the Earth's crust) and **lava** (molten rock that reaches the surface through a volcano or fissure). There are two types of igneous rocks – plutonic and volcanic. Plutonic or intrusive rocks occur when magma cools and crystallises slowly within the Earth's crust – granite is a good example of this. Volcanic or extrusive rocks such as basalt form when lava solidifies on the Earth's surface.

△ Fig. 1.1 Combestone Tor, Dartmoor, UK – an exposed granite intrusion.

△ Fig. 1.2 Giant's Causeway, Northern Ireland, UK – polygonal columns of basalt.

Sedimentary rocks

Sediment refers to particles of rocks, minerals and the remains of plants and animals. Rocks are constantly being broken down into smaller pieces or sediments by the physical and chemical processes of **weathering**, for example, the freeze-thaw action of water, which widens cracks and causes the rock to eventually break apart. Sediments are then transported to new locations by the forces of **erosion** such as the wind, rivers and ice. At the bottom of seas and oceans, soft and loose sediments of mud, silt, sand and gravel deposited by rivers, and the skeletons of sea creatures, can build up into thick layers. As new layers of sediment are added above, lower layers are compressed over millions of years into strata of hard rock. This process of rock formation is called cementation.

△ Fig. 1.3 Limestone is made up largely of calcium carbonate from the shells and skeletons of marine creatures such as this scallop. Limestone forms in clean, warm shallow seas where there is an abundance of life.

△ Fig. 1.4 Sandstone, such as this in Nevada, USA, consists almost entirely of small sand grains, usually quartz, cemented together by substances such as clay.

△ Fig. 1.5 Shale is consolidated mud, silt and clay. It is finely stratified, which means it splits easily into flat pieces.

Metamorphic rock

Sometimes the Earth's movements cause existing igneous and sedimentary rocks to be heated up and put under great pressure. This can cause a chemical change in their minerals and the formation of new metamorphosed rocks. Slate forms in this way from shale, and marble forms from limestone. Both rocks have important uses in construction and interior design.

△ Fig. 1.6 Slate being used for roofing.

△ Fig. 1.7 Marble being used for a kitchen surface.

The rock cycle

The rocks of the Earth's crust are constantly being changed and recycled. As soon as any 'new' rock is exposed to the physical, chemical and biological forces of weathering, it begins to be broken down into sediments. For example, physical weathering through exfoliation causes the surface layers of rocks to disintegrate as a result of constantly being heated and cooled. Rainwater containing dissolved CO_2 will remove limestone rock particles (chemical weathering) and the roots of trees and plants will, over time, pull apart joints and cracks in rock and cause biological

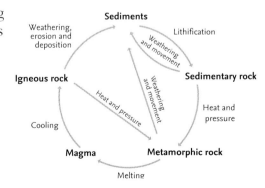

△ Fig. 1.8 The rock cycle.

weathering as they search for water. Sediments of all sizes are transported away by wind and water erosion and can be deposited a long way from where they originated. If sediments accumulate in hollows beneath seas and oceans then **sedimentation** begins, which in time will create new sedimentary rocks. If these rocks become buried deep inside the Earth, then a combination of heat and pressure can change them into **metamorphic rocks** – or they might even melt entirely to become magma. This magma may then solidify below the surface or above ground as lava to form new igneous rock, which will immediately come under attack once again from the forces of weathering. In this way, the whole dynamic and unending cycle of rock creation, weathering and recreation begins again.

△ Fig. 1.9 Sandstorms in the Negev Desert – wind is a powerful force of erosion.

EXTRACTION OF ROCKS AND MINERALS FROM THE EARTH

Rocks and the minerals of which they are composed are vital to modern life; they are what physically support us as we go about our lives. If something does not come from a plant or animal then it is mined or quarried from the rocks of the Earth's crust. Rocks are the source of all soils upon which plants rely and upon which we depend to grow food crops and rear livestock. Stones and rocks are the most important source of building materials in the world after wood. An average person in North America uses over 500 000 kg of stone, sand and gravel each year (in construction and cement) and 12 000 kg of clay (in the manufacture of ceramics, bricks and pipes). Minerals like galena, bauxite, sphalerite, malachite and uraninite are made up of valuable chemical elements such as (in the correct order) lead, aluminium, zinc, copper and uranium, which provide industrial metals and fuels. For example, the element aluminium is found in the mineral bauxite, which is commonly contained in igneous rocks such as granite and basalt. From the dawn of time, the decorative beauty of precious stones has been admired and valued by cultures everywhere.

△ Fig. 1.10 The mouth of the Connecticut River depositing sediment into Long Island Sound.

△ Fig. 1.11 Diamond is a very hard mineral composed of a crystallised form of the chemical element carbon.

There are two main methods of extracting rocks containing minerals from the Earth's crust: **surface mining** and **subsurface mining**.

△ Fig. 1.12 The mineral malachite contains the element copper.

Surface mining

This approach can only be used when the rocks containing the mineral (the ore body) are found relatively close to the surface and the surrounding area is not heavily built up. Sometimes referred to as open-cast, open-pit or strip mining, the soil and rock overlying the ore body (called the overburden) is first removed by specialist earth-moving heavy machinery. Once exposed, other equipment such as massive dragline and bucket wheel excavators dig out and remove the ore body from flat terraces or benches that circle the mine at descending levels.

△ Fig. 1.13 Bucket wheel excavator in an open-cast mine.

△ Fig. 1.14 A diamond open-cast mine in Russia.

Subsurface mining

Subsurface mining removes the mineral through underground mining methods such as declines, vertical or inclined shafts and tunnels, and adits. The overlying rock remains in place. Declines are wide tunnels that descend in a circular manner down to and around the ore body. The ore is hauled to the surface in huge trucks. When the ore body is too deep to be reached by inclines, tunnels are sunk down adjacent to the ore body, which is then removed by lifts. Adits are horizontal rather than vertical shafts excavated into the side of a hill or mountain following level layers of ore.

△ Fig. 1.15 Subsurface coal mining.

△ Fig. 1.16 An underground excavator in a decline tunnel of a salt mine.

Factors affecting the mining of rocks and minerals

If a mining company has no existing knowledge of mineral deposits in an area, but believes that potential ore bodies may be present underground, it may begin the process of mineral 'greenfield' exploration. A number of surveying techniques are then commonly used to determine the geology of the underlying rock and identify patterns indicative of certain mineral deposits. These include detecting radiation, measuring magnetism and variations in magnetic field, and **remote sensing** satellite imagery combined with geological seismic mapping using artificially created shock waves. Only if initial results appear encouraging will drill rock samples be sent for geochemical analysis.

△ Fig. 1.17 The Molycorp rare-earth elements mine and processing facilities in California cost over US$500 million to set up.

△ Fig. 1.18 A geologist in Mali carrying out a seismic exploration study.

Opening a new mine is very expensive and time consuming. Finding mineral deposits is no guarantee that they will be extracted. Mining will only be considered if it is economically profitable. This means that the price the company receives for the metal or fuel it produces (the market price) must be greater over the lifetime of the mine than the costs of exploration, setting up the mine (**capital** costs) and of extracting, refining and transporting the ore (operating costs). The major economic factors that have to be taken into account when reaching a decision are as follows:

- The ore grade – how much of the mineral is composed of the chemical element desired.
- The amount or reserves of ore present underground and how long they will last once mining begins.
- The scarcity and likely long-term demand for the element – the greater the demand then the higher the market price will be for supplying that demand. As long as demand increases, there will always be a market from which the mine can profit.
- The geological difficulties associated with mining, for example, can the ore be extracted relatively cheaply by open-cast methods or will more expensive deep underground tunnels and shafts be required.
- Whether new and expensive refining plants will have to be constructed on site compared perhaps with the costs involved in transporting the ore to existing refineries further away.
- The location's suitability for mining, such as how accessible it is, its **climate** and vegetation cover. The more remote and hostile the **environment** then the higher the costs will be in overcoming problems, for example, building transport and communication links, creating water and power supplies and constructing housing for employees.
- The costs of meeting the requirements of **environmental impact assessments** undertaken by local government in the host country, for

example, installing new water filtration systems to avoid **pollution**, compensating the local **community** for loss of farmland or preserving areas of primeval forest.

- Any expense associated with obtaining health and safety and environmental protection permits.
- Whether financial support may be available from the national government to help set up and open the mine in return for the jobs created and the tax it will receive each year from the company.

IMPACT OF ROCK AND MINERAL EXTRACTION

Economic impacts

Mining can create wealth and prosperity in the communities where it is located. In Alaska, 4400 direct jobs and a further 4300 indirect jobs have been created by mines producing gold, lead, silver and zinc as well as construction materials such as sand, gravel and rock. This means that for every job at the mines, another has been created in companies supplying the mines, for example, with machinery or services such as catering, cleaning and security. This is known as 'the **multiplier effect**'. Mining companies pay their employees US$620 million a year. In turn, workers spend their wages buying products and services in the local community, which helps to create further jobs, for example, in restaurants or sports centres and as new businesses move in. This is called the '**trickledown effect**'. In addition, the state government receives US$139 million a year in income and property taxes from the mining company and its employees. Much of this money is used to improve living standards for people locally, such as building new schools and hospitals.

△ Fig. 1.19 Limestone quarry, Texada Island, British Columbia.

Further south, the Mining Association of British Columbia in Canada estimates that 21 112 direct and 24 590 indirect jobs rely on the mining **industry**, and a further 15 000 job opportunities will be created by 2017. The state government receives US$495 million a year in taxes from companies and their employees and calculates that for every US$1 invested by mining corporations, US$1.73 of wealth is created in local communities.

Social impacts

A mining development can have both positive and negative effects on the wellbeing of individuals and families within the community in which it is based.

Examples of possible social benefits	Examples of possible social problems
Better-paid work raises living standards for many and improves prospects for their families, for example, being able to pay school and college fees for their children.	Sudden rises in disposable income can lead to higher rates of alcohol and drug use, social nuisance and crime.
Local councils use tax income to improve services for the community, for example, health visitors for the elderly.	Divisions may arise in the community between those who benefit from the mine and those who do not, such as small scale miners who can no longer work.
The new infrastructure of transport, communication networks, water supplies and waste disposal systems built for the mine also improves the quality of life for local people.	Resentment can arise in situations where people are displaced from their land and properties to make way for the mine.
People may also benefit directly from social community development projects paid for by the mine, for example, a new sports hall or playing fields.	When mining corporations fail to understand the cultural and spiritual importance of the environment to indigenous groups, conflict can arise.
Employees and their families may have cheap or free access to mine facilities such as its hospital, school or sports facilities.	Maintaining traditional ways of life can become difficult when many outsiders arrive with different lifestyles that may be very attractive to the young.
Mine workers may be entitled to free or subsidised housing as part of their benefits.	A lack of regulation can sometimes mean poor health and safety standards for workers in mines.
Employees often receive career development training at the mine, which enables them to be promoted to other positions in the company nationally and internationally.	The community may have to cope with air, noise and water pollution, and power shortages associated with the mine.

△ Table 1.1 The possible social benefits and problems of a mining development.

Environmental impacts

Most mining operations are huge primary industries requiring massive earthworks. If such mines are poorly regulated, they can cause great environmental damage.

Habitat and biodiversity loss – The clearing of huge areas of land for the mine, and also adjoining areas for refineries, offices, housing, roads and railways, can cause a catastrophic decline in the range of plants, trees, birds and animals that are able to survive in surrounding aquatic and terrestrial habitats.

△ Fig. 1.20 Forest clearance around Carajas iron ore mine, Brazil.

Water pollution – Toxic chemicals such as cyanide and arsenic are frequently used during refining to separate the valuable mineral elements from the waste rock in which they are contained. When water is contaminated with these pollutants and other **heavy metals** such as mercury and lead, this is known as acid rock drainage. This water can run off the surface into nearby rivers or seep underground until it reaches the **water table**. Poisoned water can have devastating effects on both wildlife and humans, especially pregnant mothers, babies and the young.

△ Fig. 1.21 Water polluted by copper mining in Geamana Lake, Romania.

Air pollution – The excavation, crushing and refining of mineral ore can release huge quantities of dust containing dangerous heavy metals such as lead into the **atmosphere**. Mining often exposes sulfide minerals such as pyrite that release high levels of iron and sulfate when contact is made with air or water.

△ Fig. 1.22 Dust pollution from stone crushing, Myanmar.

Soil erosion and sedimentation – Once soil has been disturbed to make way for the mining operation, it can be very quickly eroded by rainfall and the wind. Soil can be carried in solution into rivers by rainwater, where sedimentation leads to a shallowing of the river, a decrease in aquatic life and the increased likelihood of flooding.

Visual and noise pollution – Visually, mining operations can be very intrusive. They are huge and noisy complexes, operating 24 hours a day, all year round. Once constructed they completely change the makeup of the landscape and can be seen for miles

△ Fig. 1.23 Sediment builds up at the mouth of the Huang He (Yellow River), China.

around. As well as noise, local people often have to cope with floodlighting at night and the fact that it is rarely dark enough to sleep adequately.

△ Fig. 1.24 Potgietersrus platinum mine, Limpopo, South Africa.

MANAGING THE IMPACT OF ROCK AND MINERAL EXTRACTION

In over 100 countries, regulations now require an environmental impact assessment of how a mining company intends to return the land to an environmentally acceptable standard and productive use when the mine is decommissioned. This has to be agreed before permission to begin mining is granted and often consists of details on **remediation**, **restoration** and **reuse**.

Remediation

This involves ensuring that the site is made safe by demolishing the plant, removing machinery, stabilising the ground, draining pipelines and disposing of any hazardous waste. Waste rock that contains minerals in concentrations too low to be extracted and refined profitably will nevertheless also contain toxic sulfides. Generally this waste will be covered in clean topsoil and planted out with vegetation. In some cases it may be used as underground backfill to increase the stability of mine shafts. Tailings consist of finely ground particles of rocks and minerals that result from ore processing and contain poisonous chemicals such as arsenic. They are usually mixed with water and disposed of in specially prepared tailing ponds enclosed by dams. Contaminated water is often dealt with at water treatment plants set up on site. Toxic chemicals are extracted, leaving a residue or sludge that is usually disposed of underground. Bioremediation may also be used to treat water contamination. This process encourages naturally occurring pollution-eating single-celled bacteria (prokaryotes) that already live on site to degrade contaminants in soils and water. Although this will not work for pollutants such as cadmium, which are poisonous even to the microbes, it is often a safer and less expensive alternative to incineration or landfill.

Restoration

Many mining sites are returned to their pre-mine use, which in the majority of cases is open countryside. Care is taken to rebuild the **ecosystem**, through establishing native trees and plants close to that

△ Fig. 1.25 Tailing ponds for mineral waste, Utah, USA.

which existed before the environment was disturbed. Nature reserves may also be created, incorporating lakes that have formed in open-cast mining areas and the steep rugged cliffs around quarries and open pits.

△ Fig. 1.26 Stanwick Lakes nature reserve, UK, created from a disused gravel quarry.

△ Fig. 1.27 Butchart Gardens, Canada.

Reuse

Recent years have seen a trend of reusing decommissioned mines and quarries so that they continue to contribute economically to the local community. Such schemes take advantage of the existing transport infrastructure, which makes the locations very accessible. Some sites are used to dispose of domestic landfill waste that otherwise would have to go to 'greenfield' locations, while visitor attractions have been set up at others. The new Gotland Ring 28-km motor racing circuit in Sweden, and Butchart Gardens in Canada, have both been constructed within old limestone quarries. In Ghana, the disused Homase gold mine is the centre of an **aquaculture** project including fish farms, livestock rearing, leafy vegetable growing and **ecotourism**. At the Martin Lake lignite mine complex in Texas, USA, 65 sq km of reclaimed land is now used for commercial forestry (37 million trees have been planted since 1975), 50 sq km for wildlife habitat, 20 sq km for livestock farming and 8 sq km for industrial uses.

SUSTAINABLE USE OF ROCKS AND MINERALS

Rocks and minerals are not **sustainable** resources because they exist in fixed amounts and are **non-renewable**. Supplies will eventually run out. For example, if the **consumption** of copper continues to increase at its present rate then it is estimated that existing global reserves will be exhausted between 2050 and 2070. On the other hand, sustainable resources such as the wind are infinite and **renewable** and will continue to exist indefinitely whatever the rate of human consumption.

Rocks and minerals are essential to support **economic growth** and to maintain and improve the prosperity and quality of life of people everywhere. The fact that they are of finite size and will not regenerate presents great challenges in a world that will see its **population** grow by another 4 billion by 2100. For example, if the production of uranium continues at the present rate, known reserves will be consumed by 2085, while for indium (a rare-earth element used in the manufacture of solar panels), the reserves will be consumed by 2035.

Faced with this situation, many countries have already introduced conservation or **resource management** plans for rocks and minerals to help ensure their long-term existence. These plans are based on the principle of **sustainable development** – improving economic growth and lifestyles on the one hand while preserving the **natural resources** and ecosystems on which everyone depends on the other. Sustainable development planning focuses on two areas: increasing the life of known mineral reserves and discovering new sources of minerals so as to increase available supplies.

Measures that help to extend the life of existing mineral reserves

- The use of modern technology to extract minerals more efficiently from ore bodies that previously were not economical to exploit, and also from waste rock and tailings at existing mines. This will become increasingly profitable to mining companies in the future as commodity prices rise as a result of increasing demand.
- Substitute the use of scarce minerals in **manufacturing** with more common minerals or non-mineral alternatives. For example, aluminium can be used instead of copper in power lines and fibre optic cables can replace copper in communication lines.
- Increase the amount of minerals recovered through recycling from discarded and obsolete products. Metals recycled from scrap will need to make up a larger proportion of metals used in manufacturing in the future. Recycling other minerals must become common practice. The EU has recently introduced rules requiring member states to recycle at least 65% of all electronic equipment by 2019 to recover rare-earth elements such as dysprosium and neodymium.
- Increasing pressure is being placed on businesses to use minerals more efficiently both during manufacturing and by redesigning their products to ensure they have a longer operational life and can be more easily repaired and reused.
- Governments frequently encourage conservation and efficiency in mineral use through enacting laws, for example, that mineral waste

must be used as road aggregate or additives in cement manufacture or through providing easily accessible recycling centres for both domestic and commercial waste. In Scotland, land with known reserves of unexploited economically important minerals is protected from any other form of permanent development.

Measures to increase available mineral reserves

The search to discover new mineral reserves using advanced technology, including geophysics, seismic and remote sensing and geochemistry, is being carried out by mining corporations all over the world. Because of the rising price of minerals it is now possible to consider the potential of locations such as sea and ocean beds where previously operations would not have been economical. The extraction of minerals from seabed manganese nodules, sea mud and sulfurous mounds that gush hot water from

△ Fig. 1.28 Manganese nodules from the Baltic Sea.

fissures associated with volcanic activity at **tectonic plate boundaries**, are becoming a focus of exploration. Found at depths of 4000–5000 metres, nodules contain nickel, copper, cobalt and manganese, and sea mud (6000 metres) contains gold, silver and zinc.

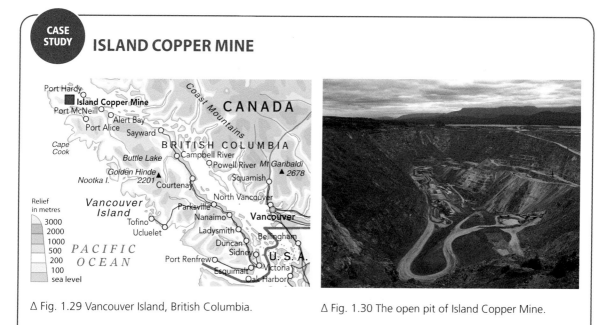

CASE STUDY

ISLAND COPPER MINE

△ Fig. 1.29 Vancouver Island, British Columbia.

△ Fig. 1.30 The open pit of Island Copper Mine.

Development

Island Copper Mine, at the northern end of Vancouver Island, beside the Pacific Ocean, began operation as an open pit mine in 1971 and was worked until 1995, by which time the remaining ore reserves had become unprofitable to extract. During its lifetime it became the third largest copper mine in Canada. Over 1 billion tonnes of rock were excavated from the site, which created a huge oval pit that dropped to 400 metres below sea level. Excavated ore was mostly ground up, mixed with water and then processed in slurry on site to remove the minerals.

Impact and management

- The mine employed 900 people and turned the tiny community of Port Hardy into a town of 5000.
- 1.3 million tonnes of copper, 31 000 tonnes of molybdenum, 336 tonnes of silver, 31.7 tonnes of gold and 27 tonnes of rhenium were extracted and processed at the mine.
- Waste rock was dumped in piles around the pit and also along the shore of an inlet from the ocean.
- Rather than being disposed of in ponds and lagoons on land, the mine tailings were placed on the seabed, as it was considered that this would have less environmental impact.
- Since 1985, sea life has been monitored through environmental management plans to ensure there have been no adverse effects from tailings dumped on the marine ecosystem. Recent surveys suggest that the numbers and diversity of bottom dwelling animals have returned to pre-mining levels.
- In 1986, serious acid rock drainage pollution (water containing toxic metals) flowing from the waste rock dumps occurred through both surface run-off and percolation of polluted water underground. Management programmes were immediately introduced to control further run-off and drainage of polluted water through recycling schemes at the metal processing plant.
- Detailed plans as to how the closure and restoration of the mine would be managed were submitted and agreed two years in advance of the mine opening in 1969.

Restoration

Environmental components of restoration

- Nearly 10 sq km of waste rock dumps and disturbed land were covered in fresh topsoil and planted with native species of trees, plants and grasses to recreate the woodland wildlife habitat that existed in the area before mining began.
- Waste rock dumps along the shore were reshaped to create coastal habitats for marine life.
- The huge open pit was flooded with sea water in 1996 to create a very special 330 metre deep lake covering an area of 2.2 sq km. The lake is meromictic, which means its surface and deep layers of water never mix. The bottom layers of water in the lake are anoxic, or oxygen free. Polythene pipes inject acid rock drainage water into the lake at a depth of 220 metres. Here, microscopic bacteria, for which sulfur is a source of energy, slowly separate the sulfides and heavy metals from the water, which eventually precipitate out as solid waste that settles on the bottom of the lake.

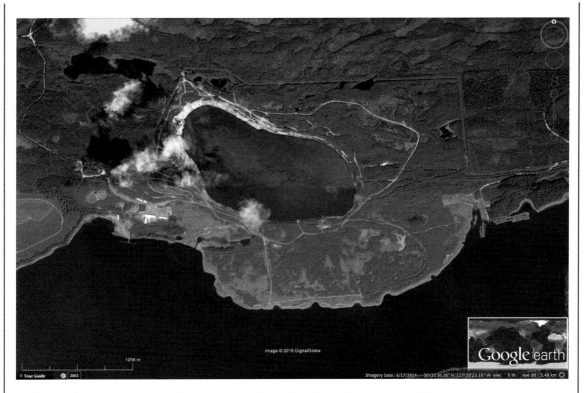

△ Fig. 1.31 Google Earth image of the meromictic lake at the disused Island Copper Mine.

Economic reuse components of restoration

To help ensure that the site continues to be economically sustainable and benefits the local community (including previous employees), the machinery, buildings and dock facilities that formed the 0.9 sq km ore processing plant were entirely remediated. This means that they were completely decontaminated and then inspected by government officials to ensure compliance. The docks, buildings and much of the machinery were sold on to several local businesses that moved in and set up wood processing and aquaculture (fish cultivation) operations.

△ Fig. 1.32 Salmon is farmed at 130 sites along the coast of British Columbia.

△ Fig. 1.33 Salmon hatchery.

End of topic checklist

Key terms

biodiversity, capital and operating costs, chemical elements, conservation and resource management, costs and benefits, economically profitable, economic growth, environmental impact assessment, heavy metals, igneous, sedimentary and metamorphic rocks, infrastructure, market price, multiplier effect, quality of life, remediation, remote sensing, renewable and non-renewable resources, restoration and reuse, rock cycle, supply and demand, surface and subsurface mining, sustainability, sustainable development, trickledown effect, weathering and erosion

Important vocabulary

accessibility, aggregate, aquaculture, atmosphere, cementation, climate, commercial, communications, community, composite, contamination, crust, crystallise, decommissioned, decontamination, degrade, economic, ecosystem, exfoliation, exploration, extraction, extrusive, flood, freeze-thaw, geochemistry, geology, habitat, impact, intrusive, landfill, landscape, lava, magma, meromictic, nodule, ore, overburden, permeable, plant, plutonic, pollution, precipitate, process, recycle, refining, regenerate, remediated, residue, resource, run-off, sediment, sedimentation, seismic, sludge, social, solution, strata, tailings, tax, topsoil, toxic, transport, vegetation, volcanic, waste

During your study of this topic you should have learned:

○ Rocks are classified into three categories according to how they were formed.

○ The rock cycle describes and explains the cyclical and continuous process of rock formation, weathering and erosion, and reformation.

○ Minerals are made up of valuable chemical elements, which are necessary for modern life.

○ Minerals are found in rocks known as ores, which are extracted from the ground by using either surface or subsurface mining techniques.

○ Many different economic, social and environmental factors have to be taken into account before a decision is made to construct a mine to extract minerals from underground rocks.

○ Mining creates wealth for both the governments of countries and individuals living there – directly through employment and indirectly via the investment they make in local communities.

End of topic checklist continued

○ Poorly regulated and controlled mining can cause very serious environmental damage and social costs in the areas in which it is carried out.

○ Mining companies use remediation, restoration and reuse measures to ensure that exploited land is returned to productive use after closure and this may involve both environmental reclamation and alternative economic uses.

○ The fact that rocks and minerals are finite and not sustainable resources presents the world with very real challenges for the future.

○ Planning for how we will ensure the preservation of natural resources, such as minerals, and continue to improve living standards for everyone in the world in the future, is known as sustainable development.

The questions for Section 1 start on page 238.

Global population growth, combined with increasing levels of economic development and consumption, have led to a huge growth in the demand for energy sources over time. In 2014, world energy consumption reached a staggering 12 928 million tonnes of oil equivalent. This measure includes tonnes of actual oil consumed, as well as all other energy sources converted into the equivalent amount of oil. The vast majority of this energy demand is met by exploiting oil, coal and gas – fossil fuels that are non-renewable. The extraction, processing, transport and consumption of fossil fuels brings both benefits and costs to countries around the world. Deciding whether to exploit non-renewables or invest in renewable energy sources is a key decision facing governments across the world today.

The pattern of demand for energy across the world is uneven, as is the mixture of sources used in each country: the average North American will use 6 tonnes of oil equivalent per year, with the majority coming from oil and natural gas. Compare this with the average of countries in Africa, at between 0 and 1.5 tonnes of oil equivalent per person. Globally, in 2014 the use of renewable energy sources reached record levels, although still only accounted for just over 9 per cent of total energy consumed. How we source, transport and consume energy – and the effects of this – are key questions for the twenty-first century.

CONTENTS

a) Fossil fuel formation

b) Energy resources and the generation of electricity

c) Energy demand

d) Conservation and management of energy resources

e) Impact of oil pollution

f) Management of oil pollution

g) Case study: The Deepwater Horizon disaster

LEARNING OBJECTIVES

Describe the formation of the fossil fuels coal, oil and gas.

Classify fossil fuels, nuclear power, biofuels, geothermal power, hydroelectric power, tidal power, wave power, solar power, wind power as non-renewable or renewable energy resources.

Describe how each of these energy resources are used to generate electricity.

Describe the environmental, economic and social advantages and disadvantages of each of these energy resources.

Describe and explain the factors affecting the demand for energy.

Describe and explain strategies for the efficient management of energy resources.

Research and development of new energy resources.

Describe the causes and impacts of oil pollution on marine and coastal ecosystems.

Discuss strategies for reducing oil spills in marine and coastal ecosystems.

Discuss strategies for minimising the impacts of oil spills on the marine and coastal ecosystems.

Study the impact and management of an oil pollution event.

2
Energy and the environment

FOSSIL FUEL FORMATION

What are fossil fuels?

Fossil fuels are **non-renewable** forms of energy such as coal, oil and natural gas. In 2014, an estimated 86 per cent of the energy used globally came from burning these fuels. As demand for energy has increased over time, we are using up fossil fuels at an increasing rate. Burning fossil fuels provides humans with the energy to power homes, offices and factories and to transport ourselves and goods around the world. However, burning coal, oil and gas releases carbon back into the **atmosphere**, which is changing global temperatures and also contributing to air **pollution** around the world.

Oil, coal and natural gas are hydrocarbons that were formed hundreds of millions of years ago from the remains of organic (living) matter like plants and animals. Three hundred million years ago the Earth's **climate** was warmer than today, which led to extensive plant growth. There were large areas covered with shallow swamp-like conditions and flooded forests. When the flora and fauna died, they decomposed in the water and were buried under layers of sediment. Over time, the sediment deposited would have built up into layers of mud, **rock** and sand – sometimes

△ Fig. 2.1 An offshore oil rig.

thousands of metres thick. In some places, variations in the sea level meant these sediments were covered by ancient seas, which then receded. Over millions of years, the dead organisms decomposed while being heated by the pressure of being buried in layers of rock and slowly formed into fossil fuels. Different types of fossil fuel were formed depending on the combination of plants and animal debris, the temperature and pressure that existed while they were decomposing and the length of time the material was buried. These factors gave rise to different fossil fuels like coal and oil, as well as different types of coal and oil with variations in the amount of carbon or sulfur present.

Formation of coal

Coal formed from the dead remains of trees, ferns and other plants that lived in the **Carboniferous period** of Earth's history, 300–400 million years ago. In some areas, coal formed in swamps that were covered by seawater containing a large amount of **sulfur**. As sea levels changed, the sulfur was deposited as part of the **sedimentation** that buried the decomposing remains. Today, coal from these areas contains much more sulfur than in other areas. This pollutant is released when the coal is burned. Other coal deposits were formed from **freshwater** swamps that contained very little sulfur, so coal from these areas releases much less sulfur when burned. This is important because the sulfur, when mixed with rainwater, turns to weak sulfuric acid, which falls as **acid rain**.

There are several key stages in the formation of coal:

△ Fig. 2.2 An open-cast coal mine.

- Decomposing vegetation is buried under layers of sediment. This keeps the decomposing matter out of the oxygen and, as time passes, the pressure and temperature increases and gradually 'cooks' the matter – transforming it into coal.
- Firstly, **peat** is formed. Peat consists of partially decomposed vegetation in which you can see roots and branches.
- Secondly, the peat is compressed and heated and turns to lignite, which contains more carbon than peat but still contains a high content of decayed wood. Lignite makes up the largest proportion of the world's coal reserves.
- Next, with increased temperatures, pressure and time, sub-bituminous coal is formed, followed by bituminous coal. These contain up to 86 per cent carbon and are burned in industrial boilers to make coke – a processed coal used in steel making.

△ Fig. 2.3 A close up of anthracite coal.

- Finally, anthracite is formed. This is the hardest type of coal and contains the most carbon. When it is burned, it produces the most heat. It has taken the longest time to form.

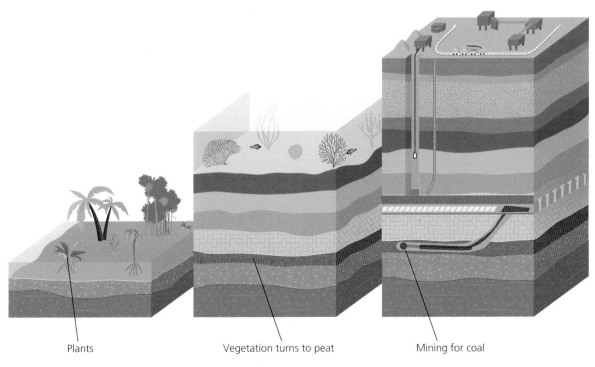

| Plants | Vegetation turns to peat | Mining for coal |

△ Fig. 2.4 The formation of coal.

Formation of oil and natural gas

Oil and natural gas were created from organisms that lived in the water. They are often found together in sedimentary rocks. The common microscopic organisms, such as plankton, fell to the bottom of the sea and were buried by layers of mud. Due to the lack of oxygen they did not decay completely and accumulated in a layer of mud that was rich with organic matter. As with coal, over time, pressure and temperature increases 'cook' the organic matter and transform it into oil. The high temperatures (100–160 °C) gradually break down the matter into chains of hydrocarbons, which form oil and natural gas in the source rock. The oil and gas are less dense than water, so begin to rise up through the porous (sponge-like) rock.

It took millions of years for the oil and natural gas to migrate only a few kilometres upwards. In places where the **permeable rocks** containing oil and gas were covered by a 'cap rock' of **impermeable** rock, the oil and gas would collect in reservoirs kept in place by the structure of the rocks underground. Geologists use sound waves to identify the shape of the rocks and from there, they can begin to search for oil using exploration drilling rigs.

Oil is also produced from less conventional sources, such as shale rocks and tar sands. Shale rocks are hydraulically fractured or 'fracked' to release oil and gas, whereas **tar sands** found in Canada are dug out from the soil and processed to produce oil. Both of these methods are not without controversy due to the damage they cause to the **environment**.

Plankton falls to the seabed.

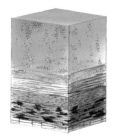

Organic matter is cooked.

Oil migrates upwards.

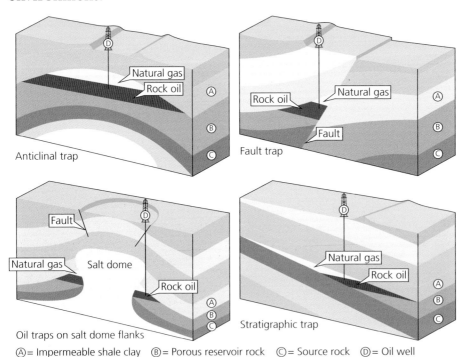

Anticlinal trap

Fault trap

Oil traps on salt dome flanks

Stratigraphic trap

Ⓐ = Impermeable shale clay   Ⓑ = Porous reservoir rock   Ⓒ = Source rock   Ⓓ = Oil well

△ Fig. 2.5 Different ways that oil is trapped.

Oil and gas is extracted.

△ Fig. 2.6 The formation of oil.

ENERGY RESOURCES AND THE GENERATION OF ELECTRICITY

Renewable and non-renewable energy resources

From powering our laptops and smartphones, to heating our houses and boiling our water, we are all using an increasing amount of energy each year. Global **population** increase and rising levels of **economic development** mean that this pattern is repeated across the world.

Humans use a wide range of sources to provide us with energy for heating, power and transportation. Much of our power is generated by using energy sources to create heat. This heat is used to turn water into steam, which turns giant turbines that make electricity. This is known as **thermal power generation**. The sources of energy available to a country vary around the world. Countries with plentiful supplies and the technology to use them are described as **energy secure**.

Each different energy source has advantages and disadvantages to people, economies and the environment when it is used. The table below classifies each type of energy source shown on the energy landscape in Figure 2.7. We can classify all of the energy sources into two groups.

Renewable energy sources can be used again and again	Non-renewable energy sources will eventually run out
Biofuels (bioethanol, biogas and wood)	Coal
Geothermal power	Oil
Hydroelectric power	Natural gas
Tidal power	Nuclear power using uranium
Wave power	
Solar power	
Wind power	

△ Table 2.1 Renewable and non-renewable energy sources

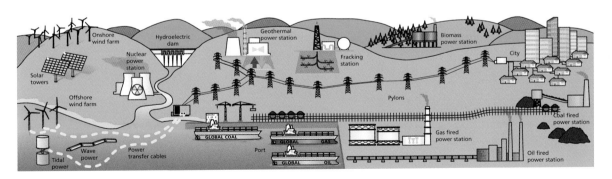

△ Fig. 2.7 The energy landscape.

Generation of electricity

There are a range of different methods used to generate electricity. Power stations use different energy sources to turn turbines, which in turn drive a generator. The most common method is thermal power generation.

1. Water is heated in a boiler to produce steam. **Nuclear** reactions, burning fossil fuels, and **geothermal** and **biofuel** power are all used to produce steam.

2. The steam turns a turbine.

3. The turbine drives a generator.

4. The generator produces electricity.

5. The electricity is distributed to homes and industries.

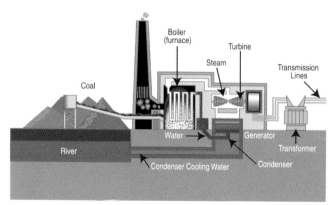

△ Fig. 2.8 A coal-fired thermal power station.

△ Fig. 2.9 A wind farm in Europe.

Other energy sources harness moving water, the tide, waves, wind or the sun – either by turning turbines or converting sunlight directly into electricity using solar panels. These renewable sources of energy have a number of environmental advantages over fossil fuels, but they rely on having the technology available to harness them as well as the suitability of different locations around the globe. Governments, energy companies and local communities have to take into account a range of factors when deciding on how to meet their electricity needs. The range of sources a country uses to generate electricity is referred to as the **energy mix**.

Energy sources compared

Each energy resource can be compared by looking at how it is harnessed to produce electricity and the range of advantages and disadvantages this brings. Both renewable and non-renewable energy sources are compared in Table 2.2.

Energy source	How is it used to generate electricity?	Advantages	Disadvantages
Oil and natural gas	Fuel oil and natural gas are burnt in conventional thermal power stations to heat water into steam. The steam turns turbine blades to produce electricity. Both fuels can also be burned under pressure with the exhaust gases being used to turn turbines blades. Combined-cycle plants use exhaust gases to turn turbines and waste heat to turn water to steam – maximising the efficiency of the fossil fuels.	• Oil is a highly useful energy source that can be refined into hundreds of products. • It is relatively easy to store and transport. • Electricity from oil and gas is reliable and can respond quickly to demand. • Oil and gas provides thousands of jobs globally. • Natural gas produces 70 per cent less CO_2 emissions compared to other fossil fuels.	• Both are finite non-renewable resources which release CO_2 into the atmosphere. • Creating and managing the pipelines used to transport natural gas and oil can be costly. • Oil spills can be devastating to the marine environment. • By-products of oil can be toxic and pollute the environment.
Coal	Coal can be burned directly in boilers in thermal power stations. More efficient power plants mill the coal to create a fine powder which burns quickly at a high temperature. The hot gases and heat energy turn water to steam. The steam is under high pressure, causing turbine propeller blades to turn at high speed. This has a shaft connecting it to a generator which produces high voltage electricity.	• Coal is an affordable energy source because of a stable price compared to other fuel sources. • Coal is easy to burn. • It produces high levels of energy upon combustion. • Coal is one of the most abundant sources of energy – more so than oil and natural gas. • Coal energy is a reliable energy source. • Coal exports provide valuable income for some countries.	• Coal is a finite non-renewable resource. • Coal is highly polluting and releases greenhouse gases when burned. • Coal mining can scar the landscape and the equipment used for mining is large and noisy which may affect local wildlife. • Transporting coal can also add to atmospheric pollution. • Mining coal can be dangerous and lead to health problems.
Nuclear power	Nuclear power uses uranium or plutonium to create controlled nuclear fission reactions in thermal power stations. Nuclear fission occurs when a neutron splits a uranium atom, releasing energy in the form of heat and radiation. This chain reaction is controlled in a power station reactor to produce a desired amount of heat. Uranium fuel rods are kept cool in water. If more heat is needed, they are lifted out.	• Nuclear power does not depend on fossil fuels. • It uses significantly fewer raw materials than coal or oil. • CO_2 emissions are limited. • Countries could close older coal-fired power stations. • Nuclear power provides jobs in design, construction and operation. • Local economies benefit from the investment.	• Nuclear power stations are very expensive to build. • Uranium and plutonium are finite resources so will run out eventually. • Mining, refining and transporting uranium and plutonium causes environmental impacts. • There is no current satisfactory long-term solution to where we put toxic radioactive waste, which lasts for thousands of years. • A by-product of power generation is material used to create nuclear weapons.

Energy source	How is it used to generate electricity?	Advantages	Disadvantages
Nuclear power continued	A sealed water source is then heated to produce steam which turns turbines to make electricity.		• A nuclear accident (like at Chernobyl or Fukushima) is devastating. • Nuclear power stations are built at coastal locations – possibly vulnerable to sea-level rise.
Wind power	Wind turbines use wind to make electricity. The wind turns the blades, which spin a shaft that connects to a generator to make electricity. The electricity is then fed into the power grid. When turbines are clustered together they are known as wind farms. These can be located onshore or offshore.	• Wind energy uses a clean, renewable, energy source. • Wind turbines are cheap to operate once built. • There are zero emissions, which benefits health and carbon emission levels. • This reduces the reliance on fossil fuel imports – providing more energy security for the future.	• If there is no wind, there is no power. • Some people oppose wind turbines if they live nearby. • One unit of electricity generated from wind costs more than from fossil fuels. • The windiest places are remote (hill tops or offshore) so maintenance can be challenging.
Wave power and tidal power	It is possible to generate electricity from the ocean by harnessing the movement of the waves and the incoming and outgoing tide. There are four methods: • Nearshore wave power – harnessing wave energy as the waves break. • Offshore wave power – harnessing wave movement in deeper water. • Tidal stream power – turbines harnessing the tide as it moves past. • Tidal range power – trapping the high tide behind a barrage and releasing it to generate electricity.	• Both generate clean, renewable electricity. • In some countries there are multiple suitable locations for wave power. • This creates jobs in environmentally friendly industries. • Wave and tidal power both reduce carbon emissions.	• There are high upfront costs involved with tidal power and there are fewer suitable locations than for wave power. • Tidal and wave energy could disrupt marine life. • Tidal energy is difficult to transport and is intermittent, although predictable. • Wave energy can be very intermittent. • Offshore wave farms could disrupt marine navigation. • Nearshore wave farms have a visual impact on the coast.
Solar power	Solar energy can be harnessed by: • Photovoltaic cells, or solar panels.	• A renewable, clean energy source with no air pollution. • Reduces reliance on foreign energy imports.	• The initial set-up cost is high. • Solar potential varies between and within countries.

Energy source	How is it used to generate electricity?	Advantages	Disadvantages
Solar power continued	• Concentrated solar power – using parabolic mirrors to focus solar energy at the top of a tower filled with fluid. The fluid is heated to produce steam which turns a turbine to make electricity.	• Easy to maintain. • Silent in operation and can be small scale.	• It is intermittent and can be hard to store the energy. • Solar energy cannot produce electricity as quickly or as cheaply as fossil fuels.
Geothermal power	Geothermal power harnesses the heat of the Earth's crust to generate electricity. This is quite straightforward in some places – in Iceland for example, which sits on a constructive plate boundary and a hot spot. This heat can be harnessed to generate electricity by drilling boreholes and pumping high-pressure heated water up to the surface and converting it to steam to drive the generator turbines. These flash steam plants then cool the steam, which condenses to water. It is then injected back into the ground to be used again.	• A renewable energy source that reduces reliance on fossil fuels and energy imports. • It is low carbon, so helps to reduce CO_2 emissions from electricity generation. • It has very low running costs so produces cheaper electricity.	• Drilling operations can be disruptive. • Limited large-scale potential in many countries – not everywhere is suitable. • High installation costs. • Drilling and operations may release harmful gases.
Hydro-electric power (HEP)	HEP uses the power of moving water to turn turbines which generate electricity. Schemes can be small- or large-scale. Humans have used HEP for centuries to run mills. There are two distinct ways of generating HEP from rivers: • Building dams. • Building run of the river systems that use the change in height of a river as it moves downstream.	• A renewable source of energy. • No pollution or greenhouse gases are emitted from HEP generation. • A dam is often a multipurpose scheme: it helps flood control, water supplies and irrigation, and creates leisure, recreation and tourism opportunities. • Water can be stored and used to generate power when demand is high. • HEP schemes are long lasting, so can be relied upon for decades.	• Dams are very expensive to build and maintain, and will disrupt river ecosystems. • Dams flood large areas behind them after completion, causing social impacts. • Dams can also cause conflict between countries where rivers cross international borders. • Run of the river systems can disrupt river environments and natural processes.

Energy source	How is it used to generate electricity?	Advantages	Disadvantages
Biofuels (bioethanol, biogas and biomass)	Bioethanol is plant matter that has been fermented to produce a petrol substitute. Biogas is gas made from the decomposition of organic matter from landfill sites, plant waste or sewage waste. The gas can be burned in thermal power stations. Biomass from wood is burned in thermal power stations.	• Biomass fuel is cheap and renewable. • Crops absorb CO_2 while growing. • Biogas is produced from waste so is usually cheap. • Power stations that burn fossil fuels can be easily converted to burn biofuels.	• Burning biofuels still releases CO_2 into the atmosphere. • Land given over to biofuel production takes land away from food production – increasing food prices. • Using biogas on a large scale is difficult as collecting the gas is inefficient.

△ Table 2.2 The advantages and disadvantages of different energy sources.

ENERGY DEMAND

Globally there has been a significant increase in the demand for and **consumption** of energy over the last 100 years. Although a significant amount of this rise is caused by global population growth, the greatest increases have been driven by increased consumption. As technology capabilities increase and economies grow, there are ever more devices and gadgets in our homes that use electricity. As we demand more products, industrial demand will increase – as will the energy consumed by transporting these goods. Humans are an energy-hungry **species**; Figure 2.10 shows the global pattern of energy use.

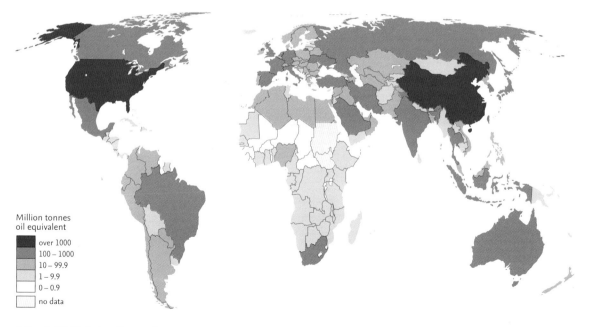

Million tonnes oil equivalent

- over 1000
- 100 – 1000
- 10 – 99.9
- 1 – 9.9
- 0 – 0.9
- no data

△ Fig. 2.10 Global patterns of energy use.

There is a clear disparity across the world, for example, the USA uses 10 000–20 000 kg of oil equivalent per person per year, whereas large parts of central Africa use less than 499 kg per person. Figure 2.11 shows how the use of different sources of energy has changed over time.

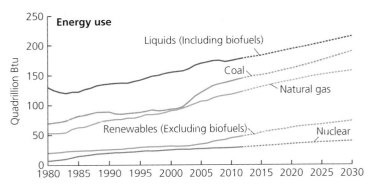

△ Fig. 2.11 The relative use of different energy sources.

In 2012, 52 per cent of the energy consumed globally was used by **industry**, 26 per cent by transportation, 14 per cent by residential properties and 8 per cent by commercial properties. There is a range of factors that affect the demand for energy across the world: domestic demand, industrial demand, transport, personal and national wealth, and climate.

Domestic demand

At home we are using increasing amounts of energy to power, light and heat our homes. Domestic demand is made up of the following:

• heating
• cooling
• water heating
• running appliances (washers, dryers, refrigerators etc.)
• lighting
• electronics (computers, games consoles, TVs, DVD players, etc.).

As levels of income increase, we purchase more products and consequently our energy consumption increases.

Industrial demand

Globally, industrial demand uses over 50 per cent of all the energy consumed each year. Much of this demand is driven by increasing levels of income and demand for **consumer** products. The main areas of industrial demand come from producing the following:

• iron and steel
• chemicals and petrochemicals
• metals
• paper
• food
• machinery
• **minerals**.

Many of these products go on to be assembled into finished goods that consume yet more energy in production. If the global economy grows, industrial energy consumption will also increase.

Transport

Humans are increasingly mobile and this, along with our demand for goods from across the world, can be seen in the rising demand for energy used in transportation, which has doubled since 1970.

The main areas of energy demand are:

- shipping
- passenger vehicles
- road freight
- air travel
- rail.

The vast majority of the energy demand comes from individual cars and trucks on the road. Globally, there are now over 1 billion cars on the road.

△ Fig. 2.12 An overcrowded road in Bangkok, Thailand.

Personal and national wealth

Increasing levels of personal wealth can lead to increased demand for energy as people are likely to consume more and purchase more goods that require electricity. They may also purchase larger houses, which need more energy to light, heat or cool them.

An increase in levels of national wealth will also lead to an increase in energy consumption as countries will build more power stations and **infrastructure** (schools, roads, hospitals, water pipes), all of which consume energy.

Climate

It is also important to consider the role that weather and climate play in influencing demand for energy. Long periods of cold weather will lead to more energy consumed to heat houses. Conversely, a warm spell may reduce energy consumption in some countries as people will be outside more and heating their homes less. However, in hotter regions nearer the equator, more energy may be consumed cooling houses with air conditioning and fans.

CONSERVATION AND MANAGEMENT OF ENERGY RESOURCES

The rapid increase in demand for energy driven by consumption, population growth and economic development is currently being met by fossil fuels. These finite, non-renewable energy sources will run out in the future. Their use, while providing many benefits, causes significant environmental management challenges – from **climate change** to water and air pollution, as well as conflicts between and within countries. Much of the energy we use is wasted through inefficient use, so it is vital that people around the world conserve and manage energy resources. Given the global need to reduce **carbon dioxide emissions** and that some countries are not energy secure, there are several key strategies being used:

- Change the energy mix by moving to more renewable sources of energy.
- Reduce consumption through use of energy-efficient technology and education.
- Research and develop existing and new energy sources.
- Use government policy to reduce energy demand from transport.

△ Fig. 2.13 High energy consumption in Tokyo at night.

Changing the energy mix

By shifting electricity production toward renewable energy sources, countries can reduce their demand for non-renewable energy sources. However, this requires significant investment and not all parts of the world have the same potential for using renewable energy. Currently, despite the obvious advantages of cleaner and renewable fuels, many of the decisions are influenced by the relative cost. Fossil fuels are currently cheaper and easier to use, although this will not remain the case for ever. Some governments offer incentives like loans and grants to install renewable energy sources in homes, which encourage people to reduce their reliance on fossil fuels.

Reducing consumption

Houses – Increasing or shifting energy supplies to a more renewable mix can take time and money, and may not be possible in some countries. However, all countries can work on their methods of reducing consumption. Key to this is the development of more energy-efficient technology and new building design and planning that takes into account energy use.

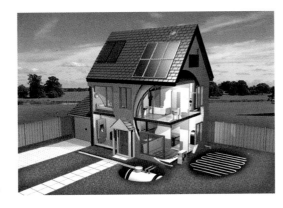

△ Fig. 2.14 An energy-efficient house.

In some cities, large buildings are connected to the control rooms of the national supply grid. These smart buildings can reduce consumption quickly to manage a sudden increase in demand elsewhere. Reducing lighting, shutting down elevators and turning off air conditioning or heating temporarily will lead to reductions in energy consumption.

Education – Reducing consumption through technological fixes is important as it takes decisions out of the hands of consumers. However, saving energy only to keep wasting it through inefficient behaviour is still unsustainable. This is why education is vital. Educating consumers about strategies to reduce consumption by changing their behaviour can lead to dramatic results. Many schools and companies around the world are working toward reducing energy use by conducting energy audits and identifying areas that can be addressed. For example:

- Leaving lights, heating or air conditioning on in empty rooms.
- Leaving electronic items like TVs, DVD players and computers on standby.
- Leaving heating on, but opening windows when it feels too hot.
- Leaving taps running.
- Boiling too much water in a kettle.

Educating people from a young age about the need to save energy will help transform behaviours and ultimately lead to a reduction in energy use. However, it is important to remember that the number of devices, appliances and vehicles is increasing, so although there are gains from education these could be outweighed by the number of new devices that need power. To address this, countries must change the energy mix and develop new technologies to reduce demand alongside education programmes.

Vehicles – We have already seen that passenger vehicles are responsible for a significant amount of the global energy demand each year, as well as air pollution and congestion in cities and towns. It is possible to make significant reductions in energy consumption by increasing the fuel efficiency of vehicles – making them go further for every litre of fuel burned. Making cars out of lighter materials will also allow them to use less energy as the fuel taken to accelerate will be reduced. Furthermore, taxing of older, less-efficient and more-polluting vehicles, will lead to people shifting toward more fuel-efficient vehicles, which in turn can lead to reduced energy demand.

However, all of these changes relate to cars that burn petrol, which is refined from crude oil. It is possible to reduce energy consumption in these cars by moving toward biofuels. Biodiesel can be made from waste vegetable oil. Oil is collected from factories and shops that use vegetable oil in large quantities, processed and then used to create a mixture of diesel and vegetable oil. The resultant fuel can then be used in adapted diesel vehicles. This reduces oil consumption but only currently operates on a small scale. The most successful biofuel is bioethanol, which powers every light vehicle in Brazil, with a mixture of up to 22 per cent ethanol (made from sugar cane) and petrol. The USA is also a world leader in using ethanol to power vehicles.

Perhaps the most significant way of reducing oil consumption in cars is to increase the development of hybrid and electric vehicles. Hybrid cars use a

△ Fig. 2.15 A hybrid electric bus.

petrol engine that charges an electric power unit and the car will switch between each unit to maximise fuel consumption. Some cars now feature kinetic energy recovery systems that collect the energy used in braking and feed it back into the power system – reducing the energy consumed. There are also fully electric vehicles available with no petrol engine at all. These require charging every day and use electricity, which may come from fossil fuels. They use less energy than other cars and cause less pollution. Increasingly, charging points for electric cars are visible in towns and cities. There is an increasing number of hybrid and fully electric vehicles on the roads today.

△ Fig. 2.16 An electric vehicle charging point.

Government policy

Obviously not everyone is driving an electric car today. The current situation across the planet is that cities are dominated by petrol- and diesel-powered vehicles. Some cities have decided to take action to reduce the number of cars on the road. In London, UK, there is a **congestion charge** for all vehicles entering a clearly marked zone. The daily fee was designed to force people to car share, use public transport, walk or cycle to work. This was

△ Fig. 2.17 The London congestion zone.

successful, although 10 years on, the number of vehicles entering the city has risen to a level higher than before it was introduced. Without the charge it would probably be higher still. In Singapore, the government introduced a highly successful **MRT (mass rapid transit)** system of underground trains that run cheaply and efficiently, alongside ERP (electronic road pricing) and a variable tax rate for vehicles where owners have to buy 10 years of road tax up front – making cars very expensive to buy in Singapore. Both schemes have been successful in encouraging greater use of public transport and reducing demand for energy.

Research and development

Another option for managing energy resources is increasing the supply of energy. Huge sums of money are invested into both developing new energy sources and further exploiting existing sources. However, the success of these schemes is reduced if fossil fuel energy prices are low, as there is less incentive to make more energy due to the costs of research and development. In 2016, global oil prices were at a low of around US$40 a barrel – US$100 less than in 2007. When the price is high, looking for alternatives becomes economically viable. We are now beginning to see the impact of the high oil price in the last decade with alternative energy sources being produced:

- Oil from tar sand in Alberta, Canada.
- **Fracking** is the hydraulic fracturing of gas and oil rich shale rocks. They are fractured by injecting high pressure chemicals and fluid into wells. The shale rock fractures releasing the hydrocarbon from that location back to the surface.
- Deep water oil production off the coast of Brazil.
- Innovation in the development of solar panels.
- Developing larger-scale wave generation schemes.
- Researching methods to extract oil from deep in wells that cannot be accessed through current techniques.

△ Fig. 2.18 Tar sands extraction in Alberta, Canada.

In the future, there will be an increasing need for engineers and scientists to develop innovative methods of energy generation to replace our reliance on fossil fuels. There is debate and uncertainty over when they will run out, but expanding consumption of finite resources will lead to an inevitable exhaustion of supplies.

IMPACT OF OIL POLLUTION

Causes of pollution

Global demand for oil is high, but the largest consumers of oil are not always the largest suppliers. Sometimes the oil is in inaccessible locations, such as deserts or offshore in deep water, and often the main population centres are some distance from the oil fields and refineries. This means that oil needs to be transported from the source to the refinery and from there onwards to a variety of distribution networks. Oil is transported across the oceans in large ships or across land using pipelines. From extraction to transporting to refining, there are a number of places that oil can enter marine or coastal **ecosystems** and cause significant pollution: offshore oil extraction, pipelines and shipping.

Offshore oil extraction – When oil is discovered and extracted offshore, there is a greater risk of an uncontained oil spill than on land. Although oil rigs are fitted with safety valves that shut the well if an accident occurs, sometimes these fail. Oil can enter marine and coastal ecosystems if the oil-well head on the seabed is damaged, and fixing these is very challenging and time consuming in deep water. There can also be leaks if the equipment is outdated or poorly maintained. Oil can also be spilled when being transferred to ships or through pipelines to shore. Oil rigs are also vulnerable to strong winds and there have been examples where spills have occurred following hurricanes in the Gulf of Mexico.

Pipelines – Oil pipelines are the most common method of transporting oil on land. They sometimes run for several thousand kilometres, crossing a range of terrain, climates and even countries. The largest pipelines are capable of transporting over a million barrels of oil each day along vast distances powered by pumps that are controlled by monitoring stations. The pipes sometimes leak due to corrosion, metal fatigue and human error in construction. They are also vulnerable to accidental collisions and there have been pipelines that have been attacked and disabled

△ Fig. 2.19 An oil pipeline in Alaska, USA.

during conflicts – leading to oil entering the local ecosystems. There have been hundreds of recorded pipeline spills across the world, with the largest of these in North America, spilling hundreds of thousands of litres of oil into nearby rivers – with devastating effects.

Shipping – Pipeline spills are more common, but oil spills caused by maritime accidents are more commonly reported in the media. There have been a number of high-profile oil tanker spills that dumped large quantities of crude oil directly into the sea. These were caused by the weather, metal fatigue, collisions and navigation errors.

The largest oil spill from tankers happened in 1979, when two ships collided in the Caribbean sea, spilling 333 million litres of oil. However, much of the oil did not wash up onto the nearby coastline, but was carried away by **ocean currents**. Perhaps the most widely known oil tanker spill is the Exxon Valdez, which in 1989 – through human error – ran aground in the pristine Prince William Sound in Alaska, USA. This oil spill comprised 42 million litres of crude oil, killing an estimated 250 000 seabirds, 2800 sea otters and 300 seals. While not the largest spill in history, the environmental impact and clean-up efforts were massive. The oil company was eventually ordered to pay US$500 million in damages to the locals, fishermen and businesses damaged by the disaster.

△ Fig. 2.20 A ruptured pipeline leaking into the sea.

The impact on marine and coastal ecosystems

Oil floats on salt water and usually spreads out rapidly to form an oil slick. Eventually the slick thins out to leave a thin sheen of oil on the water. The oil itself is poisonous to birds, mammals and fish that come into contact with it on the surface and when it washes up onto beaches and coral reefs. The clean-up operations can also be harmful to ecosystems due to the detergents used. Each oil spill is different in terms of type of oil, weather conditions, location and scale, but there are key impacts of many spills that are shown in Figure 2.21.

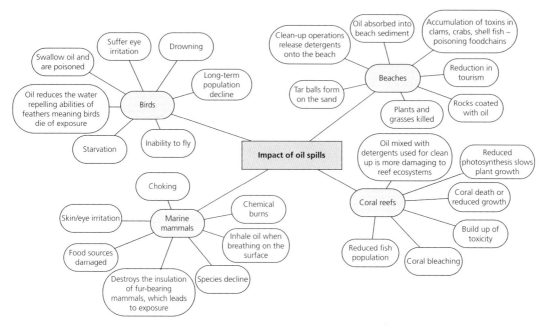

△ Fig. 2.21 The impact of oil spills on marine and coastal ecosystems.

MANAGEMENT OF OIL POLLUTION

Oil pollution has a devastating effect on ecosystems, which can take many years to recover. Due to rising demand for oil over time, by 2013 the global oil tanker fleet comprised about 11 000 tankers weighing 490 million tonnes when empty. Between 2000 and 2013, overall capacity increased by over 70 per cent. There are also around 500 offshore rigs that are drilling for new oil resources and countless production platforms globally. In 2012, there were over 1.78 billion tonnes of oil transported by ship; this is a significant amount of oil, so there is an increased risk of spills. Given the environmental, economic and social costs of oil spills, there have been many attempts to develop strategies for reducing oil spills in marine and coastal ecosystems.

MARPOL (International Convention for the Prevention of Pollution from Ships)

In the mid-20th century, ships regularly dumped waste oil at sea with little regard for the impact. A number of high-profile oil spills led to the development of a new international marine **treaty** in 1973, which was amended in 1978. **MARPOL** was designed to eliminate marine pollution in the sea. The treaty has six sections, each addressing a different kind of marine pollution. Section one relates to oil pollution and specifically bans ships from releasing oil waste from engines and tanks into the sea. Ships are now fitted with oil discharge monitoring equipment – a **GPS** tracking system than reports oil released into the sea.

Double-hulled oil tankers

MARPOL has been effective at reducing deliberate oil discharge into the sea. The treaty also includes provisions on reducing the consequences of accidents, such as ships running aground, colliding or sinking. Modern ships use GPS and accurate charts to navigate so the risk of running into rocks has been reduced, but not removed. Collisions can also occur in busy ports and shipping lanes. In 1992, MARPOL was updated to include regulations that require oil tankers to now be fitted with double hulls that protect the cargo in the event of a collision. Furthermore, single-hulled tankers have been phased out and there are strict regulations on how oil should be carried, including a ban on carrying oil in the front of the ship where it is most at risk from a collision.

Dealing with oil spills

△ Fig. 2.22 Booms deployed to stop an oil slick in the Gulf of Mexico.

△ Fig. 2.23 High-pressure hoses tackling an oil spill in Thailand.

Even with new technology and international laws, accidents do happen and oil enters marine and coastal ecosystems. Each spill is different in terms of the amount and type of oil, the environment affected and the clean-up options. Some spills disperse naturally, but others require significant intervention to minimise the impact on ecosystems and to clean up the oil. There are several methods that are deployed in most oil spills:

- Booms – temporary floating barriers to oil which can prevent the oil from spreading. These are less effective in high waves.
- Chemical dispersants and biological agents – these break down oil into very small droplets, which can then biodegrade. They are delivered by specialised boats and planes.
- Skimmers – boats that skim (collect) spilled oil from the water's surface for processing and recovery.
- Sorbents – materials like peat moss, which are used to absorb oil.

- Controlled burning – a method of burning freshly spilled oil, usually while it is floating on the water surrounded by booms.
- High-pressure hoses – for washing oil off beaches.
- Vacuum trucks – to remove spilled oil from beaches or the water's surface.

△ Fig. 2.24 Chemical dispersant being dropped onto a slick in the Gulf of Mexico.

CASE STUDY

THE DEEPWATER HORIZON DISASTER

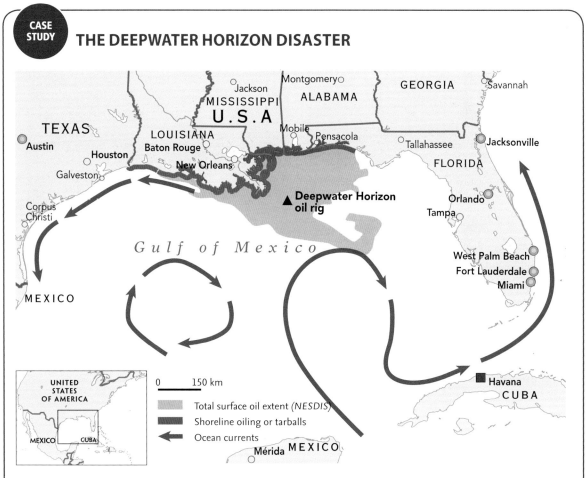

△ Fig. 2.25 The extent of the Deepwater Horizon oil spill.

How did the Deepwater Horizon disaster impact the Gulf of Mexico?

Causes

In April 2010, the BP-leased oil rig Deepwater Horizon was only days away from sealing a new oil well in the Gulf of Mexico, ready for handover to a production platform that would pump the oil to the surface. On 20 April, the well suffered from a blowout and a series of catastrophic failures occurred. Gas pressure in the well built up and the cement seals failed – leading to the gas escaping. The fail-safe blowout preventer did not operate and the oil rig was flooded with gas. The rig exploded, killing 11 men working on the platform and injuring 17 others.

The well-head on the seabed began leaking oil from the well uncontrollably. In total, 795 million litres of oil spilled into the Gulf of Mexico for three months. This was the largest accidental marine oil spill in the history of the oil industry.

Despite numerous attempts to stop the leak, it took 3 months to bring it under control, by which time it had leaked 4.9 million barrels of crude oil. An estimated 53 000 barrels each day escaped before it was stopped.

△ Fig. 2.26 The Deepwater Horizon oil rig on fire in the Gulf of Mexico.

Effects

Environmental effects

- Marine and coastal ecosystems were devastated, with thousands of birds, mammals and sea turtles affected.
- Large stretches of coastline, wetlands and estuaries were polluted.
- Significant numbers of birds and mammals were immediately affected.
- Long-term effects are still being studied, but evidence suggests that oil and dispersant are being found in the food chain 5 years later. Polluted migrating birds' eggs were found in northern USA.

- Mass beaching of dolphins and whales with diseases attributed to oil.
- Fish with deformities are still being discovered.
- Areas of gulf coral death.
- Reports of a dead zone around the well, with oil found in large quantities on the seabed.

Immediate responses

- The rig fire was tackled by fire boats, but the rig sank after 3 days.
- Attempts were made to contain the spill at sea using booms and burning.
- Various attempts were made to close the leaking well from the top, but they failed. Plans were made to drill a relief well.
- Preparations were made for oil coming ashore along the Gulf Coast of the USA.
- Emergency funding was released to pay for the clean up.
- Satellite imagery was used to predict the flow of oil.

Economic effects

- There was a ban on new drilling.
- Fishing and tourism collapsed.
- US$23 billion was lost in tourist income.
- The oil price increased temporarily.
- BP share price values were damaged.
- The economies of the Gulf Coast went into a decline.

Short-term responses

- The oil was cleaned up with dispersant, burning and skimming.
- The spread of oil was monitored.
- The affected wildlife was cleaned up.
- Fishing grounds were closed.
- The oil was cleaned up as it washed ashore.
- New drilling was banned.
- The leaking well was sealed after 3 months.
- Compensation was paid to the local people affected.

Social effects

- Levels of unemployment increased and incomes reduced.
- Health problems for Gulf shore residents and clean-up workers.

Long-term responses

- There were governmental investigations into the causes of the incident.
- There is ongoing monitoring using satellites and digital maps.
- A comprehensive scientific study was carried out.
- BP were hit with record-breaking fines.
- New regulations on deep-water offshore drilling to prevent new drilling in the Arctic Ocean.

Deepwater Horizon disaster fact file

Fact file

Location: 66 km off the coast of Louisiana, USA in the Gulf of Mexico

Depth of water: 1522 m

Depth of oil well: 5486 m

Date of explosion: 20 April 2010

Total volume of oil leaked: 4.9 million barrels

Oil slick size: 176 100 sq km

Coastline affected: 1770 km

Recorded animal deaths within 3 months: 4768

Vessels used in the clean-up operation: 7000

People involved in the clean-up operation: 47 000

Methods used to control the oil slick: booms, skimmers, burning, chemical dispersant

Length of boom deployed: 3 048 000 sq m

Amount of chemical dispersant used: 7 million litres

Area of fishing ground closed: 225 290 sq km

Fine for BP: US$18.7 billion

Total cost to BP of charges associated with the spill: US$53.8 billion

End of topic checklist

Key terms

anthracite, biofuels, boom, carbon, carboniferous, coal, congestion charge, dispersant, energy mix, energy secure, fossil fuels, fracking, geothermal, GPS, hybrid car, hydrocarbons, hydroelectric, impermeable, MARPOL, million tonnes of oil equivalent, MRT, natural gas, non-renewable, nuclear, oil, oil slick, organic matter, peat, permeable, porous, renewable, skimmer, smart metering, solar, sulfur, tar sands, thermal power generation, tidal, treaty, vegetation, wave, wind

Important vocabulary

accident, conflict, construction, consumption, costly, crust, decomposition, demand, dense, devastating, development, drilling, electricity, emissions, energy-efficient, environment, expensive, exploration, factors, finite, generator, geologist, harnessing, health problem, infrastructure, innovative, intermittent, leak, marine, mining, multipurpose, offshore, oppose, pipeline, pollution, population, potential, pressure, recreation, reliable, reliance, reserves, reservoirs, spill, supply, tankers, technology, temperature, tourism, transporting, turbine, uranium, wealth

During your study of this topic you should have learned:

○ How fossil fuels form, and how coal and oil form through different processes.

○ How to classify energy sources into renewable and non-renewable resources.

○ How each of these sources is used to generate electricity and the advantages and disadvantages of each source.

○ How countries around the world have a different energy mix depending on the energy sources accessible. This affects their energy security.

○ There is disparity in global energy consumption.

○ Fossil fuels meet nearly 90 per cent of the world demand for energy.

○ Energy demand is influenced by a range of factors.

○ It is possible to reduce demand for energy by using a combination of technology and education, at the same time as moving to more sustainable supplies.

○ Governments can affect energy demand through green transport policies and taxation.

are absorbed mostly through their root hairs in the form of ions (electrically charged atoms or groups of atoms), which are found in salts dissolved in soil water. The most important minerals required by plants are nitrogen, phosphorous, potassium and magnesium.

Mineral ion	Mineral element	How they are used in plants
Nitrate NO_3^-	Nitrogen (N)	Combines with glucose to form amino acids, which in turn bond together to create proteins required for cell growth.
Phosphate PO_4^{3-}	Phosphorous (P)	An important component of DNA and cell membranes and is required for **respiration** and growth.
Potassium K^+	Potassium (K)	Must be present for the enzymes required for **photosynthesis** and respiration to function effectively.
Magnesium Mg^{2+}	Magnesium (Mg)	Used for manufacturing **chlorophyll** (each chlorophyll cell contains one magnesium atom) without which photosynthesis would not occur.

△ Table 3.1 The use of minerals in plant growth.

In addition to **mineral ions**, organic matter in soil is the other natural source of plant nutrients. Organic matter is the remains of a plant or animal that was once alive and which has returned to the soil and been decomposed into humus by bacterial microorganisms. These and other **decomposers** such as worms and fungi function as an integral part of the nutrient or **carbon cycle**. The organic content of soil is very important:

- It functions as a reservoir of nutrients, which are constantly being released into the soil and absorbed by plants. Every 1 per cent of organic matter in the soil will release between 9–14 kg of phosphorous pentoxide and 1–2 kg of sulfur a year.
- It greatly improves the water-holding capacity of soil. It can store up to 90 per cent of its weight in water, which it releases slowly and evenly over the course of a year. This even release helps to prevent plants becoming waterlogged in very wet periods and also to survive dry spells.
- It helps to bind or clump soil into aggregates that improve soil structure, allowing it to take up and hold water better. Permeability, which is the ease with which water is able to infiltrate or move through the soil, will also improve with better soil structure.
- It plays an important role in preventing **soil erosion**. Increasing organic matter in soil by only 1 per cent can reduce erosion by between 20 and 33 per cent. Organic matter helps to stabilise soil and promotes stronger plant root growth, which also has a binding effect. It enables increased water **infiltration**, which prevents the soil drying out and becoming vulnerable to wind erosion.

How easily plants can absorb nutrients from mineral ions and organic matter dissolved in soil water is affected by the soil pH. This is a measure of how acid or alkaline the soil is. Soil pH is measured on a scale of 1 to 14. Soils with a pH value of below 7 are considered acidic. Values above 7 are alkaline (the opposite of acidic) and readings of around 7 are considered neutral. If the soil solution is too acid or alkaline, some nutrients will not dissolve easily and therefore will not be available for uptake by plant roots. This can lead to plants suffering from nutrient

△ Fig. 3.5 Organic matter in soil.

deficiency. A soil solution pH of between 6 and 7.5 is considered optimal for plants because most nutrients in the soil will dissolve easily in water at these levels. When the soil is acidic the nutrients of phosphorous, molybdenum, calcium and magnesium will not dissolve easily. As a result, concentrations of metal ions such as aluminium, manganese and iron may become disproportionately high and even reach toxic levels. Under alkaline conditions, plant growth can be restricted by a lack of iron, manganese, phosphorous, zinc, copper and boron in the soil water. In addition, high levels of calcium in alkaline soil water may also decrease the solubility and uptake of potassium and manganese by plants.

△ Fig. 3.6 Signs of manganese deficiency in a potato plant growing in acidic soil.

△ Fig. 3.7 Signs of iron deficiency in a raspberry fruit plant growing in alkaline soil.

Over time the tendency will be for the pH of most soils to decline and for the soil to become naturally more acidic. Rainfall weathers soils, washing or leaching out calcium and magnesium, and leaving behind more stable materials rich in iron and aluminium but with a low nutrient level. Even without rain, soil acidity naturally increases over time due to the decomposition of organic matter that naturally adds acid to the soil. **Environments** rich in humus, such as forests with thick litter layers of decaying organic matter, will naturally tend to have more acidic soils than places such as hot deserts with little rainfall, sparse vegetation cover and decaying matter. Human activity can also contribute to raising soil acidity. The burning of coal and other **fossil fuels**

△ Fig. 3.8 Tropical rainforests tend to have acidic soils.

releases sulfur and nitrogen oxides as waste gases into the **atmosphere**, where they combine with water to form acids. When this water condenses and falls as rain, acidic hydrogen is added to soils. Soil acidity can also be increased through the use of chemical-based fertilisers on farms.

△ Fig. 3.9 Alkaline soils are common in hot desert areas.

Adding ground limestone or calcium carbonate with magnesium (called liming) is the most common method used by farmers to raise the pH levels of acid soils to the more neutral levels in which most plants will grow. Adding large quantities of organic matter such as natural manure compost and sulfur to alkaline soils has a similar effect of lowering pH levels to more neutral readings.

Sandy and clay soils present different challenges to farmers. Sand particles are large and fine in texture compared to most soils and this is a benefit because its air content tends to be high as there are plenty of open spaces between the particles. This is an advantage to plants because their roots are able to use the large pore spaces to move easily through the soil. However, the same open spaces mean that water drains through sandy soil rapidly. This is a benefit during heavy rain periods because the soil will only rarely become waterlogged. In times of little rainfall, however, the same soil will dry out very quickly. Because water drains quickly through sandy soils they tend to become acidic and infertile as many nutrients such as calcium are leached out. Their light texture and loose open structure combined with the fact that they dry out quickly means that sandy soils are easy to plough and can be worked early in the growing season because they warm up more quickly than other soils. To make sandy soils easier to cultivate and support a wide range of crops, organic matter such as compost, manure, leaf mould or some clay is often added. This not only increases the nutrient-holding capacity and pH levels of the soil, but also improves its structure and water-holding capacity.

In comparison, clay has the smallest particle size of any soil. As a consequence the pore spaces are minute. Compared with the granular texture of sandy soils, clay tends to be smooth because its individual particles are too small to create a rough surface. Its small particle size also means that clay soil is often very compact and difficult for plant roots to spread through. Together these qualities create a thicker and heavier soil, more difficult to cultivate than sandy soils. Clay takes much longer to warm up in the spring because of its heavy density, and because its particles are very small, any water takes much longer to drain than in sandy soils. Clay particles will also absorb water as a result of capillary attraction causing them to expand, further reducing the size of the soil pores and slowing water flow even more. Such poor drainage means that in times of heavy rain clay soils can become waterlogged and heavily compacted, and during dry periods they may contract and become a hard and cracked sheet. When rain returns, water tends to run into the surface cracks rather than moistening the soil and plant roots. An advantage of clay soils is that although they tend to be alkaline, they are potentially very fertile because high concentrations of nutrients get trapped between their fine particles. Adding bulky organic matter, which helps to coalesce the fine clay particles into larger separate clods, is often required to release the nutrients for uptake by plant roots. Creating clay clods also helps to reduce compaction, improve drainage, and make the soil warmer and easier to plough.

AGRICULTURE TYPES

Agriculture or farming is the **cultivation** of the soil for the growing of crops and the rearing of animals. There are an estimated 570 million farms worldwide, covering 38 per cent of the planet's land surface. One-third of the world's **population** of economically active people obtain their livelihood in some form or another from agriculture and its associated food processing industries.

The United Nations (UN) estimates that 475 million farms (83 per cent of the global total) operate at a subsistence or semi-subsistence level and support 2 billion people on plots of land smaller than 0.02 sq km. Subsistence agriculture is self-sufficiency farming in which farmers concentrate on growing or rearing enough food to feed themselves and their families, with perhaps a little surplus generated occasionally. Subsistence farms are found mostly in countries in Asia and Africa and are home to half the world's undernourished people and the majority of people living in **absolute poverty**.

△ Fig. 3.10 Slash and burn being used to prepare fields in a wooded area of the Zinave National Park in Mozambique.

Slash and burn is a form of **subsistence farming** used by 200–500 million people, mainly in **tropical** regions of the world, and involves **shifting cultivation**: clear felling and burning forest and scrub to create fields for crops such as maize and rice and to sometimes graze small numbers of cattle. The ash from burned trees provides an initial fertility boost but heavy rains quickly erode and leach the soils of nutrients. This leads to the clearing being abandoned and new areas of virgin forest being cleared and burned. It is a highly unsustainable form of agriculture and ecologically very damaging to forest **ecosystems**.

Although commercial farms exist in far fewer numbers than subsistence farms, they tend to be much larger and therefore account for over 80 per cent of the world's agricultural land. **Commercial farming** is farming for a profit – growing crops or rearing animals to sell at market. Almost all farming in **MEDCs (more economically developed countries)** around the world is commercial. Commercial farms may be arable (the production of food, fodder and industrial crops), pastoral (rearing animals for meat and/or animal products such as wool) or mixed (both arable and livestock). They are often intensive operations where farmers make large investments of **capital** and technology to achieve high yields or outputs. Commercial farms use the most modern machines and technologies such as GIS systems when planting and feeding crops, and computer-operated milking parlours that prepare feeds for the requirements of individual cows while their milk output is collected and registered.

△ Fig. 3.11 A farmer in a milking parlour using a computerised system to feed the cattle.

△ Fig. 3.12 Intensive commercial farms such as this arable farm in Canada require few workers to manage huge areas of land.

INCREASING AGRICULTURAL YIELDS

Commercial farmers constantly seek to improve their profits by increasing the yield or productivity of the crops they grow and the animals they raise. For arable farmers this may mean increasing the amount of grain or fruit they produce each year from each unit of land. If the average production of wheat this year is 8 tonnes per 10 000 sq metres, and the farmer manages to raise this to 8.5 tonnes per 10 000 sq metres next year, they will have increased yield by 6.25 per cent. Similarly if livestock farmers succeed in raising milk production from an average of 7800 litres from each cow this year to 8200 litres next year, they will have increased yield by 5.12 per cent. **Agricultural yields** have risen steadily during the course of human history both by bringing new land under cultivation and also by applying greater levels of science and technology to existing farms so that more can be produced from the same area of land. Since 1961, the global production of cereal crops has more than doubled – an average of 2.3 per cent per year. Intensive farming techniques used to increase agricultural yields include **rotation**, fertilisers, **irrigation** and controlling pests and diseases.

Rotation

The practice of rotation is not a modern one. There is evidence of it being used by farmers in the Middle East at least 8000 years ago. Rotation involves regularly changing the crop that grows in a particular place on a farm according to an agreed sequence. For example, if maize has been grown one year then this might be substituted with rice the next year, potatoes the year after and peas and beans in the fourth year. In the fifth year the field might be used for maize again.

Growing the same crop in the same field year after year will quickly deplete the soil of the range of nutrients that a particular plant requires to yield well. With rotation, a crop that draws upon one kind of nutrient is followed in the next growing season by a crop that draws mostly on another range of nutrients or a crop that actually returns the depleted nutrient to the soil through a process known as nitrogen 'fixing'. Crops such as clover, are able to add nitrogen to the soil because their roots have special nodules attached. The nodules contain bacteria that feed by 'fixing' or

△ Fig. 3.13 Evidence of crop rotation on a farm in Germany.

extracting nitrogen from the atmosphere to produce nitrate chemical compounds. Clover, along with plants such as peas, beans and alfalfa, are from a family called 'legumes'. They all provide subsequent crops with substantial amounts of nitrogen. Leguminous crops in the rotation are also often used as a fodder crop on which livestock can graze. This has the added advantage of animal manure being available for ploughing back into the soil. In addition to maintaining soil fertility and improving crop yields, rotation can also bring other benefits. It helps to control the build-up of bacteria, fungus or parasites that might cause plant disease or insect pests that might feed upon them. In turn this saves the farmer money because they will need to use fewer chemical **pesticides**. If deep-rooted crops are alternated with shallow-rooted crops in the rotation then this will help to improve soil structure.

Fertilisers

A fertiliser is any natural or synthetic substance that is added to soils to supply one or more nutrients removed by growing crops. When plants are harvested and removed from the soil, an important link in the carbon or **nutrient cycle** is broken – that of decomposition. In natural ecosystems the nutrient ions present in plants are allowed to decompose into the soil as plants die back at the end of the growing season. Plant remains are decomposed by bacteria, which break down organic molecules and release nutrients back into the soil. Removing part of or all

△ Fig. 3.14 A farmer spraying liquid fertiliser onto a rice crop in Indonesia.

harvested crops exhausts the soil's mineral ion content, particularly nitrogen, phosphorous and potassium. Heavy ploughing also accelerates decomposition of organic matter and increases the release of mineral ions from the soil. Without intervention by the farmer, the humus content of the soil eventually drops to a point where it cannot supply enough nutrients to feed the crop adequately.

Fertilisers are used to replace lost nutrients and maintain the productivity of the land through constantly providing optimum conditions for plant growth. The government of New Zealand has estimated that without replacement fertiliser, the soils of the country's farms would only be able to support half of the crops they currently grow. The primary nutrients that plants remove from soils are nitrogen, phosphorous and potassium. On intensive commercial farms, synthetic chemical-based fertilisers made by pharmaceutical companies in laboratories are commonly used to replace these nutrients. They are either mixed with water and sprayed onto the land or scattered over the soil as small nodules that slowly dissolve when it rains. Organic farmers who seek to farm in an environmentally **sustainable** manner replace lost soil fertility through the use of rotation, including nitrogen fixing legumes, composted waste produced on the farm and natural animal manures rather than chemical fertilisers.

△ Fig. 3.15 A farmer spreading fertiliser nodules in a lemon grove in Spain.

△ Fig. 3.16 Animal manure is one form of fertiliser applied to soils on commercial organic farms.

Serious environmental problems can arise from the overuse of both natural and synthetic fertilisers. **Eutrophication** occurs when fertilisers are washed off the land by rainwater into rivers and lakes. High concentrations of nitrate and phosphate build up in the water and can cause very rapid algae growth known as 'blooms'. Such algal blooms can be devastating to aquatic life because they cover the water surface entirely and prevent light and oxygen reaching other water plants, fish and insects. Bacteria then break down the dead plants and aquatic creatures, which can leave the river or lake completely devoid of life.

△ Fig. 3.17 A blue-green algal bloom in the Copco reservoir in California, USA.

Overuse of chemical fertilisers – particularly nitrogen – can lead to soil acidification and contributes to **greenhouse gas emissions** and **global warming**. When nitrogen fertiliser is applied to soils, a powerful greenhouse gas called nitrous oxide is released. Recent studies in China have indicated that farmers could use 30 per cent less nitrogen fertiliser without reducing crop yields.

Irrigation

Irrigation is the artificial supply of water (as opposed to rain-fed watering) to agricultural land and is an important method of increasing yields and productivity on farms. It is used by commercial and subsistence farmers alike and currently an estimated 4 million square kilometres of farmland around the world receives irrigation water (a total area larger than India). Irrigation was first used in Mesopotamia and Egypt 8000 years ago when canals were cut from the Tigris, Euphrates, and Nile rivers to divert flood waters on to fields. These canals and irrigation techniques such as the shaduf developed at the same time are still commonly used by farmers in these areas today.

△ Fig. 3.18 The valleys of the Indus and Ganges rivers in Pakistan and India form one of the largest single areas of irrigation in the world.

△ Fig. 3.19 Modern day farmer in the Nile Valley in Egypt using the traditional shaduf to irrigate his fields.

Irrigation is practised by more than half the farmers in the world because they need more water for their crops and livestock than is available from rainfall alone. It is particularly important in regions with marked dry seasons. The great advantage of irrigation is that it enables a farmer to control precisely how much water is taken up by plant roots and when. As a result, yields obtained from using irrigation are almost always higher than yields obtained from relying on just natural rainfall. The main types of irrigation include surface irrigation, localised irrigation, sprinkler irrigation, sub or seepage irrigation and in-ground irrigation.

Surface irrigation – This is the most common but least efficient system of irrigation and is often called flood irrigation. It involves covering the entire cultivated area with water. Terraced rice fields (rice paddies) use this technique with the movement of water from one field to another being controlled by mud dikes or embankments and narrow channels. Water loss through **evaporation** is considerable.

△ Fig. 3.20 Irrigated rice paddies in northern Vietnam.

Localised irrigation – This is a much more precise and targeted approach, and is highly efficient because evaporation is minimised. Drip irrigation, which delivers small drops of water to the roots of each plant through a network of narrow rubber pipes located above, on or just below the soil surface, is a good example of localised irrigation.

Sprinkler irrigation – This system seeks to imitate natural rainfall. Water is piped through a hose to a central location where it is then distributed over the fields in a fine spray from overhead high-pressure sprinklers. The sprinklers rotate slowly, which avoids any one area becoming waterlogged. Such sprinkler systems are often mounted on wheels to enable easy movement from one field to another.

Sub or seepage irrigation – This system provides plant roots with water from beneath the soil. It can only be used effectively in areas of the world such as Florida in the USA where the **water table** (the level below which the ground is saturated with water) is close to the surface. A combination of pumping stations, canals and weirs are used to raise the water table enough to dampen plant roots from below. It is much less wasteful of water than both surface and sprinkler irrigation systems as there is little evaporation and the farmer has a lot of control over raising and lowering the water table. However, it needs very careful management to avoid waterlogging the soil. All crops require air in the soil (specifically oxygen) and will quickly start to die back if air is prevented from entering. Waterlogging will also cause **salinisation** – build-up of the dissolved salts of sodium, magnesium and calcium in the soil.

In-ground irrigation – This involves burying the entire irrigation system of pipes, sprinklers, drippers and valves underground. It is costly to set up and to maintain, and for this reason is usually confined to servicing individual properties and streets in residential areas. It is not suited practically or financially to farms with fields that may cover many square metres.

△ Fig. 3.21 Drip irrigation of young vine plants in New South Wales, Australia.

△ Fig. 3.22 A potato field being irrigated from a pivot sprinkler system made up of several sections of aluminium pipes; these are fed by water from a central pivot point around which the sprinklers move in an arc to cover the entire field.

△ Fig. 3.23 Sub-irrigation is a common method of artificially watering sugar cane fields in Florida, USA.

Controlling pests and diseases

If crops are attacked by pests and diseases, or if invasive weeds are allowed to grow up unchecked, then agricultural yields will fall. Intensive commercial farmers spray their crops with a wide range of chemicals produced synthetically in laboratories and designed to kill or control specific weeds, insects or **pathogens**. These are known as pesticides. There are three main types of pesticide: fungicides, **herbicides** and **insecticides**.

Fungicides, worth over US$20 billion, are sold by pharmaceutical companies to farmers every year to kill fungi that attack plants. For example, 14 different varieties of fungicide are available in the USA to control soya bean rust – a windblown disease that attacks the crop's leaves causing lesions and eventually killing the plant. Spraying young soya bean plants with fungicide can increase crop yields by as much as 20 per cent compared with untreated plants.

△ Fig. 3.24 Young soya bean plants being sprayed with fungicide in spring.

Herbicides are chemical sprays, used against weeds, which absorb the toxins through their roots or leaves. Most herbicides are selective in that they act only on specific **species** of weeds leaving the farmer's crop unharmed. The most widely used herbicide is glyphosate. More than 300 glyphosate herbicides manufactured by forty different companies are registered for use in Europe alone. It is sprayed on cereal crops including wheat, barley, oats, rye and maize.

Insecticides kill insects that attack crop plants. The most widely used insecticides are called neonicotinoids and are designed especially to kill sap-feeding insects such as aphids. Neonicotinoids are systemic, which means that the chemical is taken up by the plant either from its roots (as a seed coating before planting or soil drench) or through its leaves. The toxin remains active in the crop plant for many weeks, protecting it throughout the growing season. Aphids that eat any of the plant foliage are poisoned.

△ Fig. 3.25 A worker spraying glyphosate on a palm oil plantation in Malaysia.

While there is no doubt that the use of pesticides have increased agricultural yields and helped the world to feed a rapidly growing population, their use has had some serious ecological impacts. Non-selective or broad spectrum pesticides can cause considerable environmental damage because they destroy not just the target weed or insect but also harmless and potentially useful non-pest species.

For example, spraying a broad spectrum insecticide on cereal crops will kill aphids but also destroy ladybirds – a small beetle that is harmless to the crop plant and actually feeds on aphids. Destroying the ladybirds then breaks the **food chain** for birds such as swallows and swifts, which rely on ladybirds for an important part of their diet.

△ Fig. 3.26 English grain aphid on a barley plant.

Another serious ecological problem known as **bioaccumulation** can be caused by the use of **systemic pesticides**. This is the gradual build-up of pesticide-spread toxins in organisms in increasing amounts up the food chain. It particularly affects top predator animals and birds.

DDT was one of the first chemicals to be used as a pesticide in the 1950s. It was sprayed onto plants (**producers** at the lowest **trophic level** of the food chain) such as potato plants, which absorbed small quantities. Insects such as the potato beetle (a primary **consumer**) were poisoned when they began to eat the plant but did not die immediately so the concentration of toxins built up in their systems. Secondary consumers such as birds like the robin then ate many of the beetles, which meant that even higher levels of the toxin built up in their bodies. Finally, top consumers or apex predators such as the peregrine falcon, which consumed hundreds of robins, ingested the highest amounts of DDT of all because they were at the top of the food chain. The ingested DDT made it very difficult for the falcons to absorb calcium and the lack of calcium made the shell of their eggs very thin. As a result many eggs broke during incubation and populations of peregrine falcons were decimated.

△ Fig. 3.27 A plane spraying DDT in Georgia, USA, during the 1950s.

△ Fig. 3.28 Bioaccumulation of the DDT pesticide resulted in a catastrophic fall in peregrine falcon numbers.

The overuse of pesticides can lead to insects and weeds becoming resistant or immune to the toxins they carry. This means that pesticides may only be effective for a short time before a new one has to be synthesised, often containing higher levels of toxin than the previous one. For example, resistance can build up in an insect population if just a few of the target insects are able to survive the first spraying with the insecticide. Insect species reproduce rapidly, having many generations a year and as a result, the individuals that have survived quickly pass on their resistance to their offspring. If the same insecticide continues to be used too often, then most of the insect population will quickly develop immunity and the once-effective insecticide can no longer control the target insect at all.

On organic farms, alternatives to synthetic chemical-based methods of controlling pests, diseases and weed growth are used, for example:

- Pests are controlled by encouraging their natural predators to attack them. In Thailand, farmers attract tiny wasps on to their farms in order to kill the mealybugs that eat cassava plants.
- Rotation includes a regular fallow period so that pest populations are not allowed to build up in particular fields.
- Crops are grown in mixed cultures (with other crops) rather than in **monocultures** (on their own). Planting a variety of plant crops in a field increases the distance between plants of the same species, making it harder for pests to locate their main food crop.
- Labour intensive methods of weed and pest control can be used to avoid chemicals, such as hand pulling and hoeing and picking insects off plants by hand.
- Pesticides are available that use naturally occurring substances such as pyrethrum, an insecticide made from the dried flower heads of two species of chrysanthemum.

△ Fig. 3.29 Hoe weeding tomatoes on an organic farm.

Mechanisation

The use of machines and computer-based technologies as a substitute for human labour has enabled commercial farmers to significantly increase the productivity of their land. In the USA in 1940, the average farm fed 19 people; today it would feed 155 people. Machinery has helped to make farm work easier and faster and enabled land that was previously impossible to farm to be brought into cultivation. Farms have become larger and more efficient because they need fewer workers. Increasingly, modern farms use satellite imagery and GPS guidance in combination with robotically controlled machinery as a means of increasing agricultural yields. This is known as precision agriculture. Large areas of land often contain different soil types, moisture content and levels of nutrients. The use of **remote sensing** (the scanning of the Earth from satellites) and the generation of infra-red images of the land combined with GIS and GPS systems means that farmers can precisely identify what inputs – water, fertiliser, pesticides etc. – are needed for the different parts of their farm rather than treating all of the land as if it were the same. This enables farmers to both reduce costs and to increase yields.

Selective breeding

Selective breeding or artificial selection enables farmers to increase yields through only breeding from certain individual animals or plants. A dairy farmer may identify those cows that are producing the most milk in a herd and only breed from those animals. These cows then pass on their genes to their offspring and in time the farmer will have a whole herd of high-yielding cows. Similarly, an arable farmer may crossbreed a high grain-yielding variety of rice with a variety that is highly resistant to disease to create a hybrid that combines both advantages. The IR36 hybrid variety of rice was created by crossbreeding a high-yielding species,

△ Fig. 3.30 A field of high yielding hybrid paddy rice plants that do not require flooded fields in which to grow.

that suffered from lodging or falling over, with a strong-stemmed dwarf variety. The result was a high-yielding dwarf plant that no longer collapsed in the wind or when heavy seed heads developed. This hybrid formed part of what was known as the **Green Revolution** in farming.

Genetic modification (GM) or engineering

GM involves artificially changing the genetic structure of the cells of farm crops or animals by swapping genes within and across species to improve yields. It is selective breeding done in the laboratory rather than naturally. Genes can be introduced from one plant to another plant, from a plant to an animal and from a microorganism to a plant. For example, if a wild grass is discovered to possess a gene which makes it resistant to a chemical herbicide, then that gene could be introduced into a crop plant such as wheat. In the future this would mean that the herbicide for controlling weeds could be sprayed all over the wheat field and only kill the target weeds. About 85 per cent of the maize now grown in the world has been genetically modified to ensure that it is resistant to the herbicide glyphosate.

Controlling growing environments

One way of increasing productivity on a farm is to remove plants and animals entirely from the natural world and cultivate or tend to them in artificial conditions. The farmer then has complete control over all growing conditions: water, light, heat, the availability of food, and fertiliser. A greenhouse is a good example of a controlled environment. In the Netherlands, massive greenhouses are used to grow peppers in constant light conditions, which reduces their growing season by four weeks. This reduces the farmer's cost and increases profits. If extra carbon dioxide is pumped into the greenhouses then plants such as tomatoes will photosynthesise faster, which has the effect of increasing sugar production, improving flavour and yield. Hydroponics involves immersing plant roots only in a water solution of minerals and nutrients within a greenhouse. As no soil is involved, it offers farmers the possibility of high yields at reduced costs, which boosts profits. Hydroponics also enables the farmer to isolate growing plants from outside pests, diseases and weeds, which further

△ Fig. 3.31 Chickens in battery cages laying eggs.

reduces costs because less pesticide is used. Housing huge numbers of egg-laying hens permanently indoors in confined spaces in battery cages is a controlled farming environment that has generated opposition in recent years from many who support animal welfare and compassion in farming.

IMPACT OF AGRICULTURE

Overproduction and waste

The widespread use of intensive production methods in MEDCs (particularly in the USA and the countries of the European Union (EU)) means that more food is often produced than consumers require. The UN estimates that as much as one-third of all the food produced in the world each year is never consumed by people. When this figure is converted to calories, this means that about one in four calories intended for **consumption** never gets eaten. Around 550 billion cubic metres of water are wasted globally in growing crops that never reach the consumer. There are several reasons for the overproduction of food in MEDCs:

- In the USA and the EU, farmers receive guaranteed minimum prices for what they produce, irrespective of how much they produce. This system of paying **subsidies** is designed to protect the income of farmers if the prices of food products drop on the world market. The US government spends about US$10 billion a year on farm subsidies. If farmers produce more of a commodity than they can sell then the government buys up the surplus at the agreed price.

- Demand for food in many MEDCs is not increasing because of low population growth, which means the market for most farm products is saturated. For the last 20 years, the rate of global food production has increased faster than the rate of global population growth. The world already produces enough food to feed a population of 10 billion people – the global population is only supposed to reach 9.7 billion by 2050.

- Produce may not be harvested by farmers because of damage caused by pests, disease, and weather, or because its quality does not meet the exacting standards of retailers, especially multinational supermarket chains. Each year farmers in Europe are forced to throw away millions of tonnes of perfectly healthy and nutritious fruit and vegetables because they do not meet the 'cosmetic standards' (for example, without any blemishes or bruises and being the perfect colour, size and shape) required by supermarkets. 'Ugly' produce is rejected and wasted. As a result as much as 30 per cent of fruit and vegetable crops are never harvested.

As well as overproduction, another serious problem in many MEDCs is the wastage of food by consumers. Up to half of all the food that is bought in Europe and the USA is thrown away. Every year people in MEDCs waste almost as much food (222 million tonnes) as the entire food production of the countries of Sub-Saharan Africa (230 million tonnes). Some of this wastage is due to supermarket promotions such as 'buy one get one free' offers, which encourage consumers to buy more than they need. Poor packaging and consumer knowledge about storing foods at home is also a factor. If all fresh meat was sold by supermarkets in packaging that could be resealed, its fridge life would be extended significantly. Date labelling also leads to food wastage when consumers confuse 'use by' and 'sell by' dates and consequently throw away perfectly edible food.

Cash crops replacing food crops in LEDCs

In MEDCs almost all farms produce food in order to generate income for the farmer. In most **LEDCs (less economically developed countries)**, the majority of farmers own smallholdings of less than 0.02 sq km, which they operate on a subsistence or semi-subsistence basis. For these farmers, converting their land to produce a **cash crop** such as coffee – which can be exported for profit to MEDCs – has many attractions. A cash crop farmer will have cash to buy food locally, employ relatives and pay for family expenses such as medical and school bills. However, making the change can also have serious consequences for the farmer's family, the local **community** and the environment:

- Farmers have little power to set the price for their cash crops. This is determined by the wholesalers who act as buyers for large manufacturers and retailers in MEDCs. Wholesalers will always seek to reduce purchase prices to a minimum.
- Farmers are very vulnerable to changes in demand (and therefore prices) for cash crops in MEDCs. For example health advice to consume less refined sugar, give up smoking and drink less coffee will affect sugar cane, tobacco and coffee farmers in LEDCs if demand falls.
- If cash income drops, farmers may not be able to buy enough food from other sources and their families may suffer from **malnutrition** or be forced to migrate to work in towns and cities.
- Because small plots of land are not really viable for cash crop production, many farmers allow their land to be absorbed into large estates or plantations that then have the power to control what they produce and where they live.

- Converting from subsistence farming to cash-crop monoculture can have serious impacts on the ecosystem. Cash crops (especially fruit production) require much greater volumes of water than subsistence crops like maize. As a result, local water supplies may become depleted. Planting the same crop every year quickly removes the particular nutrients required by the plant and expensive chemical fertilisers are then required to replace them. These may pollute water tables through run-off and further reduce the profits of the farmer.

CAUSES AND IMPACTS OF SOIL EROSION

Causes of soil erosion

If not managed carefully, intensive farming can lead to both the **overcultivation** and **overgrazing** of the land. Both factors can cause serious soil erosion when topsoil is washed or blown away by heavy rain or strong winds. Overcultivation is the continuous and excessive use of farmland for crops to a point where soils are depleted of nutrients and the soil structure is severely broken down by a lack of organic matter. Overgrazing degrades the land by stripping away its vegetation cover as a result of the density of livestock being greater than the **carrying capacity** of the soil. Removing the protective cover of vegetation and its roots, and allowing the soil structure to disintegrate to a point where the land no longer has an economic or ecological value, is termed land degradation. Often, land degradation leads to soil erosion (the removal of topsoil). It is estimated that the world has already lost almost half of its topsoil through erosion in the last 150 years.

Overgrazing by increasing numbers of livestock farmers is a particular problem in many dry regions of the world such as the Sahel in Africa. Higher density farming means that cattle herds now tend to be fenced into confined areas and are no longer allowed to roam in search of fresh pasture and water. The situation is made worse by the construction of boreholes at specific locations to bring underground water to the surface and create waterholes. This allows animals to stay all year in places that previously they may have only grazed for a few months. Consequently they gather around the borehole and overgraze the surrounding area causing serious soil erosion and **desertification**.

Impacts of soil erosion

Topsoil layers contain most nutrients, so soil erosion quickly removes essential nutrients from the land. Soil nutrients are also lost from degraded soils through leaching, which is the soaking away of soluble nutrients because, as a result of overcultivation or grazing, there are too few plant roots in the soil to absorb the nutrients and lock them away in plant tissue.

Soil erosion in dry regions can lead to once fertile land coming to resemble a desert. As water tables drop, salinisation (contamination by soluble salts) of the remaining soil water occurs and surface water features such as rivers and lakes disappear. This process is known as desertification. The United Nations estimates that as a result of desertification, 24 billion tonnes of fertile topsoil disappear from around the world every year. This amount of soil could support the growing of 20 million tonnes of food grain. A total of 110 countries are vulnerable to the effects of desertification.

As well as desertification, other serious environmental impacts of soil erosion include **habitat** loss and the silting up of rivers. Exposed soil is easily washed off the land into nearby streams and rivers by heavy rainfall – a process known as **sedimentation**. In Central America, soil eroded from plantations and farmlands in Honduras, Guatemala, Belize and Mexico is carried as sediments by rivers into the Gulf of Honduras. Here the sediment is causing serious damage to the Mesoamerican barrier reef which stretches for over 1000 km along the coast. Damaging pesticides and fertilisers are also dissolved in the sediment. The Mesoamerican Reef is the largest barrier reef in the western hemisphere. As well as a dazzling array of coral, the reef is a habitat for hundreds of fish species, marine turtles and sharks. Along its shores, mangrove swamps provide a habitat for fish and shore birds and the trees protect the people of the coast from the effects of hurricanes.

△ Fig. 3.32 Map of the Mesoamerican Reef.

△ Fig. 3.33 Coral of the Mesoamerican Reef.

Soil erosion can also lead to the displacement of people when they are forced off the land they have been farming because of desertification. A good example is the infamous *Dust Bowl* event of the dry High Plains region (especially the states of Texas and Oklahoma) of the United States in the 1930s which forced tens of thousands of farmers and their families

△ Fig. 3.34 A dust storm of eroded soil in Kansas in 1933.

△ Fig. 3.35 A farming family from Missouri escaping the Dust Bowl in 1937.

to abandon the land. For the previous ten years, farmers had been deep-ploughing the grassland and removing the natural vegetation cover of deep-rooted grasses which held the soil in place. This exposed the light, sandy, loose soils. In the 1930s, three long periods of **drought** combined with fierce winds removed the region's topsoil. The unanchored soil turned to dust and was carried away in huge clouds known as 'black rollers' which travelled across the country as far as New York.

In 2012, millions of people of the Sahel region of Africa faced **famine** as their crops failed and livestock died. The Sahel is a dry region, 1000 km wide, which lies to the south of the Sahara Desert and stretches for 5500 km from the Atlantic Ocean to the Red Sea, incorporating areas of over a dozen countries. In 2012, a natural event in the form of a prolonged drought combined with human factors such as overgrazing, over cultivation and the removal of forest cover for fuelwood, to cause serious land degradation, soil erosion and desertification. The United Nations World Food Programme stepped in to distribute emergency food supplies to over ten million people.

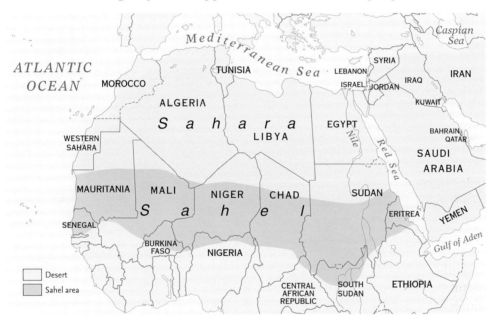

△ Fig. 3.36 The Sahel region.

△ Fig. 3.37 Drought in the Sahel region of Mali.

MANAGING SOIL EROSION

There are a number of measures that farmers can take to reduce the likelihood of erosion and to conserve the soil. If the risk of erosion is to be managed successfully, it is very important for the farmer to know the capability of the soils and terrain of the land really well and to decide upon different land uses accordingly, for example, growing pasture on steeper slopes with shallow soils and only ploughing lower flatter land with deeper soils. The Dust Bowl disaster shows what can happen when farmers have unreasonable expectations of soils.

Vegetation cover

This is the most effective way of preventing soil erosion. Plants and trees build root systems that anchor the soil in place, and add decaying organic matter that improves water retention. Vegetation cover also reduces the speed of water run-off and the likelihood of the wind removing soil particles. Regularly adding a mulch of organic matter such as manure to the soil is also effective as it allows the soil to soak up water slowly, protects it from raindrop impact and encourages soil to clod. This is the amalgamation or joining together of smaller soil particles into larger pieces more resistant to erosion. It is very important for a farmer to maintain as much of the existing vegetation cover such as hedges on the farm as possible. Grubbing up hedges (digging up hedges from the ground) to make larger fields more easily accessible by machinery may improve profitability but will also make the land more vulnerable to soil erosion. Hedges not only protect the soil as natural wind breaks, but are also the habitat of insects and birds that will prey on crop pests such as aphids. In addition to conserving existing vegetation cover, farmers can also use strategic planting of new vegetation, such as native trees on areas like steep hillsides and river banks most vulnerable to erosion. Wind breaks are commonly used to help prevent soil erosion. These are lines of trees planted to face the **prevailing wind** and filter out 50–60 per cent of its strength. A windbreak will significantly reduce wind on its leeward side to a distance of ten times its height. In order to combat erosion, many farmers will also ensure, through using cover crops, that soil is never left bare at any time. Cover crops such as clover and oats also help to suppress weeds and improve soil quality.

△ Fig. 3.38 A windbreak of trees beside a wheat field.

△ 3.39 Field hedges act as an important wind break.

Cropping systems and ploughing techniques

The decisions a farmer makes about the type of crops to grow and the pattern and sequence in which they will be grown are important when it comes to reducing the risk of soil erosion. Choosing to rotate crops between different areas of a farm as opposed to mono-cropping will significantly reduce the risk of soil erosion. Soils in fields that are regularly rotated benefit from higher levels of fertility and an improved structure compared with those in mono-cropped fields.

△ Fig. 3.40 Turmeric plants intercropped with coconut trees in Pakistan.

Intercropping (growing two or more crops in the same field or area) also helps to reduce the risk of soil erosion. Mixed cropping is the simplest form of intercropping and involves the intermingling of plants randomly over the area with no row arrangement, such as the practice of commonly growing maize, beans and squash together in the countries of Central America. Row or strip cropping is more structured and involves different crops being planted beside each other in alternate rows. The alternating plants need to be carefully selected to complement each other in order to gain the maximum erosion protection, for example, crops with wide shallow roots are planted alongside crops that are deeper rooted. Soil fertility and structure can also be maintained by planting crops together that draw upon different mineral ions or have growing seasons of different lengths. The decaying organic matter of the first crop to be harvested can then be left to provide nutrients for later maturing crops. The intercropping of leguminous nitrogen-fixing crops such as beans and peas alongside cereal crops will help ensure the continual replenishment of nutrients in the soil.

Contour ploughing is an important technique for preventing soil erosion. It involves ploughing furrows across rather than down slopes, following the natural contours of the land. This creates furrows that curve around the land and are mostly level. Natural water breaks are then created by the furrows, which allow rainwater more time to soak into the soil and prevent rapid run-off along gullies down the slope. In addition, a farmer may construct a bund along the contour to slow down the seepage of water and soil down the slope and encourage greater water uptake by the soil. A bund is made of stones or soil and the steeper the slope, the closer they tend to be. A common type of bund is the terrace commonly used by rice farmers in countries of Southeast Asia. These have the effect of evening out the slope of the land around each contour to create flat steps or benches in the hillside upon which the crop is grown.

△ Fig. 3.41 Rice terraces in Vietnam.

SUSTAINABLE AGRICULTURE

Sustainable agriculture is farming that seeks to balance profitable yields of crops and livestock with protecting and conserving the ecosystems upon which all life depends, ensuring the fair and ethical working conditions and remuneration of workers and safeguarding the health and welfare of consumers and all farmed species. This form of agriculture is guided by the principle of **stewardship** rather than the exploitation of **natural resources**. It enables farmers to produce food in a way that does not compromise the ability of future generations of farmers to do the same. In this sense, sustainable agriculture is a good example of **sustainable development**. Farmers look to work with the natural processes of the ecosystems in which they operate to enrich and protect soils and fight pests and diseases. They also commit to animal welfare standards and ensure that their workers are paid at least the legal minimum wage of the country in which they farm.

Crop rotation is central to the operation of sustainable farms. It enables soil fertility to be maintained and increased and soil structure to improve naturally through growing different crops in succession. Ensuring that leguminous crops such as soya beans are part of the crop rotation cycle has the effect of adding or fixing nutrients, particularly nitrogen, in the soil. For example, maize grown in a field that last season grew soya beans will need much less added nitrogen than if maize was grown continuously. Rotation also helps in the natural management of crop pests and diseases without the use of chemical pesticides. Continuous cropping of one plant species in the same place guarantees pests that feed and reproduce on that crop a source of food and habitat year on year and so their populations grow. If their host crop is not grown for a year as part of a rotation then their reproductive cycle will be broken and their numbers will decline. Using cover crops to ensure that soil is protected at all times will naturally help to control weeds and reduce the need for pesticides.

Rotational grazing of animals is practised on sustainable farms for the same reasons as crop rotation. Continuous grazing on the same pasture season after season results in declining yields, such as of milk or meat, because the forage (crops grown to be eaten) never has time to regain lost nutrients and energy levels. Rotational livestock grazing involves a farmer dividing pasture into different paddocks. Only one paddock of pasture is then used by the animals at any given time. Livestock is moved from one paddock to another in sequence. Being left to 'rest' enables the forage crops to restore lost energy reserves and vigour and deepen their root systems.

When enriching the soil to replace lost nutrients, sustainable farmers rely upon naturally occurring materials and avoid synthetic fertilisers. Approaches include leaving decaying crop remains in the soil after harvest, ploughing cover crops into the soil, ensuring nitrogen-fixing legumes are part of the rotation cycle and adding composted plant material and animal manure.

The **biocontrol** of crop pests and diseases on sustainable farms often begins with a farmer selecting crops that are well adapted to the specific site conditions of the farm. This could, for example, be a crop selectively bred to be drought-resistant if the farm is in a dry region. Crops may also be grown that have been crossbred to be resistant to a particular range of pests and diseases. The Alizze and Harnas hybrid varieties of oilseed rape have a high degree of natural resistance to canker and leaf spot disease and the XL6 strain of hybrid rice offers resistance to blast and sheath blight. Other pest control measures include using farming practices that encourage healthy populations of birds and insects on to the farm. These 'natural enemies' include insects such as ladybirds, spiders and hoverfly larvae, which feed on plant-eating pests such as aphids and caterpillars. For centuries, the African bollworm has fed on a wide range of crops, including cotton, tomato, potatoes and maize. In recent years a wasp called trichogramma has been bred in laboratories and released in huge numbers when bollworm eggs are identified on crops. The wasp is parasitoid in that it lays its eggs on or in other insects, including the bollworm. When the wasp larvae hatch, they feed on and kill their host. In Europe, the bird-cherry oat aphid is a common pest on cereal crops; in Sweden, encouraging natural predators, including ground-dwelling beetles and spiders, to attack the aphids has resulted in a 303 kg (15 per cent) increase in spring barley yields per 10 000 square metres.

Naturally occurring chemical pathogens that kill pest fungi, bacteria and viruses can be obtained from diseased insects and incorporated into bio pesticides. One example is a virus pathogen called PlxyGV that is used as a bio pesticide to kill diamond moth caterpillars – a serious pest of brassicas including cabbages and cauliflower.

Agriculture is the major consumer of water, accounting for 70 per cent of the planet's **freshwater** withdrawals each year. Sustainable farmers look for ways to increase their water-use efficiency and protect water in the environment:

- Targeted drip irrigation systems waste little water and are less affected by **evapotranspiration** than other forms of irrigation.
- Low-pressure sprinkler systems for larger areas, and scheduling the timing of applications reduces waste and evapotranspiration losses, for example, during the night and avoiding windy times when water will drift into areas that do not need watering.
- Rainwater run-off from roofs can be harvested to use as 'grey water' for cleaning yards or irrigation. A roof area of 1800 square metres receiving 600 mm of rain a year will yield a harvest of 1188 cubic metres of rainwater, which is equivalent to 6000 average-sized baths.
- Earthen irrigation channels can be replaced with concrete linings, and fields levelled off, to reduce water loss through seepage.
- Technology such as neutron probes can be used to detect the existing moisture content of soils before irrigating. The amount of water applied will then precisely meet plant needs and minimise waste.

THE ARAL SEA

The Aral Sea, straddling the border of Kazakhstan and Uzbekistan in central Asia, once covered an area of 68 000 sq km (equivalent in size to the island of Sri Lanka). At one time it was the fourth largest inland water body on Earth. Since the 1960s, the sea has been steadily shrinking in size, and by 2007 it had been reduced to just 10 per cent of its original area. The accumulation of soluble salts such as sodium, magnesium and calcium through salinisation means that today the open dry seabed area is a salt desert

△ Fig. 3.42 Location of the Aral Sea.

and a source of salt dust. In 2010, a NASA satellite captured the process of desertification occurring as wind eroded and transported away millions of tonnes of salty soil from the dry eastern basin of the Aral Sea. In 2014, this area was renamed Aralkum.

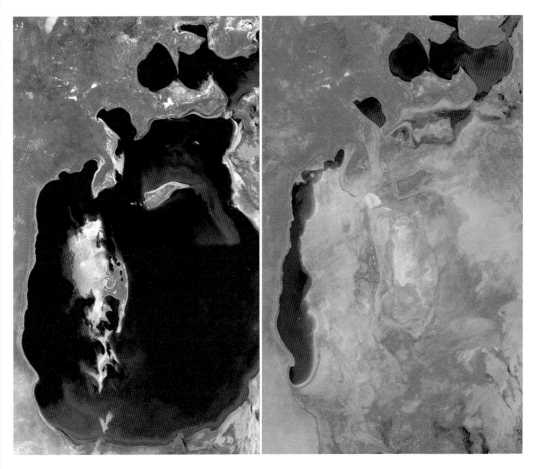

△ Fig. 3.43 Desertification of the Aral Sea in 1989 and 2009.

The causes of the desertification of the Aral Sea began in the 1960s when water was diverted away from its two main tributary rivers by the former Soviet Union (over 100 million cubic metres every year) to irrigate cotton fields and arable crops in the surrounding region. Between 1960 and 1980, traditional fishing communities employing tens of thousands of people living in communities around the Aral Sea, together with 90 per cent of its fish species, were wiped out. In the same time period, 80 000 sq km of irrigated land were established and water entering the Aral Sea declined by 80 per cent. The drop in the volume of water also resulted in an increase in the concentration of chemical pesticides (used in the monoculture of cotton) in soils, which then contaminated drinking water and poisoned the land many semi-subsistence nomadic farmers relied upon for their survival.

△ Fig. 3.44 Windblown soil erosion occurring in the eastern basin in 2010.

△ Fig. 3.45 Cotton plants with bolls ready for harvesting.

△ Fig. 3.46 Fishing boats in the desert that was formerly the Aral Sea.

Since 1994, some progress has been made to combat desertification and restore the Aral Sea. An international project is focusing on colonising the dry, sandy and salty Aral Sea bed with plants to create vegetation cover to stabilise the soils and improve fertility. The restoration project uses phytomelioration techniques involving the planting of halophyte (salt-tolerant) plants adapted to growing in deserts and dry steppe regions such as those in central Asia. Over 200 species of halophytic plants have now colonised the saline soils of the bare seabed. It is anticipated that conserving the soils of the Aral Sea in this way will take many decades but ecologists are encouraged to see colonisation of new areas now occurring through natural seed dispersal from plants that were originally placed in the ground by hand.

△ Fig. 3.47 Vegetation cover of between 30 and 40 per cent will begin to stabilise the soil and increase its fertility.

End of topic checklist

Key terms

absolute poverty, acidification, acid rain, agriculture, algal bloom, atmosphere, bioaccumulation, biocontrol, carbon cycle, cash crop, commercial, desertification, drainage, economically active, ecosystem, environment, erosion, eutrophication, evapotranspiration, famine, farming, food chain, fossil fuel, genetic engineering, Green Revolution, grey water, habitat, hydroponics, irrigation, land degradation, mechanisation, mineral ion, natural resources, nutrient cycle, nutrient deficiency, overcultivation, overgrazing, overpopulation, permeability, photosynthesis, precision agriculture, productivity, remote sensing, respiration, rotation, salinisation, sedimentation, selective breeding, shifting cultivation, slash and burn, soil solution, soil structure, stewardship, subsidy, subsistence, sustainable agriculture, sustainable development, weathering

Important vocabulary

acid, acidic, adaptation, aggregate, alkaline, arable, bind, biopesticide, borehole, broad spectrum, bund, carbon dioxide, chlorophyll, clay, clump, consumer, contamination, crop, cultivate, decomposition, deficiency, deplete, disease, displacement, drainage, efficient, enzyme, ethical, farm, fertile, fertiliser, fodder, fungicide, gene, glucose, greenhouse, halophyte, herbicide, humus, hurricane, hybrid, infertile, infiltrate, inorganic, insecticide, intensive, leaching, leguminous, loam, malnutrition, manganese, market, migration, mineral, mono-cropping, mulch, nitrogen, nomadic, non-selective, nutrient, optimal, organic, oxygen, particle, pastoral, pathogen, pesticide, phosphorous, phytomelioration, plantation, potassium, predator, producer, protein, remuneration, reservoir, Sahel, sand, sediment, sedimentation, silt, steppe, synthetic, terrace, topsoil, waste, waterhole, water table, welfare, windbreak, yield

During your study of this topic you should have learned:

◯ Soil is made up of organic matter, inorganic materials, water and air.

◯ Clay, silt, sand and loam are soils with very different properties.

◯ Nitrogen, phosphorous, potassium and magnesium are essential for plant growth in different ways.

◯ Organic matter in soil performs four very important functions.

End of topic checklist (continued)

○ The pH of a soil solution will have an important effect on how well plants absorb the nutrients they require.

○ Farms are subsistence or commercial and the differences between them.

○ Commercial farms are mostly arable, pastoral or mixed.

○ Commercial farmers are able to increase the yield or productivity of their farms through the use of many different intensive farming methods.

○ A number of serious environmental problems can result from poorly managed intensive farming.

○ Overproduction of food is occurring in many MEDCs.

○ There are costs and benefits associated with subsistence farmers in LEDCs converting their farms to produce cash crops for export.

○ Soil erosion has many causes and soil degradation can lead to desertification.

○ Farmers can use a number of strategies to protect and conserve the soils on their farms.

○ Sustainable agriculture involves farming the land in a way that produces profitable food while at the same time protecting and conserving the environment for future generations.

○ The Aral Sea is an example of how the overexploitation of the land can lead to desertification and long-term projects are now underway to restore its environment.

The questions for Section 3 start on page 244.

Human life depends on a tiny fraction of the world's water, which is constantly recycled between the oceans, land and atmosphere. Freshwater reserves are unevenly distributed, which creates water-rich and water-poor regions (in which shortages occur). Millions lack access to both safe drinking water and improved sanitation facilities and are affected by water-borne diseases as a result.

Improving water quality and sanitation for the poorest requires sustainable development that uses appropriate technology and the expertise of local communities. Diseases contracted from contaminated water such as malaria and cholera are being effectively controlled in many areas.

Water pollution such as marine oil slicks is a worldwide environmental issue and many countries have responded by introducing laws and agreeing to international conventions to prevent it.

CONTENTS

LEARNING OBJECTIVES

Describe the distribution of the Earth's water.

Describe and interpret the water cycle.

Describe the sources of fresh water used by people.

Describe the different ways fresh water can be used.

Compare the availability of safe drinking water (potable water) in different parts of the world.

Describe and evaluate multipurpose dam projects.

Describe the sources of water pollution.

Describe and explain the impact of pollution of fresh water on people and on the environment.

Describe and explain strategies for improving water quality.

Describe the life cycle of the malaria parasite.

Describe and evaluate strategies to control malaria.

Describe strategies to control cholera.

Describe the impact of a named multipurpose dam scheme.

Describe the causes, impact and management of pollution in a named body of water.

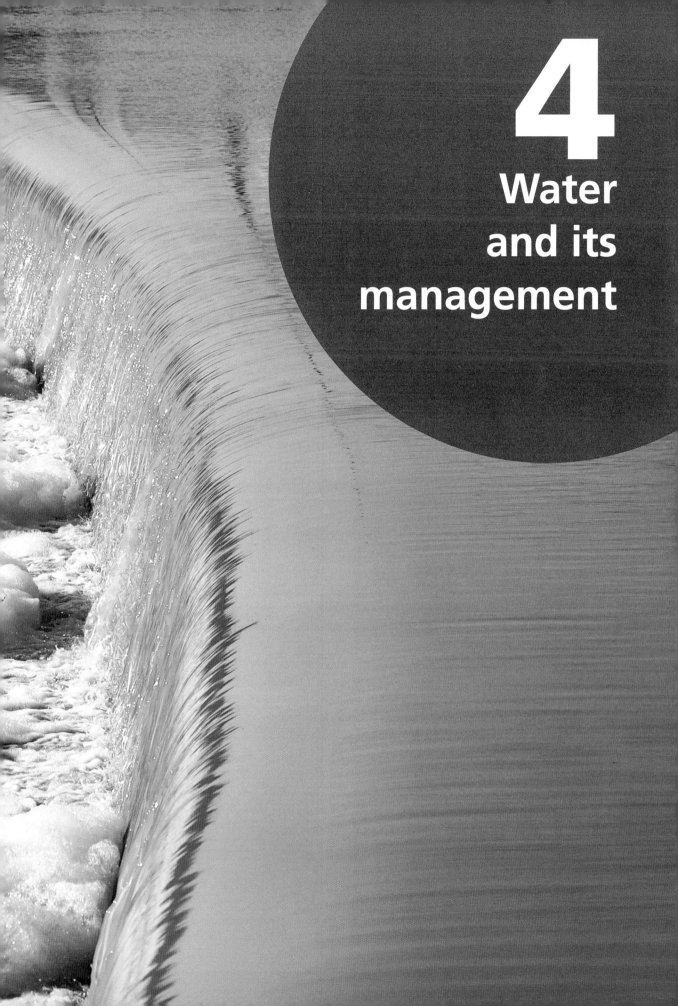

4
Water and its management

GLOBAL WATER DISTRIBUTION

The world's total water supply amounts to approximately 1386 cubic metres. Figure 4.1 (first bar) shows that over 97 per cent of this water is saline and mostly located in the oceans. Only a tiny proportion of this total (2.5 per cent) is the **fresh water** that humans require to sustain life (middle bar). Of this fresh water, over two-thirds is locked up in glaciers and ice caps and almost all the rest is stored as **groundwater** (water in the soil or held in pores of **rock**). Surface fresh water (third bar), which is the source of the water people consume around the world, represents only slightly more than 1 per cent of the total fresh water available (0.0067 per cent of the Earth's total water). Almost 90 per cent of the planet's fresh water is stored in ice and lakes with the remaining 10 per cent being held in five other main stores. Considering that rivers are the main source of water for the world's **population**, it is clear that human life depends on just 0.0002 per cent of the planet's total water.

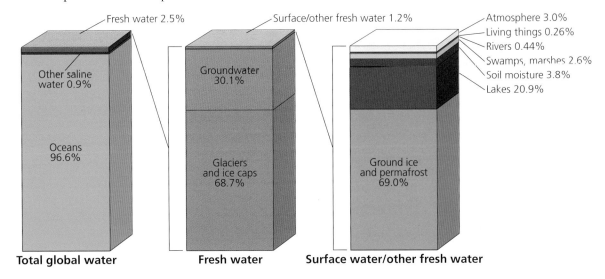

Δ Fig. 4.1 The locations of water on Earth.

THE WATER CYCLE

The volume of water on Earth has remained much the same for billions of years because it moves continuously and very efficiently around the world. The **water cycle**, driven by the sun's energy, also known as the hydrological cycle, describes this movement of water between the oceans, the land and the **atmosphere** and is summarised in Figure 4.3.

- The sun heats the water held on the Earth's surface in oceans, seas and lakes. Some of this water is turned into **water vapour** (water in the form of an invisible

Δ Fig. 4.2 Victoria reservoir, Sri Lanka – rivers are the world's most important source of fresh water.

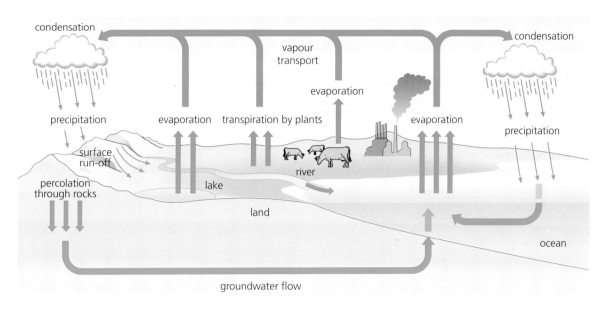

△ Fig. 4.3 A summary of the water cycle.

gas) through the process of **evaporation**. Some water vapour is added by plants through the process of **transpiration** (the evaporation of water moving through the plant from its leaves).

- This warm moist water vapour rises because it is less dense than the surrounding atmosphere. As it rises the air cools and the water vapour condenses (turns back into water droplets) into clouds, which air currents transport around the globe.

△ Fig. 4.4 Plants intercept some precipitation.

- These water droplets then fall as **precipitation** (rain, snow, fog, mist, dew) onto the land and oceans. Some will be intercepted to provide the water that plants and humans require for their survival, for example, taken up by plant roots or collected in reservoirs. Water will also be captured and stored in freshwater lakes or in ice caps or glaciers.
- Most of the precipitation, however, will flow across or run off the surface of the land and into rivers or infiltrate the ground through **percolation**. Rivers return the water to the oceans. Some of the water that seeps underground through **infiltration** will be stored in **aquifers**

△ Fig. 4.5 Ice caps such as the Greenland ice cap will capture and store some precipitation.

(layers of **permeable rock** that absorb water) while the remainder will eventually seep back into the ocean as **groundwater flow**.

WATER SUPPLY

Humans cannot live without water. Not only is it an essential **natural resource** for drinking, cooking and sanitation, it is also the basis of all food production and a great many industrial operations. The two major sources of water are groundwater and surface water.

Groundwater

Groundwater is the world's most important source of fresh water. It is found in aquifers below the land surface. An aquifer is a layer of rock that is both porous (absorbs water) and permeable (allows water to percolate through it). Some rocks such as sandstone or limestone are able to absorb and store percolating water because they have a loose structure with relatively large air gaps between the rock particles. Water collects in these spaces or pores. Generally aquifers are found at shallow depths of between 200 and 700 metres. At greater depths, groundwater becomes increasingly saline. It is estimated that the total amount of the world's groundwater is equivalent to a 180-metre deep lake covering the entire surface of the world. The water in an aquifer can be held beneath the Earth's surface for many thousands of years before eventually entering the oceans as groundwater flow. Hydrologists sometimes refer to such ancient reserves as 'fossil water'.

Water is extracted from aquifers from an **artesian well**, created by drilling an underground pipe down from the surface to the aquifer (Figure 4.6). Natural pressure in the aquifer may mean that the water rises up through the pipe without the need for pumps. Natural pressure can build up when there is an **impermeable** and non-porous rock layer such as clay above and below the aquifer. Such wells are known as 'flowing' artesian wells. Aquifers with insufficient natural pressure, or in which natural pressure has dropped, may require a pumping system on the surface.

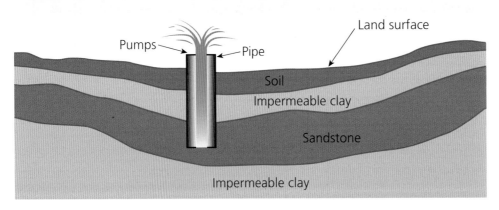

△ Fig. 4.6 An artesian well.

One of the largest aquifers, with an estimated 64 900 cubic metres of groundwater, is found beneath the Great Artesian Basin of Australia

(Figure 4.7). This basin underlies 23 per cent of the country and provides the only reliable source of fresh water for millions living in the interior.

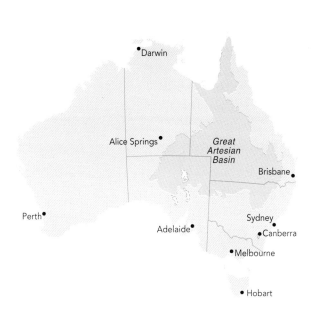

△ Fig. 4.7 The Great Artesian Basin.

△ Fig. 4.8 A windmill pumping water from an aquifer in Queensland, Australia.

In many parts of the world, pumping water out of the ground is occurring faster than the aquifers are being replenished by **surface run-off** and percolation of rainwater. This is called 'groundwater depletion'. Some of the effects can include the drying up of wells as the **water table** drops, land subsidence, and saline contamination as saltwater forces it way into the lowering aquifer when its height drops below sea level. As the depth of water increases, water must be pumped further to the surface, requiring larger pumps and more energy. This can lead to a higher cost for extracting the water than the income gained from using or selling it. Land subsidence or collapse can occur as underground rock drops because particles dry out and contract. The problem of groundwater depletion is increasingly found in areas of the world in both **MEDCs** and **LEDCs** where population is growing rapidly. The population of the state of Florida in the United States has risen from just 3 million in 1950 to 20 million today. Over 90 per cent of Florida's water used to supply households, farms and businesses comes from the Floridian limestone aquifer that sits below impermeable layers of clay. Because of increasing demand from people and **agriculture**, the aquifer level is dropping. About 450 litres of water is used by each Florida resident every day. A daily total of 4 billion litres alone is used to irrigate lawns and landscape features.

Groundwater levels in many areas of India such as Bundelkhand are also plunging as demands from households, farming and **industry** rise. For the 21 million people of Bundelkhand, groundwater pumping is free, and this, combined with the right of everyone to pump water from their land has led to **overconsumption** by farmers. The fact that the water in many rivers is unfit for drinking and that pipe leakages can result in water wastage levels of 40 per cent in towns and cities, has made the situation even worse. In the past 20 years changes in the pattern of the annual monsoon rains have resulted in less and more irregular rain – up to 50 per cent less in some districts. **Droughts** have become severe and the groundwater reserves are now being replenished at a much slower rate than previously. Water tables have dropped and deeper wells are now required to extract water for **irrigation**. Since 2010, 70 per cent of the hand pumps, tanks and ponds used for drinking have dried up.

△ Fig. 4.9 Irrigation of a golf course in Florida.

△ Fig. 4.10 A woman collecting water from a small spring in Bundelkhand, India.

Surface water

Streams, rivers, lakes and natural springs are considered surface water sources. Reservoirs, created from the damming and back flooding of rivers along their valleys, are also included in this category. Although together they account for only 1.2 per cent of the world's fresh water, they are vitally important, with millions of litres being extracted every day for domestic and commercial use.

Two million residents (and 40 million tourists each year) of the metropolitan area of Las Vegas in Nevada in the United States are almost entirely dependent on the River Colorado for their water. Only 15 per cent of the water they require is extracted from underground aquifers. Las Vegas was established in 1905 in the Mohave Desert. As the population began to grow, the Hoover Dam was constructed in the 1930s across the River Colorado to create the Lake Mead reservoir (Figure 4.11) to supply fresh water to the city.

Today Las Vegas is facing a water crisis because water extraction from Lake Mead is occurring at a faster rate than tributary streams and rivers of the River Colorado can replenish it. A 14-year drought is causing the reservoir to shrink, revealing what locals refer to as a 'bathtub ring' around the edge, which shows by how much it has dropped from its original height. If shrinkage continues at the same rate there is a danger that Lake Mead's water level will drop below the height of the intake valves and pipes that carry its water to Las Vegas.

In response, the city legislature has passed a sustainability plan to reduce its water usage by 30 per cent by 2023.

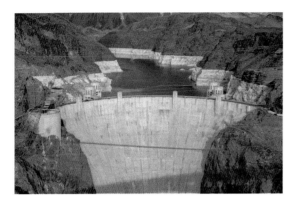

△ Fig. 4.11 Lake Mead reservoir behind the Hoover Dam revealing its 'bathtub rings'.

△ Fig. 4.12 New housing areas of Las Vegas close to the Spring Mountains.

Desalination

Global demand for fresh water is rising by 640 billion litres a year as populations grow and living standards rise. In many parts of the world, groundwater reserves are already seriously depleted and in some huge arid areas containing millions of people such as Australia and the Middle East there is no surface water in the form of rivers and lakes. This, combined with the possible effects of **climate change** making rainfall less predictable and droughts more frequent, has led to an increasing number of countries investing in **desalination** plants. Desalination involves removing dissolved salt from seawater and brackish (slightly salty) water from places such as river estuaries, and also treating waste water (mainly sewerage) to make it reusable for drinking. In 2015, a total of 18 426 desalination plants were operating in 120 countries. Together these plants provided water for 300 million people who nevertheless constituted less than 0.5 per cent of the world's population. By 2025, this proportion is expected to increase to over ten per cent. Two of the largest desalination plants in the world are at Ra's Al-Khair in Saudi Arabia and Carlsbad in California. Israel produces the highest proportion (40 per cent) of its domestic water from desalination. The main obstacle facing greater investment in desalinating water, particularly in LEDCs, is its high cost of production compared with groundwater and surface water extraction. At US$3 per cubic metre, desalination remains about twice as expensive as treating rainwater or recycling waste water because the technological processes used are very energy-intensive and require the construction of large processing plants.

△ Fig. 4.13 Desalination plant in Hamburg harbour, Germany.

WATER USAGE

The population of the world uses 9 billion cubic metres of water a year. Globally, and on average, 70 per cent of this water **consumption** occurs in agriculture, 20 per cent in industry and 10 per cent in domestic household use. However these are average figures and exactly how water is used in each of these categories in a particular country depends very much on its level of **economic development**. Generally speaking, this is true also of individual water consumption. On average, each person in the world consumes 1385 cubic metres of water a year, but in the United States, the figure is 2842 cubic metres, in India it is 1089 cubic metres and in Botswana it is 125 cubic metres. So the level of economic development of a country may determine not only how much water a person is likely to use but also how water use is distributed between the three main uses of agriculture, industry and domestic consumption.

	Africa	Europe	South America	North America
Agriculture use (per cent)	85	35	71	39
Industry use (per cent)	10	16	19	14
Domestic use (per cent)	5	49	10	47

△ Table 4.1 Water consumption by category in four regions of the world.

As the table above suggests, the most important factor affecting the distribution of water use in a particular country is its level of economic development and prosperity. Generally, LEDCs such as Zambia will use most of their water in agriculture (76 per cent) because most people are working either on **commercial farms** or as **subsistence farmers**. Irrigation methods used will also tend to be the least efficient in terms of wastage and evaporation, such as surface field flooding or sprinkler systems as opposed to drip or subsurface operations. While LEDCs may have significant primary industries, such as copper mining in Zambia, big **manufacturing** industries requiring large inputs of water tend not to form an important part of the economy. In many LEDCs, manufacturing is mostly small scale and occurs mainly in small workshops or at home and involves much less demand for water. Consequently, in most LEDCs, water use in the industrial sector is much smaller than in agriculture (7.5 per cent in Zambia). In LEDCs, the use of water in the domestic sector will tend to be much less for a number of reasons. Firstly, many people, particularly in rural areas, may not have piped water supplies and will have to rely on collecting water from wells or rivers. This can be time consuming and exhausting so only the minimum water required for drinking, cooking and sanitation is gathered, and unsurprisingly, there is little waste. Secondly, standards of living, particularly in terms of available expendable income tend to be much lower than in MEDCs. This, combined with a lack of electricity in some areas, means that there are far fewer modern domestic water-consuming appliances such as washing machines and dishwashers. In Zambia, 16.5 per cent of water is used in the domestic household sector.

△ Fig. 4.14 Children collecting water for domestic use in Zambia.

△ Fig. 4.15 A small-scale farmer irrigating his sugar cane crop, Mazabuka, Zambia.

Country	Zambia	Belgium
Gross national income per person (US$)	1112.8	46784.7
Employment in industry (per cent)	7.1	23.4
Employment in agriculture (per cent)	72.2	1.2
Average life expectancy at birth (years)	57.5	80.5
Infant mortality rate per 1000 live births	65.5	3.2
Access to safe water (per cent)	63.2	100
World Bank wealth ranking (of 183 countries)	135	21

△ Table 4.2 Comparing selected economic and social development indicators: Zambia and New Zealand.

In many MEDCs such as Belgium, the pattern of water use moves away from agriculture (4 per cent) and is dominated more by the industrial (62 per cent) and domestic (34 per cent) sectors. Belgium earns only 2 per cent of its national income each year from agriculture compared with 98 per cent from manufacturing industries and services such as banking and insurance. Farming in Belgium is intensive, which means that it relies heavily on modern machinery and technology and is very efficient when it comes to water use, ensuring that both the volume used and wastage is very low compared with LEDCs such as Zambia. Belgium is a highly-**industrialised country** and many of its large-scale manufacturing industries such as food processing, chemical production and steel making require huge quantities of water compared with farming. Over 50 per cent of Belgium's electricity is generated from **nuclear power** stations, which is another example of an industry that requires huge quantities of water for steam generation and cooling.

As one of the wealthiest countries in the world, living standards are high and homes and lifestyles reflect this. Not only are water-consuming items such as dishwashers common in homes, but many also have multiple showers, baths and toilets in additional bathrooms. Millions of litres of water are also used each year to water gardens and fill ponds. Outside of the home, many leisure and convenience activities such as swimming pools or car washes also consume large quantities of water.

△ Fig. 4.16 A petrochemical manufacturing plant at Antwerp, Belgium.

△ Fig. 4.17 Cooling towers of a nuclear power station at Doel, Belgium.

WATER QUALITY AND AVAILABILITY

There are 42 800 billion cubic metres of freshwater reserves available on Earth, which amounts to an average allocation of 5925 cubic metres per person a year. However, this figure assumes an even distribution of freshwater reserves across all of the regions and countries of the world, which is far from the case, as seen in Table 4.3.

Region	Water reserves (billions cubic metres)	Available water reserves per person per year (cubic metres)
Latin America and Caribbean	13 867	22 162
East Asia and Oceania	10 096	4525
Europe and Central Asia	7071	7866
North America	5668	15 993
Sub-Saharan Africa	3883	3987
South Asia	1982	1152
Middle East and North Africa	231	554

△ Table 4.3 Distribution of global water reserves by region.

Because of this uneven distribution, the world has **water-rich** and **water-poor regions**. South America and the Caribbean, with 500 million inhabitants or 8 per cent of the world's population, has 31 per cent of the world's freshwater reserves. North America is another water-rich region, with 13 per cent of the freshwater reserves but only 7 per cent of the planet's residents. In fact just two countries – Brazil and the United States – possess 25 per cent of the world's water reserves. Compare this with Asia where over 4 billion people live (60 per cent of the world's population) but only have access to 28 per cent of the world's freshwater resources. The most water-poor regions of the Middle East and North Africa contain only 0.5 per cent of freshwater reserves and as home to 5 per cent of the globe's population, have the lowest available water reserves per person in the world.

Such an uneven distribution of water resources means that inevitably some countries experience either physical or economic water shortages, while in others there is no scarcity at all, as Figure 4.18 shows.

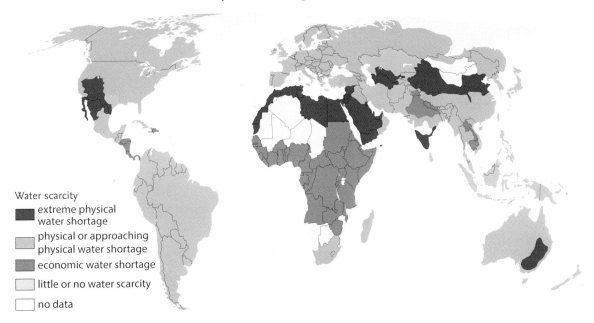

Water scarcity
- extreme physical water shortage
- physical or approaching physical water shortage
- economic water shortage
- little or no water scarcity
- no data

△ Fig. 4.18 Water scarcity by country.

A physical water shortage occurs in a country when all available reserves have been exploited and demand continues to rise. An economic water shortage means that people have insufficient water even though there are adequate water reserves available. This is often the case in the world's lowest income countries, which commonly do not possess the **capital** or technology to invest in fully exploiting their water reserves. This is true in many Sub-Saharan countries of Africa. Angola is ranked by the World Bank as 116th in terms of wealth out of 183 countries and Angolans have an average **life expectancy** of just 50 years. Despite having potential water reserves of over 6000 cubic metres per person, less than 10 per cent has so far been exploited.

△ Fig. 4.19 Cachoeiras waterfall, Angola.

Because water is the world's most valuable natural resource, serious disagreements and even conflicts can occur between countries when its ownership and use is disputed. When in 2013 Ethiopia began construction of the Renaissance Dam project on the Blue Nile, one of the major tributaries of the River Nile, the government of Egypt threatened to declare war. The River Nile (Figure 4.20) is fed by waters from 11 countries, and 40 million farmers in Egypt – the last country to be reached by the river before it flows into the Mediterranean Sea – rely upon it for all of their water supply.

Ethiopia responded by declaring that building the dam, which will generate 6000 megawatts of power and provide irrigation water for tens of thousands of square kilometres of land, was essential for the economic development of the country and work would not stop. The government of Ethiopia stressed that they were only taking their fair share of the priceless water reserves of the River Nile and this entitlement would transform people's lives in a drought-stricken country. When complete, the US$5 billion dam project will be the largest **hydroelectric** plant in Africa and the eighth largest in the world. After three years of tension, the two countries finally signed a deal to end the dispute when Prime Minister Hailemariam of Ethiopia gave assurance that the dam would 'not cause any harm to downstream countries'.

△ Fig. 4.20 The course of the River Nile.

△ Fig. 4.21 One of the objectives of the Grand Ethiopian Renaissance Dam is to provide irrigation to dry lands.

△ Fig. 4.22 Forty million Egyptian farmers depend on irrigation water from the River Nile.

Potable water, also known as improved drinking water, is water safe enough for drinking and food preparation because it has been treated to ensure that it is free of external contaminants and harmful bacteria. Globally, 700 million people (one in ten) do not have access to an improved water source. Figure 4.23 clearly shows that most of these people live in the countries of Sub-Saharan Africa, where the average is 63 per cent with potable water compared with a global figure of 91 per cent. Most non-potable water will be untreated water extracted directly from wells, rivers and lakes, which may be contaminated by **faeces** and may cause chronic **diarrhoea** as well as bacterial diseases such as botulism, dysentery and typhoid, and viral infections including hepatitis A and poliomyelitis.

An estimated 1.5 million people a year die from the effects of diarrhoea and **water-borne** diseases caused by a lack of access to safe water and **improved sanitation** facilities. Over 90 per cent of these deaths are of children under the age of five. This is the number one cause of deaths amongst children worldwide and the relationship between

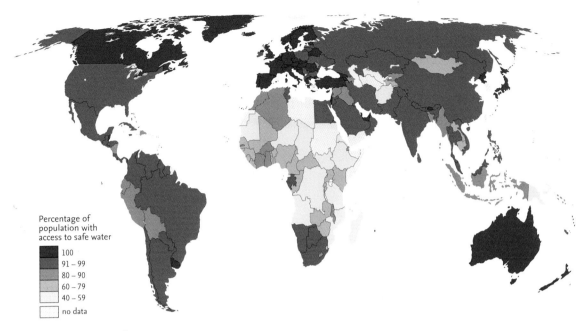

△ Fig. 4.23 Access to safe water.

infant mortality shown in Figure 4.24 and access to safe water shown in Figure 4.23 is striking. Every year, 160 million people are infected with bilharzia from ingesting parasitic worms and tens of thousands die as a result. Another 500 million people are at risk of contracting trachoma, a bacterial infection of the eye; over 150 million people worldwide are blind or have serious sight impairments as a result of this disease. In addition to bilharzia, other intestinal helminths (parasitic worms) such as hookworm infect over 100 million people. There are around 1.5 million cases of clinical hepatitis A every year.

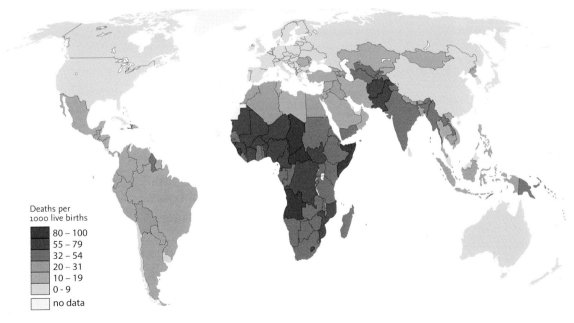

△ Fig. 4.24 Infant mortality rate.

Poor sanitation that allows drinking water to come into contact with human waste is the major cause of contamination. Over 2 billion people worldwide lack access to improved sanitation facilities and unsurprisingly, regions with poor levels of sanitation tend also to have the highest levels of contraction of water-borne infectious diseases. Only two-thirds of the world's rural dwellers have access to improved sanitation (compared with 82 per cent of all urban residents), and 80 per cent of all the people in the world without improved water also live in rural areas. Sub-Saharan Africa has the largest population of any region still without improved water sources (319 million people). Angola and Equatorial Guinea, both in this region, are two of the three remaining countries in the world in which less than 50 per cent of the population have improved water access.

△ Fig. 4.25 Equatorial Guinea is one of three countries worldwide where less than half the population have access to potable water.

△ Fig. 4.26 A child suffering from cholera is held by his mother at a treatment centre in Somalia.

MULTIPURPOSE DAM PROJECTS

A dam is a barrier constructed across a river in order to control the flow of water leading to the creation of an artificial body of water, known as a reservoir, upstream of the dam. Dams that store more than three million cubic metres of water are typically referred to as 'large dams', and there are more than 50 000 worldwide. Dams have been built since ancient times and the Jawa Dam in Jordan is the oldest known, dating from 5000 years ago. More than 70 per cent of all existing dams in the world have been built for a single purpose:

- One-third of all dams collect water that is then used to irrigate crops on adjacent land. Today, irrigated land covers about 2 770 000 sq km, that is about 18 per cent of the world's arable land, but is responsible for around 40 per cent of crop output and employs nearly 30 per cent of population spread over rural areas.

- Some dams hold back water that is then released under pressure to turn turbines and generate electricity. Worldwide hydroelectric power plants have a combined capacity of 675 000 megawatts that produce 2.3 trillion kilowatt hours of electricity each year, which is 24 per cent of the world's total consumption. Electricity generated from dams is by very far the largest **renewable energy** source in the world. More than 90 per cent of the world's renewable electricity comes from dams.

- The function of many dams is to gather and then distribute fresh water for domestic and industrial uses, especially in urban areas. Modern manufacturing industries and giant cities require huge amounts of water daily. Producing just one tonne of steel requires 281 000 litres of water. Over 12 litres of water is needed to manufacture just one litre of paint and 177 000 litres is needed to produce an average size family car. The 16 million people of Mumbai in India consume 4300 litres of water a day and the 4 million inhabitants of Melbourne in Australia require 1000 litres.

- Dams are frequently built to improve navigation along rivers and canals by ships and barges carrying cargo inland from coastal ports where it has been offloaded from much larger ocean-going vessels. Here dams are often used in conjunction with weirs and locks to control river levels and to enable vessels to avoid hazards such as rapids, ice accumulation and channels prone to **sedimentation**.

- Many dams and reservoirs have been built to protect communities from flooding by regulating river flow and water discharge to prevent flooding downstream of the dam. This is particularly important in locations that have very marked wet and dry seasons. In the wet season, surplus water can be stored in the reservoir rather than running off saturated ground to cause flooding. In the dry season, the reservoir water can then be released to avoid droughts occurring.

△ Fig. 4.27 The hydroelectricity dam at Itaipu between Paraguay and Brazil.

Developing a site for multipurpose dam projects

Most dams built today usually have more than one use and are referred to as **multipurpose dams**. For example, a water supply dam can also be used for irrigation and hydroelectric power generation. When selecting a site to construct a multipurpose dam project, a wide range of both physical and human factors must be taken into account. These are the most important considerations:

- The geology of the site must be stable, with no risks of serious Earth movements such as **earthquakes**. The rock of the dam itself and the bed and walls of the reservoir must be able to sustain huge hydraulic pressures from the volume of water so as to avoid potentially disastrous floods. For this reason, there must not be any joints or faults in the underlying rock structure. Weaker **sedimentary rocks** such as sandstone will be avoided and harder rocks such as granite are preferred. The rock structure also needs to be impermeable and non-porous to avoid seepage.

- The optimum location for a dam and reservoir is where there is a narrowing of the river within a wide and deep valley or canyon. A narrow cross-section reduces dam length and therefore building costs. A large deep valley behind the dam means that a considerable volume of water can be stored in the reservoir. Deep valleys also have the advantage that the reservoir created will have the least surface area possible, which reduces water loss through evaporation. This is particularly important in hot dry regions.

- Reservoirs need to be constructed as close as possible to the location where the water (or electricity generated) is going to be consumed, such as a city or new iron and steel works. This not only reduces water and electricity transmission losses during transport but also lowers transport costs.

- Dams need to be built in regions where the annual rainfall is sufficient and reliable enough to keep the reservoir topped up with water. The catchment of the river that is being dammed must also have enough tributary streams and rivers to supply the reservoir with the rainfall run-off required.

- Materials such as stones and binding material required for the construction of the dam should be available locally to minimise the costs of the project. The site should also have enough space for constructing housing and services for large numbers of workers.

- As far as possible, the site for the dam and the valley that will be submerged should be as cheap as possible and not contain a resident population who will have to be compensated and relocated. Avoiding high value agricultural land and important ecological, historical or cultural sites such as ancient burial sites or the **habitats** of endangered **species** will also be a consideration.

△ Fig. 4.28 Dam construction on the Marsyangdi Khola river, Nepal.

Evaluating the impacts of multipurpose dam projects

Throughout the world, constructing multipurpose dams is seen by governments as an important way of boosting economic development. Multipurpose dams are **infrastructure** projects in that they help to provide the basic facilities, services and installations a country requires to develop economically. Economic development can be defined as measures that improve the prosperity and **quality of life** of people living in a country. Examples include encouraging the setting up of new industrial businesses and jobs, increasing productivity (output) of existing industries including farming and expanding services such as banking and insurance. As the number of employed people in a country grows, so does the amount of income tax collected by the government (the tax base). Much of this will be spent by the government on improving living conditions for people such as new roads, railways, hospitals and schools. Multipurpose dams contribute to economic development through providing electricity from a renewable source, helping to regulate water levels, distributing fresh drinking water and feeding irrigation systems that support new areas of farmland that boost food production. In this way they help to ensure energy, food and water security in a country.

However many multipurpose dam projects are often highly controversial and heavily criticised for not being a **sustainable** form of development. Critics stress that while the economic benefits of the dam tend to be enjoyed widely throughout the country, it is local communities and **ecosystems** that have to cope with the potential serious environmental and social costs:

- The compulsory resettlement of people, and sometimes whole communities, from flooded areas who are forced to abandon their homes and livelihoods such as farming or forestry. It is estimated that 30 million people have been expelled from their homes worldwide as a result of the construction of multipurpose dams. These people often come from the poorest sections of society, and find adapting to new ways of life elsewhere very hard. This can lead to serious social and psychological effects, particularly when **indigenous** tribal groups in areas such as the Amazon Basin are forced out of ancestral homes. The Aswan High Dam led to the expulsion of 100 000 people in Egypt, and in China, over 1 million people were forced from their homes to make way for the Three Gorges Dam and reservoirs. Over 400 new dams for the Amazon Basin are currently in their planning or construction phase.
- There may be large-scale wildlife habitat destruction and alteration, as reservoirs flood valleys above the dam and river-flow below the dam is massively reduced. For example, the **migration** patterns of fish, such as salmon travelling up rivers to spawn, will be altered by both the construction of the barrier dam and reduction of downstream water levels. Dams can radically change the physical and biological processes of river ecosystems. As well as reducing river levels and flow rates, they block the free flow of nutrients, increase water temperatures (especially if extracted water is being used to cool electricity generating turbines) and alter oxygen levels.
- The loss of livelihood for communities locally who rely on the natural flow of water through the **environment**, such as fisheries located below the dam, can be great.
- High concentrations of nutrients can build up in reservoirs as run-off carries fertilisers from the land into the water and traps them behind the dam. Algal blooms can occur through **eutrophication**, which depletes oxygen levels and leads to such a drastic loss of crustaceans, insects, amphibians and fish that the whole ecosystem may die.

- Poorly maintained reservoirs are ideal breeding grounds for mosquitoes, snails and flies, which transmit deadly diseases such as **malaria**, bilharzia and river blindness to humans, and which affect millions of people in **tropical** regions.
- Although hydroelectric power generation produces little **carbon dioxide**, and therefore helps to reduce **greenhouse gas emissions**, large shallow reservoirs, particularly in tropical regions, often produce huge volumes of methane – a much more potent greenhouse gas. Methane is emitted as the vegetation below the reservoir water decays and ferments.

CAUSES AND IMPACTS OF WATER POLLUTION

Water **pollution** occurs when potential harmful substances are discharged into lakes, rivers, aquifers and groundwater, and the resulting contamination degrades the environment or presents a threat to human health. The most important sources of water pollution are domestic waste, industrial processes, agricultural practices, and global inequalities in sewage and water treatment.

Domestic waste

This includes sewage and waste water produced by households in urban and rural areas which, if untreated or inadequately purified, causes pollution and potential health problems when it is discharged into water bodies. For example, **pathogens** in water contaminated by faeces can cause chronic diarrhoea as well as bacterial diseases such as botulism, dysentery and typhoid, and viral infections including hepatitis A and poliomyelitis. Globally, 700 million people in LEDCs currently drink water from contaminated water sources. In MEDCs,

△ Fig. 4.29 River Mersey in Warrington, UK polluted with detergent.

chemical detergents used in the home in washing machines, dishwashers and as cleaning agents can enter water bodies through sewage treatment plants. Detergents can have poisonous effects on all kinds of aquatic life if they occur in high concentrations. For example, detergents can destroy the external mucus layers that protect fish from bacteria and parasites, as well as damaging their gills.

Industrial processes

Activities that involve the mining and transport of **minerals** and energy supplies and the manufacturing of goods from **raw materials** in factories produce a huge amount of waste. Much of this waste contains toxic chemicals such as lead and mercury, which can have catastrophic consequences if they are not managed properly and allowed to drain into water bodies. Industrial pollutants can contaminate water bodies either directly or indirectly. For example, the Deepwater Horizon oil spill of 2010 in the Gulf of Mexico resulted in 780 000 cubic metres of liquid petroleum hydrocarbon being released straight into the Gulf of Mexico (see page 46–49). The accident killed 11 people and the resulting oil spill is estimated to have resulted in the death of 82 000 birds, 6000 sea turtles and 25 000 marine mammals, including several species of dolphin.

△ Fig. 4.30 Deepwater Horizon oil slick.

Sulfur is a non-metallic compound that can be very harmful to aquatic life. It tends to pollute water indirectly by way of **acid rainfall**. Sulfur dioxide (SO_2) and nitrous oxide (N_2O) are released into the atmosphere from industrial plants and the burning of **fossil fuels**, and they can combine with water droplets to form nitric acid (HNO_3) and sulfuric acid (H_2SO_4). Natural rainwater is slightly acidic (pH 5.5) because of dissolved carbon dioxide, but the addition of sulfur dioxide and nitrous oxide increases this natural acidity to a pH value of 4.

In terrestrial habitats, acid rain damages the waxy layer on the leaves of trees, making it more difficult for them to absorb the nutrients required for healthy growth. This may lead initially to the browning and dieback of foliage, which reduces **photosynthesis** and makes the tree more susceptible to pests and disease that will eventually kill it. Acid rain can also have serious consequences for aquatic environments such as rivers and lakes. As well as adding nitric and sulfuric acid directly to the water, acid rain will also leach out toxic aluminium from the soil and carry it into rivers and lakes. The more acid the rain is, the more aluminium is released from the soil. As the acidity of a lake or river increases, the number and types of aquatic life that can survive the extreme conditions will decline drastically. Only those that can tolerate acidic waters will remain. Today some acidified

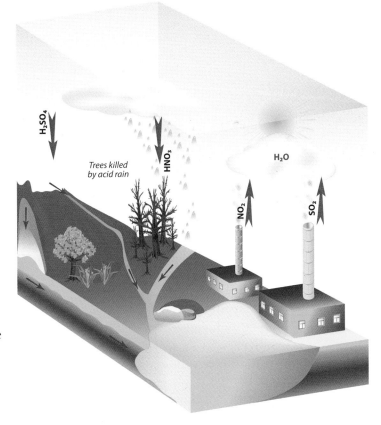

△ Fig. 4.31 Acid rain flow diagram.

lakes contain no fish at all. At a pH of 5 or below, most fish eggs cannot hatch and lower pH levels may cause some adult fish to die. Even if a particular species of animal or fish can adapt to the increased acidity, the animals or plants that it eats may not. For example, many frogs can survive pH levels of 4 but the mayflies they eat will only tolerate a maximum acidity level of pH 5. As the variety of aquatic life in an acidified lake drops, the water often appears blue and 'crystal clear'. Far from being an indication of a healthy habitat, this occurs because there is no plant life to provide a greenish tinge or animals to cloud the water due to their activities and body processes.

Agricultural practices

Farming processes have the potential to cause serious water pollution if they are not managed carefully to avoid contamination of water bodies. Leakage from slurry tanks and silage clamps, drainage of animal wastes, disposal of sheep dip and the run-off of fertilisers and **pesticides** from the land can all poison stream and river life and present human health threats. Using contaminated water sources for irrigation is another cause of pollution. If irrigation water is polluted with organic compounds and **heavy metals** from industrial processes, then crops can absorb small quantities of mercury, arsenic and lead. **Soil erosion** from deforested hillsides and poorly ploughed fields can result in the sedimentation of streams, rivers and lakes. This process can lead to the stagnation of water bodies and **deoxygenation**, causing a serious decline in aquatic life. Antibiotics and artificial growth hormones are commonly used on intensive livestock farms, either injected directly into animals or added to their feed. Large amounts of both substances are excreted by animals and can pollute water bodies; some hormones can remain functional up to 270 days after excretion. Hormones not only contribute to causing eutrophication in water bodies but have also been shown to seriously affect the reproduction of some fish species. An estimated 75 per cent of all antibiotics are excreted by animals. There is evidence that several species of antimicrobial-resistant bacteria that are highly dangerous to humans have now evolved in water courses polluted by these hormones.

In addition, the damaging effects of eutrophication when fertilisers are washed off the land by rainwater, and the serious impacts of the **bioaccumulation** of toxic substances such as DDT in **food chains**, have already been explored in Section 3. Bioaccumulation describes the process by which water pollutants increase in concentration through all the **trophic levels** of a food chain from **producers** to tertiary or apex **consumer**. For example, mercury is a toxic heavy metal that can build up in high concentrations in the sediments lying at the bottom of lakes, rivers and seas. It is known to be very dangerous to both natural ecosystems and human health, because of its capacity to damage the central nervous system. In marine areas contaminated with mercury, tiny quantities of the metal will be absorbed by countless numbers of phytoplankton such as algae as they feed by filtering both water and sediments. When primary consumers such as krill eat phytoplankton, the mercury grows in concentration within their bodies. In turn, secondary consumers including herring and salmon that feed on the krill build up higher levels of mercury still. Finally, tertiary or apex consumers like seals, killer whales and humans that may eat many herring or salmon will accumulate the highest concentrations of all.

Global inequalities in sewage and water treatment

'Sanitation' refers to the provision of clean drinking water and also adequate sewage and water treatment services for waste domestic water. Globally, 2.5 billion (four out of every ten people) lack access to improved sanitation facilities that hygienically separate human waste from human contact. These include pour-flush toilets leading to a piped sewage system, septic tanks, pit latrines and composting toilets. One billion of these people are forced to defecate in the open and have no access to soap and water to wash their hands. The majority of those without access to improved sanitation live in the poorest countries of Asia and Africa. The situation is worst of all in rural areas: of the 2.5 billion people lacking access to improved sanitation, 80 per cent live in rural rather than urban areas. Water polluted with faecal matter as a result of inadequate sanitation services is estimated to affect the health of more than 1.2 billion people each year and to contribute to the death of 15 million children annually. The provision of improved sanitation facilities is directly affected by poverty, as Table 4.4 shows. The greater the income of a country then the more likely it will be that funds will be available for investing in improving sanitation and wastewater treatment services. This in turn will contribute to improving both the health and productivity of the population as well as raising average life expectancy at birth.

△ Fig. 4.32 Modern water treatment works in the Netherlands.

Country	Population with access to improved sanitation (per cent)	Gross national income per person (US$)	Average life expectancy (years)
Austria	100	49 600	82
Burkina Faso	17	700	59
Canada	100	51 630	82
Democratic Republic of the Congo	15	380	59
Israel	100	35 320	82
South Sudan	7	970	54
Japan	100	42 000	84

△ Table 4.4 Representative development data for a sample of seven countries.

MANAGING POLLUTION OF FRESH WATER

Improving sanitation and sewage treatment

The need to improve sanitation is greatest in the poorest countries of the world, particularly in the regions of Sub-Saharan Africa and South Asia. The problem is greatest in rural areas but even in urban areas where household and communal toilets are more common, over 2 billion people use toilets connected to septic tanks that are not safely emptied or that discharge raw sewage into open drains or streams and rivers. The toilets, sewers and wastewater treatment systems used in MEDCs require vast areas of land, energy and water and they are expensive to build, maintain and operate. The challenge therefore for these poorest countries such as Kenya – where a child dies from water-borne disease every 17 minutes – is to develop less expensive and sustainable sanitation systems that rely on local resources and expertise rather than advanced technology and high capital costs. Better sanitation not only saves lives and improves child health, it also contributes to economic development and improving prosperity. Studies have shown that for every US$1 spent on improving sanitation in the world's poorest countries, at least US$5 have been generated in economic benefits. As sanitation services improve, there is less illness, which means that adults can work longer and more productively, children attend school more regularly, health care costs are reduced and life expectancy increases. To meet the sanitation challenge, it is common for governments in the world's poorest countries to work in partnership with the aid agencies of wealthier countries and **non-government organisations (NGOs)** such as charities. The aim of this collaborative work is to design and introduce appropriate and sustainable improvements in domestic toilet design, pit emptying and sludge treatment, as well as new ways to **reuse** waste.

Oxfam is an international development charity working with partners and local communities in more than ninety of the world's poorest countries. In 2011 it began a pilot project with a local organisation called 'Sanergy' to develop a sustainable sanitation service in the city of Nairobi where there were no sewers and the majority of residents did not have access to a toilet. This presented a major health problem with waste being dumped in walkways and gutters. The solution was a cheap portable 'Fresh Life' toilet that sits in the corner of each house and separates the solid and liquid waste into smaller containers. The containers are then collected daily by a local enterprise business and processed to make **biofuel** briquettes and organic fertiliser, which are sold for a profit. The briquettes are used as cooking fuel and the fertiliser enriches the soil of small vegetable gardens. To date, the sanitation project has provided 30 000

△ Fig. 4.33 An open sewer in the Mathare district of Nairobi, Kenya.

portable toilets, collected and processed 6200 tonnes of human waste that would have otherwise polluted living areas, and created 766 jobs.

During the past ten years the government of Bangladesh has invested heavily in building latrines and improving access to toilets for people in both rural and urban areas. An international NGO called Practical Action is currently working with the government and partner organisations in Bangladesh to find sustainable solutions to managing safely and productively the acute problem of treating the

△ Fig. 4.34 A mobile toilet on a street in Dhaka, Bangladesh.

huge quantities of sewage produced. This waste (faecal sludge) from latrines and septic tanks is still routinely emptied, untreated, into the local environment. This undermines any health gains made through the improved latrines and toilets. A sustainable solution was required that was effective, practical and affordable and did not affect existing toilet technology. The answer was solar-powered sludge drying beds. The benefit of these is that they use no electrical power and can be built with minimal construction skills and from local materials. The most effective design allows the dried sludge to be co-composted with woody organic material such as rice and straw which can then be used as a fertiliser and soil conditioner by farmers.

Improving water quality

Access to improved water supplies is poorest for people living in the forty-eight least developed countries in the world. Sub-Saharan Africa lags behind all other regions, with just 31 per cent of people having access to improved sanitation and 60 per cent to improved water supplies. In many of the poorest countries there is an economic rather than a physical shortage of water. An economic water shortage means that people have insufficient water even though there are adequate water reserves available. This is due to the country lacking the resources or technological expertise to invest in exploiting the resources and distributing them to those who need them. This is the case for many of the countries that make up Sub-Saharan Africa who are generally underutilising their available water resources. Estimates indicate that the groundwater storage in Sub-Saharan aquifers could be as great as 0.5 million cubic km, which is 100 times more than surface reserves in lakes and rivers. In fact, groundwater reserves comprise more than 20 times the average annual rainfall. In addition, the groundwater is of excellent microbiological and chemical quality, making it suitable for all uses. At present most groundwater extraction occurs from shallow aquifers just below the surface by way of simple hand-dug boreholes and wells. Vast water reserves in deeper aquifers remain largely unexploited because of a lack of resources and appropriate technology.

Partnership working between government aid agencies and NGOs in MEDCs is supporting the sustainable exploitation of groundwater supplies in Sub-Saharan Africa. For example Muslim Charity is drilling deep boreholes in communities in Somalia to provide safe drinking water and water for sanitation and irrigation. In places such as the city of Burao the projects are having an immediate and positive impact especially for women and girls whose responsibility it was to collect water every day for their families from streams and rivers often long distances away. The girls are now able to attend school full time and the older women can start up small businesses. The general health of the **community**, and particularly that of the children, has improved. Men are no longer too sick to work and food supplies are more reliable now that the fields are watered regularly throughout the year.

△ Fig. 4.35 Water sellers in Darro, Somalia, fill water carts from a diesel-powered borehole pump.

Water pollution control and legislation

In many countries, activities that could pollute water, such as building a new sewage treatment plant, are regulated under environmental permits that have to be obtained from the relevant government department before proceeding. For example, in the UK, people or businesses wishing to carry out these kinds of activities must obtain a permit from the Environment Agency and comply with any conditions laid down. If they do not, they will commit an offence and also have the permit withdrawn. Before granting a permit, the Environment Agency informs the people it considers are likely to be affected by the activity and invites them to submit their views. Permit applications may be rejected if the environmental impact is considered to be unacceptable or if there is a potential risk to human health and wellbeing. If the Environment Agency grants a permit then objectors can appeal the decision. Similarly, if the Environment Agency refuses a permit, the person or business who applied for it may appeal. Special rules for some activities have to be consulted by the Environment Agency when considering a permit application, such as nitrate regulations that set out lots of requirements and restrictions on how farmers can use nitrate fertilisers, and silage, slurry and agricultural fuel oil regulations that contain rules on how these substances must be stored.

As well as these rules and regulations, the UK government has passed laws to help protect the environment from water pollution. Breaking these laws is a criminal offence and can result in offenders having to pay large fines or serve prison terms. An example is the Environmental Permitting Act of 2010, which sets out water pollution offences and the responsibilities of individuals and businesses. European Union member countries must adhere to any European directives introduced to reduce and control water pollution. Two examples are the Urban Waste Water Treatment Directive, which seeks to improve water quality by laying down strict regulations about the treatment and discharge of waste water from industrial and household sources, and the Bathing Water Directive, which requires member states to monitor and manage the quality of bathing water and provide public information about it. The UK is a signatory to a wide range of international conventions designed to prevent marine water pollution, such as the International Convention for the Prevention of Pollution of the Sea by Oil and the Convention on the Prevention of Marine Pollution by Dumping of Wastes and Other Matter.

△ Fig. 4.36 Flag on a beach indicating clean water.

MANAGING WATER-RELATED DISEASE

Malaria

Each year there are over 200 million cases of malaria worldwide, resulting in approximately 400 000 deaths. Although malaria is found in over 100 countries, 90 per cent of these cases and deaths occur in countries of tropical and **sub-tropical** Africa (Figure 4.37). In addition to the human tragedy, in Africa, malaria is estimated to result in the loss of US$12 billion a year due to increased healthcare costs, lost ability to work and negative effects on **tourism**. Malaria is classified as a water-borne disease because the mosquitoes that spread it breed below the surface of warm and stagnant bodies of water such as marshes, swamps and lakes. Malaria is caused by a type of parasite known as plasmodium, which is spread by the female Anopheles mosquito that mainly bites humans at dusk and during the night.

△ Fig. 4.37 Areas of Africa where malaria is common.

The life cycle of the plasmodium parasite is shown in Figure 4.38. It begins with a female Anopheles mosquito biting a human to suck blood to get the nutrients it needs to lay eggs. If this human is already infected with the plasmodium parasite then the mosquito sucks out some of the parasites in the host's blood. When the mosquito feeds on its next human, it pierces into a blood vessel and inserts a little liquid to prevent the blood clotting, enabling it to be sucked out. The plasmodium parasite is contained within this liquid and so infects the next individual. Once in the blood stream, the parasite travels to the liver. The infection develops in the liver before re-entering the bloodstream and invading the red blood cells. The parasites grow and multiply in the red blood cells. At regular intervals, the infected blood cells burst, releasing more parasites into the blood. Infected blood cells usually burst every 48–72 hours, causing bouts of fever, chills and sweating. If malaria is diagnosed and treated promptly with appropriate medication, there is a very high chance of making a full recovery. However, malaria is a very serious illness that can get worse very quickly and can cause serious complications, including severe anaemia and cerebral malaria. Anaemia occurs where red blood cells are unable to carry enough oxygen around the body, leading to drowsiness and weakness. In rare cases, the small blood vessels leading to the brain can become blocked, causing seizures, brain damage and coma. The effects of malaria are usually more severe in pregnant women, babies, young children and the elderly.

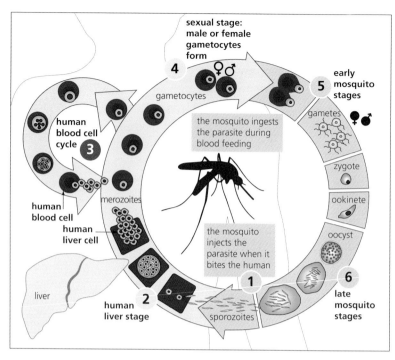

△ Fig. 4.38 Life cycle of the malaria parasite.

Various approaches to preventing and controlling malaria have been introduced globally, including antimalarial drugs known as prophylaxis in the form of tablets to prevent infection occurring once bitten by a parasite-carrying mosquito. Most provide up to 90 per

△ Fig. 4.39 Anopheles mosquito.

cent protection. Many of the same antimalarial drugs used to prevent malaria are also often used to treat the disease if infection occurs. Increasing antimalarial drug resistance as a result of genetic **mutations** amongst mosquito populations is a grave concern throughout tropical Africa. Counterfeit or substandard drug treatments and unregulated or poorly administered antimalarial drug use are both contributory factors here. While antimalarial drugs offer the greatest protection from contracting malaria and the greatest likelihood of making a full recovery in the event of infection, they are not a realistic option for most people in Sub-Saharan Africa. Their prohibitive cost combined with the need for a well-developed prescribing medical infrastructure and services such as pharmacies and health centres makes them only appropriate for visitors and tourists to the region from MEDCs.

Vector control is another common means of malaria transmission prevention. It combines the use of long-lasting insecticide-treated mosquito nets that hang over beds and cots at night, with regular indoor spraying of homes with insecticide. Sleeping under a net treated with an effective insecticide can reduce contact between mosquitoes and humans by providing both a physical barrier and an insecticidal effect. Between 2000 and 2015, over 1 billion insecticide-treated nets were delivered to countries in Sub-Saharan Africa by government aid agencies and

△ Fig. 4.40 Insecticide-treated mosquito net.

NGOs in MEDCs. During this time, the proportion of children under the age of five years sleeping under nets increased from 2 to 68 per cent. Net use can significantly reduce the incidence of malaria in communities where they are used effectively. However, for effective malaria control it is critical that sufficient nets are available to protect all community members without exception and that those families are aware of how to install and maintain them to ensure maximum ongoing protection. A mosquito requires only a tiny gap or tear in the net to gain access to a sleeping person. In 2015 only 29 per cent of households with nets in Sub-Saharan Africa had enough to protect all family numbers. In addition, most nets are designed for a life span of 20 washes or three years of constant use, after which they must be replaced. For low-income countries they are an expensive purchase beyond the means of most people. This means that they are either not replaced or people have to rely upon overseas donors continuing with aid programmes. Using indoor residual spraying of insecticide typically once or twice a year, in combination with net use every night, results in the greatest reductions in malaria transmissions. The insecticide is sprayed on indoor walls and ceilings where mosquitoes are likely to rest after feeding. However to achieve maximum impact the insecticide must be sprayed in every dwelling within a community, but coverage is presently poor. In 2015, only an estimated 16 million people (equivalent to just 4 per cent of the at-risk population) were protected from malaria transmission by indoor spraying.

Considerable progress globally has been made in controlling the transmission of malaria during the last century. In 1900, malaria was present in almost every sub-tropical and tropical country of the world. Since then the disease has been eliminated in 111 countries, and thirty-four countries are currently advancing toward elimination. Elimination is defined as less than one diagnosed case of malaria per 1000 people at risk each year in a defined geographical area (usually a country). Global incidence of malaria has dropped by 17 per cent and deaths from the disease by 26 per cent since 1900. However, ongoing transmission remains persistent in 64 countries.

Malaria eradication is the goal of achieving the permanent reduction to zero of the worldwide incidence of malaria. The Gates Foundation, an important source of funds for antimalarial research and the control effort, believes it can be eradicated by 2040. Achieving this would rank as one of the world's greatest medical advancements. Not only would it save millions of lives but billions of dollars in lost productivity and health costs in many of the poorest countries. However, the disease is very difficult to fight for a number of reasons:

- Infected humans often do not show symptoms of the disease for months and even years as the parasite lays dormant in their bodies. Mapping the distribution of active infected mosquitoes and taking timely action to control them is therefore very difficult.

- Many countries cannot afford to invest in the most modern and sensitive equipment to both collect and analyse blood samples from possible victims. Laboratory tests take over a week to complete, during which time infected mosquitoes are able to spread parasites to new victims.

- Mosquitoes and the malaria parasite have constantly shown the ability to develop resistance to both drugs and insecticides such as chloroquine and DDT. In Sub-Saharan Africa there are mutated strains of mosquitoes resistant to pyrethroids, the chemicals used in 70 per cent of house sprayings and the only type used to treat bed nets. Once a resistant strain has mutated, it spreads fast, causing catastrophic results in human populations that have no means of combatting it.

- Achieving eradication will require MEDCs (where malaria is already eliminated) to commit huge amounts of money each year for at least another 25 years. Contributions from these countries already represent 82 per cent of the US$8 billion spent on fighting malaria since 2002. The Gates Foundation projects the total cost of eradication between now and 2040 to require an additional US$120 billion of funding. In times of **economic recession** and competing demands for funding for domestic issues, there is no guarantee that fighting malaria will remain a priority for so long.

- After a decade of research and clinical trials, developing an effective vaccine to stop infections in humans or to stop infected humans becoming sick has proved very difficult and results to date have been disappointing.

- **Genetic engineering** may hold out more hope than vaccines. A genetically modified Anopheles mosquito that is highly resistant to the malaria parasite has already been developed. Mating this mosquito with wild species would pass on the modified gene to all offspring but mass release is still some years away. Other researchers have had some success in feeding mosquitoes sugar containing bacteria that blocks their ability to pass on the malaria parasite.

- In an increasingly globalised world, people are becoming more mobile as they search for work, move away to study or to live with family members elsewhere in their own nation or neighbouring countries.

Infected people can therefore transport the malaria parasite very quickly from one community to another before they have any symptoms of the disease themselves.

Cholera

Cholera is another very serious water-borne disease caused by consuming water or food contaminated by the bacterium *Vibrio cholera*. It affects the small intestine and symptoms include severe diarrhoea, stomach cramps and vomiting. Without treatment, serious **dehydration** can occur, which can lead to a massive drop in blood pressure and death. One of the main ways in which the disease spreads is through people drinking or cooking with water contaminated with the faeces of an infected person. Cholera is therefore most widespread in those regions of the world with poor sanitation, particularly parts of Sub-Saharan Africa, south and Southeast Asia, the Middle East and Central America and the Caribbean. The World Health Organization estimates that there are between 1.4 and 4.3 million cases of cholera globally every year, leading to tens of thousands of deaths. Babies, young children, pregnant women and the elderly are particularly at risk from the disease. **Natural disasters** such as earthquakes or cyclones that result in large numbers of displaced people congregating in small areas such as refugee camps often leads to cholera outbreaks as available water sources become quickly contaminated.

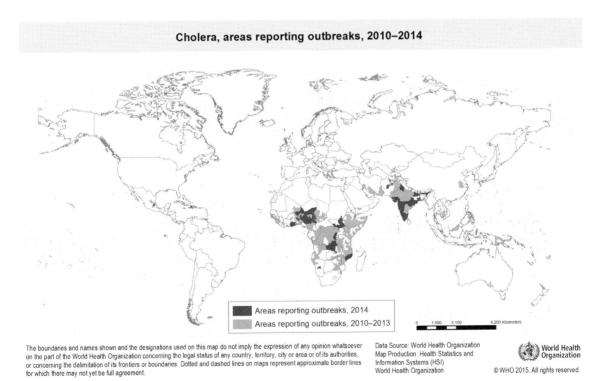

Cholera, areas reporting outbreaks, 2010–2014

Areas reporting outbreaks, 2014
Areas reporting outbreaks, 2010–2013

0   1,550   3,100   6,200 Kilometers

△ Fig. 4.41 Areas reporting outbreaks of cholera from 2010 to 2014.

Although only drinking water that has been recently boiled or disinfected through chlorination can control the spread of cholera in the short term, the only sustainable long-term solution is to ensure that everyone in at-risk areas has access to potable drinking water in ways that were outlined earlier in this chapter. Cholera **vaccination** is available in most MEDCs for people likely to be visiting endemic areas, and offers about 85 per cent protection, but this quickly declines and booster doses are required after six months. People who contract cholera can be effectively treated using oral rehydration solutions that contain a mixture of salt and glucose dissolved in purified water. When a person with cholera is severely dehydrated, antibiotics may be given by intravenous drip to stop diarrhoea and rehydrate the body quickly. As with malaria, many of the poorest countries where cholera occurs lack the resources either to vaccinate large numbers of people or to invest in expensive treatments for those infected. It is unsurprising that most of the countries where cholera outbreaks occur are also those with the lowest levels of access to improved water supplies.

△ Fig. 4.42 Refugee camp in Somalia.

> **CASE STUDY**
>
> # ENVIRONMENTAL IMPACTS OF THE THREE GORGES DAM
>
>
>
> △ Fig. 4.43 Downstream side of the Three Gorges Dam.
>
>
>
> △ Fig. 4.44 Location of Three Gorges Dam.
>
> The Three Gorges Dam, which spans the Yangtze River in China opened in 2012 at a cost of US$25 billion and amidst much controversy. It is a good example of a multipurpose dam as it has three purposes: generating hydroelectric power, increasing shipping capacity along the Yangtze and reducing the occurrence of flooding along the lower reaches of the river.
>
> The dam has had a number of positive and negative economic, social and environmental impacts.

Positive impacts

- It is the world's largest power station, generating 85 billion kilowatt hours of electricity a year from a renewable and sustainable source that does not emit greenhouse gases. This electricity replaces 50 million tonnes of coal in China's energy use. This in turn reduces both sulfur dioxide and carbon dioxide emissions, which contribute to acid rain and global warming, respectively. In comparison to coal-fired power stations, electricity generated at the dam is cheap, which allows China's industries to keep manufacturing costs down. This is a boost to the economy as it means that the price of the commodities China exports to other countries can be kept as low as possible, making them more attractive to consumers.

- For hundreds of years, serious seasonal flooding has been a problem for millions of people living along the lower course of the Yangtze River, downstream of the dam, in important cities like Wuhan, Nanjing and Shanghai. Flooding in the past has killed hundreds of thousands of people and washed away whole towns and villages. The new dam has a flood control capacity of 2215 billion cubic metres and has reduced the probability of a serious flood event occurring in the future from once every ten years to once every 100 years. An additional bonus for local people is that the reservoir provides a secure and safe source of both drinking and irrigation water.

- The presence of the dam, the reservoir, and the ship locks, which are large enough to allow 12 large ships to travel over the dam at the same time, has had a huge impact on trade in central China. For the first time, the Yangzte River is navigable for ships up to 10 000 tonnes all the way from Chongqing in the west to Shanghai on the east coast – a distance of nearly 2000 kilometres. Trade has increased five-fold as transport costs have reduced by a third along the river.

Negative impacts

- Over 1000 sites of archaeological, historical and cultural importance have been submerged below the dam waters. These include ancestral burial grounds, religious temples, fossil remains and prehistoric archaeological sites dating from the Palaeolithic era.

- Serious soil erosion leading to flooding and the silting up of the reservoir, and a decline in aquatic life, is occurring upstream of the dam where mountain slopes were stripped of vegetation during the construction phase. Sediments and silt contain valuable nutrients essential for enriching soils. The blocking of sediments behind the dam means that these nutrients are not now reaching farmland downstream of the dam.

- Although the dam produces huge quantities of electricity, most of this is distributed to factories and urban populations rather than rural communities in the more remote and inaccessible areas of China.

- As waters have risen upstream of the dam, two cities, 11 counties, 140 towns, 326 townships and 1351 villages housing over 1.5 million people have been inundated. An estimated 400 sq km of fertile farmland, which provided 10 per cent of China's annual grain harvest, has also been lost. China will now have to pay to import replacement rice from neighbouring countries. Land set aside for the relocation of displaced people has not been sufficient for everyone. There was only enough land to give to 125 000 farmers or farming families but much of it turned out to be less fertile than that which they lost. For some this has led to a decline in income and quality of life. People who were not granted land have been trained to take up new job opportunities in factories and businesses set up by the Chinese government in the area around the reservoir. This has proved difficult for many who have no other experience than working the land.

- There are over 300 species of fish in the Yangtze River. The dam has created a barrier that fish will not now be able to cross. This particularly affects fish that previously travelled upstream to spawn that are forced to follow tributary rivers less suited to breeding instead. There are forty-seven rare or endangered species in the Three Gorges Dam area that are protected by Chinese law. The greatest concern is for the baiji river dolphin, as less than 100 remained in the river before building and the construction of the dam now covers a significant proportion of the dolphin's habitat.

△ Fig. 4.45 Critically endangered baiji river dolphin.

CASE STUDY **CLEANING UP THE RIVER RHINE**

The Rhine is one of the longest rivers in Europe and the continent's most important economic waterway. From its source in the Alps it travels for 1232 km through Switzerland, Germany, France and The Netherlands before flowing into the North Sea. Between the 1950s and 1970s, the Rhine was one of the most polluted rivers in the world as a result of the largely uncontrolled disposal of industrial heavy metals and untreated sewage into the river, combined with the run-off of agricultural pesticides and fertilisers from farmland bordering the river. The impact on the ecology of the river was catastrophic and many species such as migrating salmon disappeared completely.

Today, however, the river has made a remarkable recovery thanks to international cooperation by

△ Fig. 4.46 The River Rhine.

governments and joint **conservation** efforts by all of the nine countries covered by the catchment area of the river. In 1986, all of the countries bordering the Rhine signed up to the Rhine Action Plan and committed to action to improve water quality and restore the ecology of the river. Thirty years on, progress has been remarkable. Nearly seventy species of fish, including salmon, sea trout and sea and river lamprey, have returned to the river. Since 2006, migrating salmon have reached as far upstream from the North Sea as the city of Strasbourg. Pollution of the river by heavy metals and other toxins used by manufacturing industries has been significantly reduced. The oxygen content of Rhine water and the number of microorganism species living on the bed of the river have risen dramatically. This is the result of the introduction of improved wastewater treatment plants in all of the signatories to the Rhine Action Plan. All countries have agreed to use phosphate-free detergents when treating waste water and sewage. This has reduced the amount of nitrogen entering the river each year by over 60 000 tonnes. Today the International Commission for the Protection of the Rhine coordinates the conservation work being undertaken in all of the nine countries within the catchment area of the river to improve water quality for 20 million people and restore the river ecosystem.

One example of joint working is The Rhine International Warning and Alarm System called 'Rhine Alarm'. This has been introduced at eight locations along the course of the River Rhine, which includes places in all the countries through which it flows. Water quality is constantly monitored at these sites so that information about pollution events can be communicated to all countries immediately as they happen. Regulations have also been passed requiring all major industries located along the river and that use hazardous chemicals to have large retention basins where polluted run-off water can collect in the event of an accident, rather than flowing into the river. Water pollution of the River Rhine as a result of industrial accidents has decreased by 99 per cent since the passing of these laws in 1991.

One disastrous pollution incident in 1986 led to the setting up of the River Rhine Action Plan and made governments realise that they had to take action together and quickly if the Rhine was to be saved for future generations. On 1 November 1986, a serious fire broke out at the Sandoz agricultural chemical plant near Basel in Switzerland. In the process of fighting and extinguishing the fire, members of the fire brigades attending poured millions of litres of water onto the blaze. As a result between 10 000 and 15 000 cubic metres of water mixed with thirty-two different types of insecticides, fungicides, herbicides and other chemicals, including at least 11 tonnes of highly-toxic organic mercury compounds, flowed into the nearby River Rhine. In the following two weeks, the chemical pollution travelled 900 km down the river as far as Friesland and Groningen in the Netherlands, and ultimately into the North Sea.

∧ Fig. 4.47 Chemical pollution flowing down the River Rhine after the fire.

△ Fig. 4.48 A police officer collecting dead eels from the River Rhine.

The chemical spill had a devastating ecological impact on the river ecosystem. On 12 December, the Swiss Federal Institute for Water Resources and Water Pollution Control reported that the fish population of the River Rhine had been almost entirely wiped out. Over 150 000 dead European eels alone were collected in buckets from the river. Tens of thousands of waterfowl (ducks, geese and wading birds) that were living and feeding on invertebrates in and beside the river were also killed as a result of ingesting the polluted water and eating fish and other microorganisms that had been poisoned. In Strasbourg, France, a flock of sheep died after drinking from the river.

At the time of the fire, 20 million people relied on the River Rhine for their drinking water. As a safety precaution, all River Rhine water processing plants in Switzerland, Germany, France and the Netherlands were closed down and wells were capped for 18 days. Water supplies to homes were shut off and people had to rely on water deliveries by road tankers. In addition to the water pollution, the fire also released sulfur, phosphorous, nitrogen and carbon into the atmosphere. Residents of Basel were warned to stay indoors as a red haze of pollutants settled over the city. The fire led to citizen protests in all four affected countries, and damage to property along the river totalled US$100 million.

△ Fig. 4.49 Fighting the Sandoz chemical plant fire.

The aftermath of the chemical spill proved very difficult to manage and control effectively. This was because it was a transboundary disaster – a disaster that occurs in one country and very quickly affects neighbouring countries. There were no clearly defined and agreed procedures regarding how Switzerland and Germany should notify each other when an event such as the fire occurred. The result was that Germany only received vital information about the pollution incident after it was too late to take action to reduce the ecological damage. The exchange of information was so slow and confused and German authorities could do little as the pollution moved downstream.

End of topic checklist

Key terms

accessibility, acid rain, agriculture, aquifer, artesian, bioaccumulation, catchment, climate change, commercial, condensation, culture, desalination, desert, disease, distribution, domestic, drought, ecology, economic development, economic recession, ecosystem, environment, erosion, eutrophication, fresh water, genetic engineering, greenhouse gas, groundwater, habitat, hazard, history, improved sanitation, improved water source, indigenous, industrialised, industry, infrastructure, location, manufacturing, migration, multipurpose dam, natural resources, non-government organisation, photosynthesis, pollution, potable water, precipitation, primary consumer, raw material, recycling, religion, renewable energy, run-off, rural, secondary consumer, sedimentation, services, sub-tropical, surface water, sustainability, tertiary consumer, trade, transport, trophic level, tropical, urban, water cycle, water-poor, water-rich, water table

Important vocabulary

aid, algae, antibiotic, aquatic, arable, archaeological, atmosphere, bacteria, basin, brackish, canyon, capital, charity, commodity, compensation, compost, consumer, contamination, convention, coral, dam, dehydration, deoxygenation, depletion, detergent, diagnosis, directive, disinfected, dispersant, earthquake, economic, electricity, elimination, endangered, energy, eradication, estuary, evaporation, export, extraction, faecal, fault, fertiliser, flood, glacier, hormone, hydraulic, hydroelectric, hydrologist, ice cap, impact, impermeable, infection, infiltration, insecticide, intensive, irrigation, joint, lake, landscape, latrine, law, leaching, lock, malaria, migration, mining, mobility, mosquito, mutation, navigation, nuclear, nutrient, ocean, organic, parasite, pathogen, percolation, permafrost, permeable, permit, pesticide, physical, phytoplankton, porous, productivity, prophylaxis, rapids, regulation, rehydration, remote, replenish, reserve, reservoir, resettlement, resistance, resistant, river, saline, saturated, season, seasonal, sedimentary, sewage, silage, silt, sludge, slurry, soil, spawn, spring, subsistence, tax, technology, toxins, transmission, tributary, turbine, vaccine, valley, waste, weir, wetland

During your study of this topic you should have learned:

○ All human life depends on a tiny fraction of the world's total water.

○ The water cycle describes the constant movement of water between the oceans, land and atmosphere.

End of topic checklist continued

○ Groundwater and surface water are the two main sources of water for human use.

○ Desalination involves removing dissolved salt from sea and brackish water to make it fit for human consumption.

○ Water consumption varies hugely between different regions of the world.

○ The level of economic development in a country is the main factor affecting water consumption.

○ Freshwater reserves are not distributed evenly across the world, which means that some regions can be defined as water-rich and others as water-poor.

○ Water shortage can be the result of physical or economic factors.

○ One in ten people do not have access to potable or improved drinking water and this can be the cause of serious water-borne diseases.

○ Countries with poor access to potable water also often have poor sanitation, which increases the risk of disease.

○ Multipurpose dams such as the Three Gorges Dam in China are constructed for a range of reasons, including providing energy, irrigation and drinking water and improving river navigation.

○ Multipurpose dams can have positive and negative economic, social and environmental impacts.

○ Domestic waste and industrial and agricultural practices are the main sources of water pollution.

○ Supporting appropriate and sustainable developments in the poorest countries of the world is the most effective way of improving sanitation and water supply.

○ Many countries now have strict controls and laws to prevent water pollution.

○ Water-related diseases such as malaria and cholera kill millions of people a year but a range of measures have now been introduced to combat their transmission and achieve eradication in the future.

○ Oil spills such as the Deepwater Horizon blowout can have catastrophic ecological and economic consequences, and disaster planning and management is required to minimise these effects.

The questions for Section 4 start on page 247.

From a certain angle, the Earth is entirely dominated by the Pacific Ocean, the largest of all the oceans. From this angle, the Earth looks completely covered by water; over two-thirds of its surface is made up of oceans and seas – Planet Earth is often referred to as the Blue Planet for this reason. The oceans are a vital part of the biosphere and human life depends upon them for a vast range of resources and natural services. The resource potential of the oceans is vast, with humans utilising them for food supplies, power generation, transport and tourism. With the human population expected to rise to 9.7 billion by 2050, the oceans and the resources they provide are under increasing pressure. This raises some important environmental management questions. How is our current use of ocean resources meeting our needs today? Are we harming the ability of people in the future to meet their needs from ocean resources? Is our behaviour today affecting the ability of the oceans to support life on Earth?

CONTENTS

LEARNING OBJECTIVES

Outline the resource potential of the oceans.

Describe the distribution of major ocean currents.

Explain the distribution of major marine fish populations.

Describe the El Niño Southern Oscillation (ENSO) phenomenon and its effects on fisheries along the Pacific coast of South America.

Describe and explain the impact of exploitation of fisheries.

Describe how farming of marine species reduces the exploitation of fisheries.

Describe, explain and evaluate strategies for management of the harvesting of marine species.

Examine the resource potential, exploitation, impact and management of a marine fishery.

Study an example of farming of marine species, the source of food, pollution from fish waste and impact on the natural habitat.

5
Oceans and fisheries

OCEANS AS A RESOURCE

△ Fig. 5.1 Map showing the major oceans and seas of Earth.

With two-thirds of the planet covered in water, the oceans are a significant feature of the planet and they play a vital role in the regulation of the **climate**: distributing heat from the equator toward the colder higher latitudes by way of warm and cold **ocean currents**. The oceans also absorb **carbon dioxide**, so they are an important carbon sink in the **carbon cycle** and natural greenhouse effect. Not only are oceans a vital part of life on Earth, they also contain vast resource potential, which has been and continues to be exploited.

	Area (sq km)	Percentage of total ocean area	Average depth (m)	Maximum depth (m)
Arctic Ocean	15 558 000	4.3	1205	5567
Atlantic Ocean	85 133 000	23.5	3646	8486
Baltic Sea	406 000	0.1	51	392
Mediterranean	2 967 000	0.8	1480	5139
North Atlantic	41 490 000	11.5	3519	8486
South Atlantic	40 270 000	11.1	3973	8240
Indian Ocean	70 560 000	19.5	3741	7906
Pacific Ocean	161 760 000	44.7	4080	10 803
North Pacific	77 010 000	21.3	4298	10 803
South Pacific	84 750 000	23.4	3882	10 753
South China Sea	6 963 000	1.9	1419	7352
Southern Ocean	21 960 000	6.1	3270	7075

△ Table 5.1 Fact file on the major oceans and seas.

The resource potential of the oceans can be broadly classified into the following categories: food, building materials and chemicals, power generation, **tourism**, transportation, and a source of drinking water.

Food

Perhaps the most visible use of ocean resources is the **consumption** of seafood. Seafood is comprised of aquatic plants and animals consumed by humans directly or indirectly. Included in this are fish (such as cod and herring), molluscs (such as clams and oysters), crustaceans (such as crab, shrimp and lobster), marine reptiles (such as alligators and turtles), marine mammals (such as whales) and seaweed. In 2012, nearly 160 million tonnes of fish were either caught or produced through **aquaculture** (farming). This is a rising trend, up from 140 million tonnes in 2007, and equates to 19.2 kg of food fish supply for each person. Around 85 per cent of fish is for human consumption.

△ Fig. 5.2 A fishing trawler in the North Atlantic Ocean.

Building materials and chemicals

Sea level and climate have varied over time. Erosional processes of the coast and on land have led to the formation and concentration of vast quantities of **mineral** resources that are useful to humans as chemicals or as building materials. These are either formed by marine process, but are now on land due to sea level change and tectonic uplift, extraction from seawater, or extraction from the seabed. Many of these are either being extracted today or have potential to be extracted in the future. For example:

△ Fig. 5.3 Coastal salt mining in Thailand.

- Sea salt and limestone are being mined on land today.
- Seawater contains a small proportion of dissolved solids. Tens of chemical elements have been identified, but it is mainly sodium chloride and magnesium that are currently commercially extracted.
- Manganese, phosphorites, zinc, copper, lead, silver and gold are found on the seabed or near hydrothermal vents. These are very difficult to exploit due to depth and location.
- Gold, tin, titanium and diamonds have been eroded on land and deposited in shallow coastal water sediments and on beaches.
- Sand and gravel are extracted offshore to provide aggregates for building materials for houses and roads. The removal of sediments from the natural transportation system can have significant coastal **erosion** impacts if not managed sustainably.

△ Fig. 5.4 Dredging sand for a new port.

Power generation

Offshore winds, waves and tides have vast untapped potential to meet our energy needs. Combined, they could play a significant part in meeting the current and future global demand for energy. However, there are significant environmental and economic challenges in scaling up the technology and getting the electricity from the source to the areas where it is demanded. These are the main methods for harnessing the power of the oceans:

- offshore wind farms
- offshore wave generators
- nearshore/onshore wave generators
- tidal stream generators
- tidal barrages.

Section 2 covers the main forms of **renewable energy** sources from oceans and their advantages and disadvantages (see pages 26–51).

Tourism

Globally, tourism is the largest and fasting growing economic sector, generating 11 per cent of global GDP (gross domestic product) and employing over 200 million people worldwide. An estimated 700 million people travel internationally each year, with even more visiting sites in their own countries. Due to the attraction of the coast and nearshore marine **environment** for leisure and recreation, a large proportion of these tourists head to coastal environments and have a significant impact on coastal **ecosystems**. Unsustainable tourism development can lead to mangrove and reef destruction, as well as **habitat** disruption and marine **pollution**. However, the resource potential for tourism is huge and brings many economic benefits to communities around the world.

Transportation

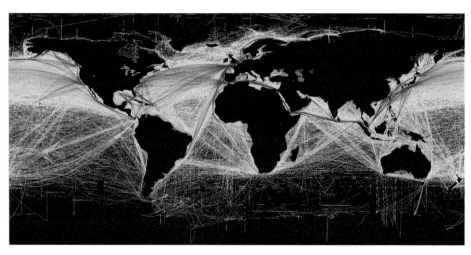

△ Fig. 5.5 Global ship movements.

The oceans play a vital role in the world economy. Transport of goods in increasingly large, fast and specialised ships is a key feature of 21st-century **trade**, with an estimated 9.93 billion tonnes of freight transported in 2013. The majority of this trade is in container ships, bulk carriers and tankers. Further to these, naval vessels, cruise ships and ferries are common. This volume of shipping is not without environmental concerns due to pollution, accidents and impacts on marine **species** – many of which are covered in Section 2 (see pages 26–51).

△ Fig. 5.6 A modern container ship.

A source of drinking water

The oceans and seas contain 97 per cent of all the water on Earth. However, the salinity level (global average is 3.5 per cent) means that the water is unsafe to meet human needs. The extraction of fresh water from seawater is possible through reverse osmosis or distillation in **desalination** plants, although it is highly expensive and energy-intensive when compared to land-based freshwater resources. Globally, around 1 per cent of all fresh water is extracted from saltwater. Over 100 countries use desalination, with Middle Eastern countries building the highest capacity plants to date. With increasing **freshwater scarcity** around the world, it is likely there will be significant investment in desalination in the future. This will make the technology more affordable and reduce the large environmental impact from waste products entering the sea.

△ Fig. 5.7 A desalination plant in Dubai, United Arab Emirates.

WORLD FISHERIES

Ocean currents

An ocean current is a continuous movement of seawater that is driven by a range of factors. These include the gravitational pull of the moon and sun in creating tides, surface currents caused by wind, and warm and cold currents driven by **thermohaline circulation** – differences in temperature and salinity. The movement of major ocean currents has a profound impact on the climate of Earth as well as on the distribution of marine species, and consequently the location of profitable fisheries.

Local currents are driven by winds and tides and how they interact with land. These play a key role in the erosion, transportation and **deposition** of sediment along the coast. Major ocean currents are complex and can be seen in Figure 5.8. There is a clear pattern of warm surface water moving away from the equator in a giant spiral motion. These **gyres** spin clockwise in the northern hemisphere and anticlockwise in the southern hemisphere.

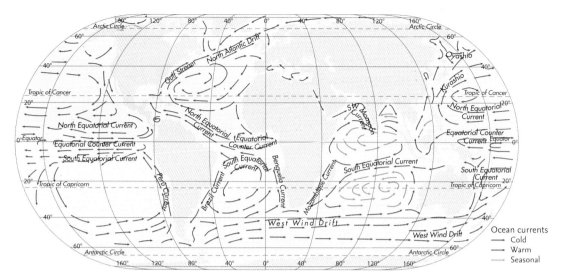

△ Fig. 5.8 The distribution of major ocean currents.

The spiral motion is caused by **coriolis effect** – the rotation of the Earth. The oceans do not have uniform temperature and salinity, so when the warm water reaches the polar regions it cools, becomes saltier and more dense, and then sinks down. These cold deep water currents move along the seabed back toward the equator. The warm and cold ocean currents combine to create a massive global conveyor belt of water (Figure 5.9) that is in constant motion, driven by thermohaline circulation. It is estimated that water takes 1000 years to complete one whole circuit around the conveyor. As the current moves, it causes nutrient-rich water to rise to the surface in various locations – a process called **upwelling**. This stimulates entire **food chains** and can explain the distribution of the most dense concentrations of marine species.

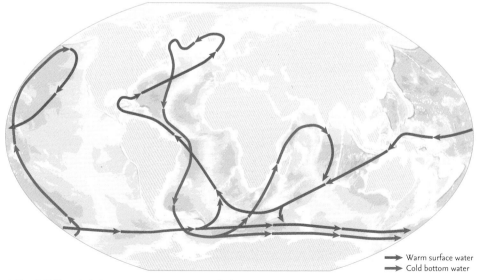

△ Fig. 5.9 The global ocean current conveyor belt.

The distribution of major marine fish populations

Over 70 per cent of all fish caught come from the Pacific Ocean, with 20 per cent coming from the Atlantic. Understanding the global distribution of marine fish **population** is complex, as many species can be located across a large geographical area. Figure 5.10 shows an innovative map developed by Aquamaps (www.aquamaps.org) that uses estimates of the environmental preferences (depth, temperature, salinity) of over 20 000 marine species to calculate the probability of their distribution. This information is cross-referenced with local observations and creates a heat map for species diversity. To explain patterns and trends in the distribution, it is important to examine the different maps in this chapter to see the links between data. Using this approach, it is possible to identify key areas where major fish populations will be found:

- in the shallow waters around the **continental shelf** where sunlight can penetrate to the sea floor
- in coastal waters
- around coral reefs
- where ocean currents cause upwelling
- around oceanic islands.

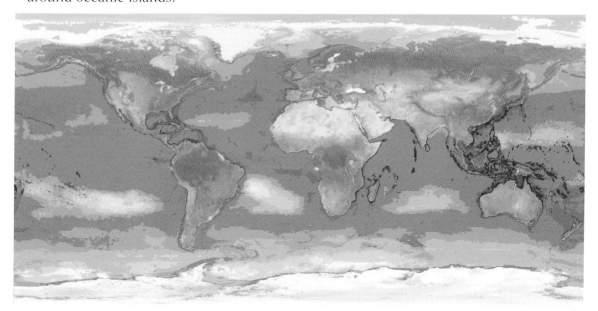

△ Fig. 5.10 The global distribution of 22 800 species of fish, marine mammals and invertebrates.

A key factor in the distribution is the relationship between marine **topography**, ocean currents and **photosynthesis**. Photosynthesis by phytoplankton will be the basis for massive **food webs**. The most productive areas with the most fish are in coastal areas, where upwelling occurs to bring nutrients to the surface. An example of this would be the Pacific coast of South America, where a combination of the continental shelf, year-round upwelling of water and high biomass production leads to high concentrations of marine species – and highly valuable fisheries.

Species No.
3209–7867
1309–3208
534–1308
219–533
90–218
37–89
16–36
7–15
3–6
1–2

△ Fig. 5.11 The location of shallow continental shelf.

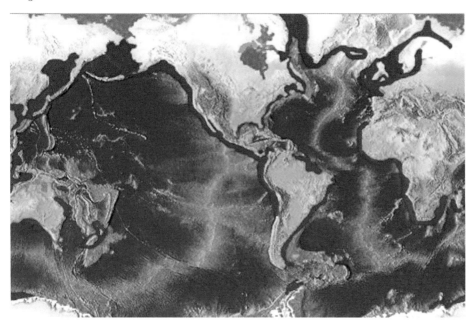

△ Fig. 5.12 Major upwelling areas around the world.

El Niño Southern Oscillation phenomenon and its effects on fisheries along the Pacific coast of South America

The Pacific coast of South America is a highly productive fishing ground that attracts boats from across the world. Coastal communities are reliant on the productivity for their livelihoods – with economies driven by catching fish for consumption, processing and export. In many places along the coast, fishing is the only **industry** to provide significant employment. Unfortunately for these communities, the Pacific Ocean experiences a climate cycle called **El Niño Southern Oscillation (ENSO)**. This is a complex oceanic–atmospheric interaction that weakens the wind and reverses the warm ocean current patterns in the Pacific Ocean. ENSO occurs on an irregular cycle that averages between two and seven years and has global effects on weather. Countries on either side of the Pacific Ocean see significant changes to the weather, with drier conditions in Asia and wetter conditions on the Pacific coast of South America. El Niño occurs when the normal easterly trade winds weaken and the warm waters they drive begin moving back toward the east, warming the ocean in the eastern Pacific Ocean. This is shown in Figure 5.13.

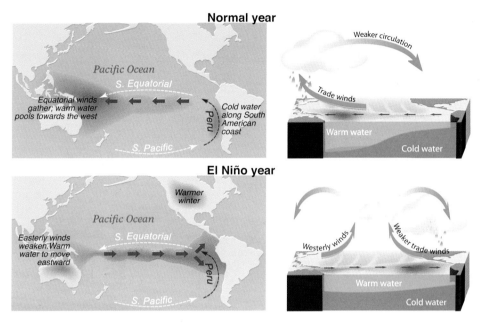

△ Fig. 5.13 The El Niño Southern Oscillation.

The warming of the eastern Pacific Ocean means the cold Humboldt current that moves up the coast of South America is overwhelmed by the warm ocean current and the sea temperatures become between 4 °C and 8 °C warmer than normal. This reduces the upwelling of cold water, which reduces the productivity of the ecosystems and causes fish to reproduce in fewer numbers or migrate elsewhere. The loss of fish has a devastating effect on the economies of countries along the coast. There have been a number of occasions where **overfishing** off the coast of Peru during an El Niño event has caused fish stocks of Peruvian anchoveta to completely collapse – with a reduction in the catch of up to 80 per cent. In Peru, an El Niño year often reduces gross national income by 5 per cent.

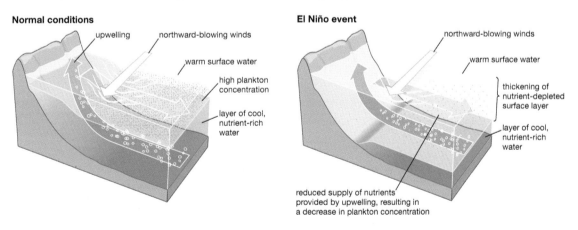

△ Fig. 5.14 The impact of ENSO on coastal upwelling.

IMPACT OF EXPLOITATION OF THE OCEANS

Overfishing

Global demand for fish and marine products in 2012 was 158 million tonnes – worth an estimated US$130 billion – making fish amongst the world's most traded food commodities. Around 12 per cent of the world's population depends upon fishing or aquaculture for their livelihoods and there are an estimated 4.7 million fishing vessels worldwide. Never before have so many marine species been caught, processed, exported and consumed. The 2014 WWF Living Planet Report identified a 39 per cent decline in marine species (birds, mammals, reptiles and fish) between 1970 and 2010. The trends vary, but the **tropical** Pacific and Atlantic Oceans and the Southern Ocean have seen the sharpest declines. The report states that in these regions, 'seabirds, sharks and many fish populations have seen declines as a result of overfishing and **bycatch**'. Overfishing occurs when more fish are caught than the population can replace through natural reproduction.

△ Fig. 5.15 A Chilean purse seine ship hauls a catch aboard.

A lack of management, increasing technology and the use of ever-larger boats has led to dangerously high levels of overfishing. In some areas, commonly eaten species are in danger of stock collapse and even extinction. As demand for fish has increased, the profits to be made from fishing have risen. Large companies can afford to build ships with increased capacity – capable of taking even more fish out of the sea with each haul. Figure 5.16 shows one of the world's biggest **pelagic** trawlers. These high tech vessels use radar and spotter helicopters to identify shoals of fish. Their massive nets – capable of containing a fleet of 12 jumbo jets – clear everything caught in them. This boat catches up to 8000 tonnes of tuna in each haul.

△ Fig. 5.16 Greenpeace disrupt the operation of one of the world's largest fishing boats.

In the Pacific, there is huge concern over the arrival of super trawlers and floating **fish factories** such as the Lafayette, a 50 000 tonne Russian-registered and Hong Kong owned ship that takes fishing at sea to a truly industrial scale. The ship does not actually catch fish, but acts as a mothership to a fleet of super trawlers. It pumps the vast catches of these trawlers and sorts, processes and freezes the fish on board. It even has 12 forklift trucks on board to move the frozen fish around, ready to be shipped off to other ships that transport the fish to land. The Lafayette rarely has to dock, so can maximise its time processing fish.

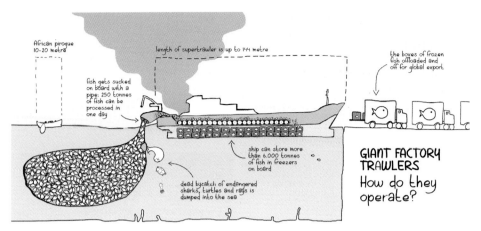

Fig. 5.17 How factory trawlers operate.

Within the image:
- African piroque 10–20 metre
- length of supertrawler is up to 144 metre
- fish gets sucked on board with a pipe: 250 tonnes of fish can be processed in one day
- the boxes of frozen fish offloaded and off for global export
- ship can store more than 6,000 tonnes of fish in freezers on board
- dead bycatch of endangered sharks, turtles and rays is dumped into the sea
- GIANT FACTORY TRAWLERS How do they operate?

Modern technology has dramatically increased the efficiency and scale of fishing fleets and, as a consequence, some species are at risk of extinction due to overfishing. Greenpeace and the Marine Conservation Society (MCS) have identified a large number of popular species that are seriously threatened by the following actions:

- catching of vulnerable species
- destructive fishing methods
- overfishing
- unselective fishing methods that create wasteful bycatch
- illegal or pirate fishing.

It is estimated that the global fishing fleet is two to three times larger than the oceans can sustainably support. In 2011, the UN report into the state of the world's fisheries reported the following:

- 28.8 per cent of fish stocks were estimated as fished at a biologically unsustainable level.
- 61.3 per cent of fish stocks were fished at capacity with no room for further growth in production.
- 9.9 per cent of stocks were underfished – with capacity to increase production.
- The ten most productive species are either fully fished or overfished. Examples include two main stocks of anchoveta in the southeast Pacific Ocean, Alaska pollock in the north Pacific Ocean; and Atlantic herring stocks in both the northeast and northwest Atlantic Ocean are fully fished. Atlantic cod is overfished in the northwest Atlantic Ocean, but fully fished in the northeast Atlantic Ocean.

The total catch of tuna and tuna-like species was about 6.8 million tonnes in 2011. There are several different species of tuna found in different oceans. The five main species are skipjack, bluefin, big eye, albacore and yellowfin. All of these are under threat in at least one location around the world. For example, skipjack tuna should not be eaten from the western Atlantic Ocean if caught by a **purse seiner**; it is at risk in the Indian Ocean, but is better if caught by hand on a pole and line in the central Pacific Ocean. Market demand for tuna is still high and there is significant overcapacity of tuna fishing fleets globally. Tuna is a highly valuable fish, which in some locations is being pushed beyond **sustainable** limits.

Bycatch and discards

Overfishing is having a significant impact on the target species that are being sought out by fishing boats worldwide. However, frequently the giant nets bring on board fish and marine species that are caught unintentionally. This bycatch can sometimes be very valuable, but at other times the bycatch is too small or of species they are not allowed to sell, so these are discarded – often dead – back into the sea. This is an appalling waste of **natural resources**. At times, the young small fish of the target species are discarded, which harms future fish stocks.

△ Fig. 5.18 Bycatch caught by a shrimp boat in Mexico.

Furthermore, marine species such as sharks, dolphins, sea birds and crustaceans are caught unnecessarily, leading to a significant impact on the **biodiversity** of the seas. Shrimp nets are the worst for bycatch, as the small nets needed for shrimp also catch a huge proportion of other species. For every 1 kg of shrimp caught, there is 5.7 kg of bycatch of other species discarded.

The role of aquaculture in managing global fisheries

Managing the biodiversity of the oceans is complex, with rising demand for food driven by population growth and increasing levels of development. One solution is to increase fish farming or aquaculture. This involves raising fish in tanks or enclosures. Aquaculture is the fastest growing food production system in the world, with China accounting for 62 per cent of the world's fish farming practice. In 2011, 66.6 million tonnes of the total 158 million tonnes of marine products came from aquaculture. If managed responsibly, aquaculture can have a significant

△ Fig. 5.19 An open water fish farm in Croatia.

impact on wild marine species, which can be allowed to recover. However, the rapid expansion of the industry has led to other environmental challenges such as water pollution and disease transfer. Furthermore, aquaculture requires a substantial amount of fish to be caught in the wild to provide food for the farmed fish – so does not immediately reduce the impact on certain caught species, or reduce bycatch and discards. However, it is clear that aquaculture has an important role to play in meeting the needs of a growing human population.

MANAGEMENT OF THE HARVESTING OF MARINE SPECIES

While aquaculture is playing an increasingly important role in global fish supply, it does not on its own provide the solution to overfishing and the impact this is having on the biodiversity of the oceans. There are many steps that have been taken to control the global fishing industry and to reduce its impact. However, this is a very complex environmental management challenge due to lack of agreement between countries, international laws and the lucrative nature of the business, which puts ever increasing profits in the short term ahead of the longer-term sustainability of the oceans as a food source.

There are a range of different strategies that are attempting to manage the harvesting of marine species and to reduce overfishing, bycatch and discards, as well as to allow fish stocks to recover. These include managing net types and mesh size, pole and line fishing, **quotas**, closed seasons, international agreements on protected areas and reserves, and **conservation** laws.

Net types and mesh size

There are a vast number of methods used to catch fish around the world, including:

- drift nets
- pelagic trawlers
- beam trawlers
- bottom dredging
- purse seining.

△ Fig. 5.20 A beam trawler hauls it nets aboard.

There are many other methods, but these are commonly associated with the greatest environmental impact in terms of overfishing, bycatch and discards. It is possible to adjust methods by changing net types or banning certain nets, such as drift nets. However, this is not a simple process as often, boats fish areas with multiple fish species present, many of which are different shapes and sizes. Efforts to reduce bycatch are focused on net design that takes into account predictable fish behaviour and changing the mesh size (the gaps in the net) to allow certain species to escape. For example, cod and haddock can be separated out into different parts of the net due to the way they react when the nets disturb the seabed. The unwanted fish can enter a part of the net with a bigger mesh size and escape.

△ Fig. 5.21 Vietnamese fishermen prepare to catch tuna using a traditional small mesh trawling net.

Changing the traditional mesh shape from a diamond to a square allows the mesh to remain open when being towed. This allows smaller fish to escape the nets and reduces bycatch. Furthermore, adding square mesh panels into the top and bottom of nets has been shown to allow certain species to either drop out of the nets or to rise up and escape – reducing catches of unwanted fish. Other nets now contain separator grids and cutaway holes that allow bigger fish to swim away, while smaller shrimp are collected.

Understanding fish behaviour, as well as the use of technology in nets and mesh design, means that in the more highly controlled fisheries of the United States and the EU, attempts are being made to manage bycatch. In the southwest of the UK, Brixham fishermen have converted 90 per cent of their boats to modified nets, with a reduction in discards by over 50 per cent across the fleet.

Pole and line

Pole and line fishing is a selective and more sustainable method used to catch naturally schooling fish such as tuna, which can be attracted to the surface by throwing live bait overboard. Poles and lines with barbless hooks are then used to hook the fish and bring them on board. This is a particularly effective method which avoids unwanted bycatch as nets are not used. Fish that are too small or unwanted can be returned to the sea.

△ Fig. 5.22 Pole and line fishing for tuna in the Maldives.

Quotas

Reducing the number of fish caught globally is very challenging due to the impact this has on incomes in the short term. However, long-term incomes are under more threat from overfishing, which causes fish stocks to collapse. Many fisheries now have strict limits placed on the total allowable catches of certain species – usually a number of tonnes of a certain species from a certain region, for example, the EU. These quotas reduce the number of fish caught and ban the catching of other endangered species. By limiting catches, more fish are left to breed, allowing the population to slowly recover. In order to prevent a race between fishermen to gain the maximum amount of fish possible in the quota, the quotas are allocated to individual vessels, fishermen or groups of fishermen. Some quotas can be bought and sold between vessels, so an inefficient slower vessel can sell its quota for a fish species to another vessel.

Quotas are usually by species and weight in tonnes. Due to net sizes and bycatch, some fishermen catch many more fish than the quota allows, so select the most valuable sized fish, discarding the rest of the dead fish into the sea. Furthermore, fishing vessels might catch fish that are not the target species and might have already reached the quota placed on numbers. Fishing vessels are forced to discard perfectly good fish to avoid fines. The quota system sometimes means that vessels sit in port, being paid not to fish. In some parts of the world, ensuring compliance is very difficult due to a lack of control over the fishing industry. Overall, the use of quotas is a controversial part of fisheries management, but an important strategy when quotas are set by individual governments for their own waters and developed alongside net changes and other sustainable management strategies.

Closed seasons

Closed seasons have been a useful strategy in freshwater fisheries and effectively ban the catching of fish in the breeding season or for a prolonged period of time. These have been extended to some coastal fisheries, where catching certain species is banned at certain times of year. For example, in Mozambique, there is now a five-month closed season for the fishing of shallow water shrimp. This relies on the compliance of fishing vessels and the use of fines as punishment. If monitored, this can be an effective strategy.

International agreements on protected areas and reserves

In areas that have been extensively overfished and stocks are at near collapse or in places that are of high biodiversity value, often the only way to protect or restore stocks is to introduce protected reserves where all fishing is banned. There are various types of protected areas, commonly known as **Marine Protected Areas (MPAs)**. Often these areas ban the removal of any resources, including fish, as well as restricting movement of shipping. However, illegal fishing does take place and enforcement requires innovative monitoring and use of **GIS**. Networks of MPAs are growing globally in response to overfishing and degrading of the marine environment through pollution. The Great Barrier Reef off the coast of Australia is a large MPA, but increasingly local communities are designating small-scale MPAs to allow fish stocks to recover and spill out into surrounding waters. MPAs are a key part of the sustainable environmental management of fisheries.

Conservation laws

Conservation laws can be a highly effective way of reducing overfishing, establishing MPAs, increasing long-term benefits from an area and ensuring the sustainability of food supply. The 1976 Magnuson-Stevens conservation law in the United States extended government control of the waters surrounding the US from 19 to 322 km and introduced fishery management plans, which included ten national standards that promote sustainable fisheries management. The law allows scientists to make annual stock assessments and to set annual catch limits that are strictly enforced. Today, 90 per cent of US fisheries catch less than their annual catch limits. UN agreements have also been made and the work of the UN Food and Agriculture Organisation (FAO) in documenting the state of world fisheries is now vital in identifying and prioritising species and regions under threat.

International agreements (implementation and monitoring)

In 1982, the United Nations Convention on the Law of the Sea (UNCLOS) allowed coastal countries to have control rights over the zone extending 322 km offshore. This **exclusive economic zone (EEZ)** lets a country ban fishing by foreign vessels, or sell permits to foreign fishing vessels. The UNCLOS agreement paved the way for the development of modern day MPAs such as the newly created Phoenix Islands Protected Area (PIPA) in the central Pacific Ocean (see the case study below). When combining enforcement of policy derived from international agreements with high-tech monitoring of vessels and fish stocks, it is possible to manage MPAs and allow the fish stocks to recover and to spill over into other areas.

CASE STUDY PHOENIX ISLANDS PROTECTED AREA (PIPA)

The island nation of Kiribati in the Pacific Ocean is a biodiversity hotspot. Covering 3.5 million sq km, the combination of warm equatorial waters and thirty-three **atolls** and reef islands separated by deep water mean that there is a huge diversity of habitats for marine species. There are 600–800 species of finfish, 200 species of coral and around 1000 species of shellfish. The species diversity is ideal hunting ground for bigger predatory fish such as skipjack, big eye and yellowfin tuna. This in turn has led to Kiribati and the waters of the western and central Pacific Ocean being considered as an economically important fishing ground. Around 70 per

△ Fig. 5.23 The location of Kiribati.

cent of skipjack tuna caught in the region are caught in the waters of Kiribati. In 2014 and 2015 there were over 44 000 days of fishing activity in the waters of Kiribati. The government sells lucrative fishing licenses to far-off fishing nations, which in 2014 accounted for 27 per cent of Kiribati's GDP.

Fishing methods traditionally use purse seine nets that are drawn together or 'pursed' (see Figure 5.24) at the bottom and the top. These are highly effective nets, but environmental concerns over bycatch – particularly dolphins – has led to the development of **fish aggregation devices (FADs)**. These man-made objects, often made up of wooden floats or buoys, are used to attract larger finfish such as tuna. These can be fixed to the seabed or left to float on the surface and attract small fish in large numbers due to the shelter they provide. This in turn attracts larger predatory fish species. The purse seine boats then encircle the fish and catch the entire shoal. This approach catches nearly one-third of all tuna caught globally, but with a high level of associated bycatch. The method of using FADs with purse seine nets has led to significant population declines in this area of the Pacific Ocean.

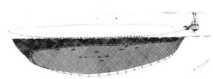

△ Fig. 5.24 A purse seine net.

Management

PIPA fact file

Location: Phoenix islands, Kiribati

Area: 408 250 sq km

Environment: total land area of 25 sq km, low-lying islands, coral atolls and **seamounts** with deep water in between.

Designation: largest MPA in the Pacific Ocean, largest UNESCO marine World Heritage site

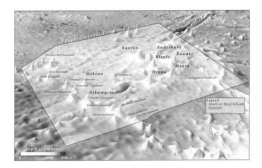

△ Fig. 5.25 Phoenix Islands Protected Area (PIPA).

Species: at least eight species of sharks, over 500 species of reef fish, 200 species of corals, and marine mammals such as bottlenose and common dolphins.

Concern over declining fish populations and the impact of bycatch of larger shark and dolphin species led to the government of Kiribati designating certain areas as protected zones. This is complex, as Kiribati needs to maintain income from selling fish licences and maintain healthy stock. This is further complicated by the vast spread of ocean that Kiribati covers, which means that due to the 322-km EEZ, Kiribati is split into three separate zones as part of a complex network of EEZs and MPAs.

△ Fig. 5.26 PIPA contains some of the last intact oceanic coral ecosystems.

In 2009, the government of Kiribati restricted fishing in 12 per cent of its total area by creating PIPA around the Phoenix islands – a unique set of seamounts and small islands that have been virtually untouched by humans. Its remote location meant that the area is a marine wilderness area. However, advances in boat technology meant that the seas around the Phoenix islands were coming under threat from the fishing industry. Other nearby areas governed by the United States were protected as 100 per cent no take zones that were monitored and policed. This led to the PIPA zone continuing to be commercially fished.

On 1 January 2015, PIPA was designated a complete 'no-take zone'. The ban on vessels is being monitored by a ground-breaking GIS called Global Fish Watch. The partnership between Google, Oceana and Skytruth allows near real-time tracking of vessels that have to use a ship Automated Identification System (AIS). Global Fish Watch combines AIS data with base maps of protected areas and ship information to identify illegal fishing and report it to the authorities. This allows accurate monitoring and for authorities to ban ships that deliberately enter protected areas to fish. The impact of PIPA using Global Fish Watch to look at fishing vessel patterns can be seen in Figure 5.27. While the ban has been effective, there was concern over the impact this would have on local economies. However, allowing fish populations in PIPA to grow causes spillover into the non-protected area and Kiribati has actually increased its revenue from selling fishing licenses. This powerful model of policy, monitoring and enforcement of international agreements can be a highly effective sustainable management tool.

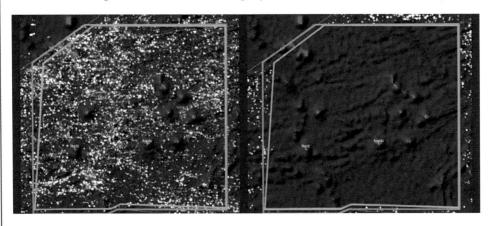

△ Fig. 5.27 The impact of the fishing ban on PIPA – the photo on the left shows fishing activity in 2014 compared to fishing activity in 2015 in the photo on the right.

CASE STUDY **SALMON FARMING ON THE ISLE OF SKYE**

Global aquaculture is the fastest growing food production system in the world. It is clear that although steps are being taken in some parts of the world to manage the stock of wild fisheries, there is a long way to go before wild fish stocks could be considered sustainable. Indeed, if current trends continue, some species will be fished to extinction. Aquaculture is one solution to reduce demand pressure on wild fish stocks. There are a range of advantages and disadvantages associated with fish farming.

One area that has seen a huge growth globally is the farming of salmon – particularly Atlantic salmon. This is a commercially valuable fish that was being overfished from wild population, and as they swim upriver to reproduce, they were being adversely affected by human activity on rivers. In the UK, the salmon farming industry has grown rapidly, with an equivalent value of over US$1 billion in 2014.

△ Fig. 5.28 Open system salmon farming on the Isle of Skye, Scotland, UK.

In 2014, over 179 000 tonnes of salmon were produced in pens or cages that are open to the sea. These are made up of nets that hang from a floating structure which are anchored to the sea bed. In the UK, the majority of open sea cage aquaculture happens on the west coast of Scotland, where a sheltered coastline and good water quality boost production. The salmon industry employs over 1700 people directly. Overall aquaculture of all fish species in Scotland employs nearly 10 000 people, making a vital contribution to the rural economy.

Advantages of aquaculture

- A global supply of marine products can increase to meet demand.
- Employment is generated in coastal aquaculture areas.
- Large profits stimulate the local economy in often rural areas, which suffer a lack of investment.
- Controlled water quality and protection against predators ensure stocks survive.
- Regular feeding and **selective breeding** can lead to more rapid growth than wild fisheries.
- Fish farming could fulfill the protein needs of millions of people in developing countries.

Disadvantages of aquaculture

- Larger farmed fish are fed pellets made of fish oil and fish meal that come from small ocean fish such as anchovy. These are small wild fish, caught with fine mesh nets, leading to bycatch.
- Every 1 kg of salmon produced requires, on average, two to three times their weight of wild-caught fish.
- Removing smaller species of fish can damage food webs, leading to impacts on larger fish.
- Waste from fish cages and uneaten food is deposited on the sea floor, causing sea floor pollution and a reduction in water quality, if unmanaged.
- There can be possible impacts on sensitive habitats and species in polluted areas.
- Fish are more closely packed than in the wild, so diseases can spread more easily.
- Open water systems can lead to fish escapes and interaction with endangered wild species.

End of topic checklist

Key terms

aquaculture, atoll, biodiversity, bycatch, climate, consumption, continental shelf, coriolis effect, current, desalination, ecosystem, EEZ, ENSO, erosion, FAD, fish factory, freshwater scarcity, gyres, habitat, latitude, MPA, overfishing, pelagic, photosynthesis, pollution, purse seine, quota, resources, sea level, seamount, tectonic uplift, thermohaline, topography, tourism, unsustainable, upwelling

Important vocabulary

capacity, closed season, collapse, commodity, conservation law, consumption, conveyor belt, cross-referenced, dissolved, distribution, dredging, exploitation, farming, food supplies, freight, Global Fish Watch, goods, gravitational pull, heat map, high concentrations, industrial scale, management, mesh and net size, migrate, minerals, pole and line, pressure, reproduction, resource potential, rising trend, rotation, salinity, scaling up, transport, trawler, waste

During your study of this topic you should have learned:

○ The oceans have a huge potential to provide humans with resources such as food, water, chemicals, building materials for energy generation and transport.

○ Global distribution of oceans and major ocean currents.

○ Ocean current and topography patterns influence the distribution of marine fish populations.

○ The El Niño Southern Oscillation (ENSO) phenomenon has a dramatic effect on fisheries along the Pacific coast of South America.

○ Exploitation of the oceans is having a significant impact in terms of overfishing and bycatch.

○ Farming of marine species reduces the exploitation of fisheries, but also leads to unwanted environmental impacts that need management.

○ Marine fisheries can be managed more sustainably through a combination of:

— developments in net type and mesh size

— the use of pole and line techniques

— the introduction of carefully-managed fishing quotas

- closed seasons

- the development of MPAs and conservation areas

- implementation and careful monitoring of international agreements.

◯ How Kiribati in the Pacific Ocean is reducing its impact and managing its fisheries.

◯ Fish farming has a range of advantages and disadvantages and these need careful management to be considered sustainable.

The questions for Section 5 start on page 251.

There are now over 7 billion humans on Planet Earth and this number is expected to rise above 9.7 billion by 2050. Increasingly, people are living in places where they face a growing risk from natural hazards. Many countries are struggling to cope with rapidly expanding populations and migration into cities. Over 50 per cent of humans now live in urban environments and it can be very challenging to develop the infrastructure rapidly enough to sustain the population expansion. Many of these places are also located in hazard zones where the people could be at risk from one or even multiple hazards (volcanic eruptions, hurricanes, earthquakes, floods, landslides, tsunamis and droughts) and the number of recorded natural disasters is increasing. It is vital in the 21st century to understand how these hazards occur, the possible effects and how humans can manage risk.

CONTENTS

LEARNING OBJECTIVES

Describe the structure of the Earth.

Describe and explain the distribution and causes of earthquakes and volcanoes.

Describe and explain the distribution and causes of tropical cyclones (storms, hurricanes and typhoons).

Describe and explain the causes of flooding.

Describe and explain the causes of drought.

Describe and explain the impacts of natural hazards on people and the environment.

Describe and evaluate the strategies for managing the impacts of natural hazards before, during and after an event.

Describe and explain the opportunities presented by natural hazards to people.

Compare and contrast the strategies for managing the impacts of tectonic events between a named MEDC and a named LEDC.

Study the strategies for managing the impacts of a tropical storm, flood or drought.

6 Managing natural hazards

EARTHQUAKES AND VOLCANOES

The structure of the Earth

The inner structure of the Earth is made up of layers with different properties. Scientists have been able to use study of **topography**, observation of **earthquake** and volcanic data, analysis of deep **rocks**, satellite imaging, measurements of the magnetic field and analysis of seismic waves to determine the relative size and density of each layer inside the Earth. Understanding how the layers work and how they interact with each other is critical to understanding the surface processes that influence humans.

The Earth is structured into three main layers that can be further subdivided into the **crust**, **mantle** and **core**.

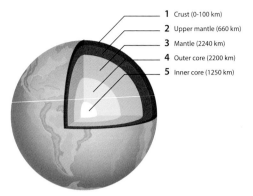

1 Crust (0-100 km)
2 Upper mantle (660 km)
3 Mantle (2240 km)
4 Outer core (2200 km)
5 Inner core (1250 km)

△ Fig. 6.1 The structure of the Earth.

Crust – The crust is the outermost layer of the Earth and is solid. It varies in thickness from 5 to 70 km. The crust is divided into thinner, but more dense oceanic crust and thicker, less dense continental crust. The thinnest crust is found under the oceans whereas the thickest crust is found under mountain chains such as the Himalayas and Andes. The crust is fractured in large **tectonic plates** that are in slow but constant motion.

Mantle – The mantle is the largest section inside the Earth, with a thickness of around 2900 km and totals 84 per cent of the Earth's total volume. The mantle can be subdivided into the upper and lower mantle. The upper mantle is beneath the crust and is mostly solid, but moves more like melted plastic in places, particularly around **plate boundaries**. The upper mantle extends to a depth of 410 km. The topmost part of the upper mantle and the crust together are known as the **lithosphere**. The semi-liquid rock in the upper mantle rises upwards from the heat of the core and lower mantle towards the lithosphere, before descending in giant **convection currents**. These currents drive the movement of the tectonic plates above.

The lower mantle extends from approximately 660 km to 2900 km. This area is hotter and more dense than the upper mantle. As depth increases in the mantle, temperature and pressure also increase.

Core – The Earth's inner core is a solid sphere that is approximately 2400 km in diameter. The core has a temperature of between 5000 and 7000 °C and is under such high pressure that the iron, sulfur and nickel cannot melt. The extreme temperature is derived from the radioactive decay of material created when Earth was formed 4.5 billion years ago.

Above this, there is a layer of liquid iron approximately 2400 km thick. This is slightly cooler than the inner core (4000–5000 °C), which allows the iron and nickel to move in swirling convection currents. This movement creates the Earth's magnetic field, which plays a vital role in protecting life on Earth from the powerful solar wind.

The distribution of earthquakes and volcanoes

The crust is broken into giant slabs called tectonic plates that are in motion. The location of the major plates and direction of movement are shown in Figure 6.2 below.

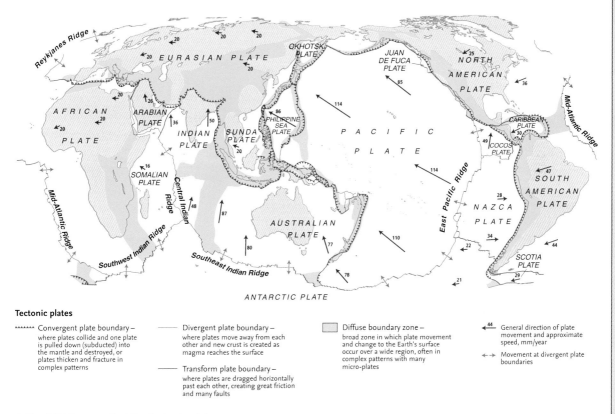

△ Fig. 6.2 Movement of the tectonic plates.

The convection currents in the mantle cause tectonic plates to move. In some places, new crust is formed and in others crust is destroyed. The edges or margins of the plates are known as plate boundaries. The interaction between the tectonic plates causes tectonic activity in the form of earthquakes and volcanoes. The distribution of major earthquakes and areas of volcanic activity can be seen in Figure 6.3.

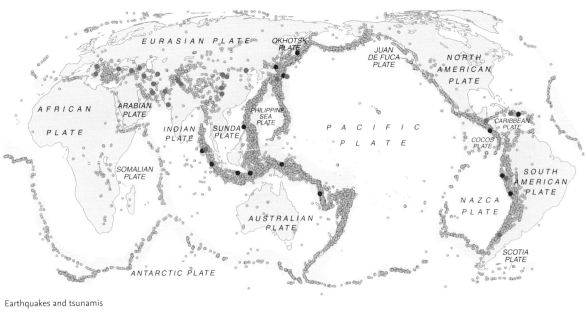

Earthquakes and tsunamis

☐ Earthquake and volcano zone
● Major tsunami since 1990

Major earthquake since 1900
● 'Deadliest' earthquakes
○ Greater than 5.5 on the
  Moment magnitude scale

The strength of an earthquake is measured using an intensity scale such as the Mercalli Scale, which measures the intensity of the shaking experienced at the surface. Other commonly used scales refer to the size and strength, or magnitude, of the earthquake. The older Richter scale and newer, more widely used and accurate Moment Magnitude Scale use very similar numbers on a logarithmic scale. A 7.0 on these magnitude scales is 10 times more powerful than a 6.0 and 100 times more powerful than a 5.0.

△ Fig. 6.3 The distribution of tectonic activity.

There is a clear relationship between areas of tectonic activity and the location of plate boundaries. There are four main types of plate boundary:

- **Constructive or divergent plate boundaries** – These occur when two plates are moving apart and new crust is formed in submarine volcanoes when **magma** rises. This most commonly occurs under oceans and is called seafloor spreading. However, it can happen on the surface. Notable examples include the mid-Atlantic Ridge and the East African **Rift Valley**. Constructive boundaries are associated with smaller earthquakes and volcanic activity.

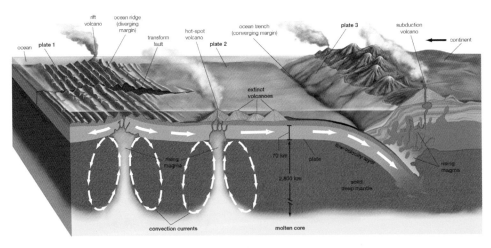

△ Fig. 6.4 Constructive and destructive plate boundaries.

- **Destructive or convergent plate boundaries** – When dense oceanic crust converges with continental crust, it is pushed down into the upper mantle at **subduction** zones. As it descends it melts, causing magma to rise and form volcanoes. The angle of descent also causes **ocean trenches** and can cause strong earthquakes and **tsunamis**.
- **Collision plate boundaries** – Continental crust can collide with other areas of continental crust. As they have the same density, the two plates are pushed upwards to form fold mountains such as the Himalayas and the Alps. These boundaries are associated with strong earthquakes.
- **Conservative or transform plate boundaries** – In places where plates run alongside one another, land is not created or destroyed. The plates do not slide smoothly so friction builds up that can be released suddenly in strong earthquakes. The San Andreas Fault in California is an example of a conservative plate boundary.

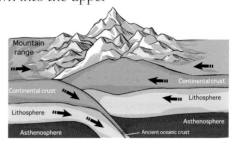

△ Fig. 6.5 A collision boundary.

△ Fig. 6.6 The San Andreas Fault, California, US.

The impacts of earthquakes and volcanoes on people and the environment

Earthquakes

When tectonic plates become locked together due to friction, pressure builds over time. This can extend to tens of thousands of years of pressure build. When the strain is suddenly released, huge shock waves of energy travel outwards from the earthquake **focus** underground towards the **epicentre** on the surface above. The shockwaves travel outwards along the surface, causing buildings and **infrastructure** to shake. Whether or not there is significant damage or loss of life depends on a range of factors:

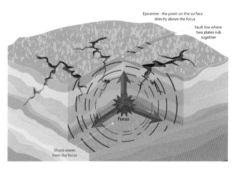

△ Fig. 6.7 The structure of an earthquake.

- The depth of the earthquake focus.
- The geology of the area – soft **sedimentary rocks** will vibrate more.
- The size or **magnitude** of the earthquake.
- The level of **vulnerability** of the **population** (wealth, building regulations, education, preparedness, emergency responses).

△ Fig. 6.8 Damage from the 2015 Nepal earthquake.

△ Fig. 6.9 A devastated Japanese landscape caused by the 2011 Tohoku earthquake and subsequent tsunami.

Mercalli intensity	Verbal description	Richter magnitude	Impacts
I	Instrumental	1–2	Detected only by seismographs
II	Feeble	2–3	Noticed only by sensitive people
III	Slight	3–4	Resembling vibrations caused by heavy traffic
IV	Moderate	4	Felt by people walking; rocking of free standing objects
V	Rather strong	4–5	Sleepers awakened and bells ring
VI	Strong	5–6	Trees sway; some damage from overturning and falling objects
VII	Very strong	6	General alarm; cracking of walls; liquefaction occurs
VIII	Destructive	6–7	Chimneys fall and there is some damage to buildings
IX	Ruinous	7	Ground begins to crack, houses begin to collapse and pipes break
X	Disastrous	7–8	Ground badly cracked and many buildings are destroyed; there are some landslides
XI	Very disastrous	8	Few buildings remain standing; bridges and railways destroyed; water, gas, electricity and telephones out of action
XII	Catastrophic	8 or greater	Total destruction; objects are thrown into the air, much heaving, shaking and distortion of the ground

△ Table 6.1 Measuring earthquake intensity.

The impact of an earthquake will vary significantly from place to place. However, there are some impacts that are commonly associated with earthquakes:

- loss of life and serious injury from collapsed buildings
- damage to buildings and loss of homes
- destroyed infrastructure (roads, rail, water and electricity services)
- fire from damaged gas pipes
- **water-borne diseases** such as **cholera**
- landslides
- tsunamis
- psychological trauma
- financial losses from damage, loss of income, rebuilding.

Volcanic eruptions

Volcanoes form at constructive and destructive plate boundaries, as well as magma hotspots. The size, shape and effects of an eruption depend on the viscosity of the **lava** that formed the volcano. Runny lava will form wider **shield volcanoes** such as Erta Ale in Ethiopia or Mauna Loa in Hawaii. Thicker, more viscous lava will build up a lava dome or, if combined with layers of ash, will form a **stratovolcano**. Fissure vents occur when lava erupts from a long thin vent. Volcanoes are described as still active and erupting frequently, dormant (temporarily

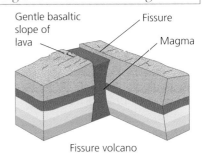

Fissure volcano

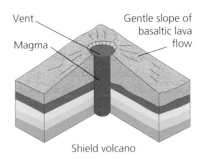

Shield volcano

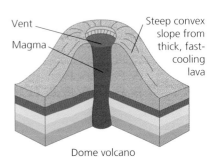

Dome volcano

△ Fig. 6.10 Types of volcano.

inactive but not fully extinct) or extinct (never likely to erupt again).

The impact of a volcanic eruption will vary significantly depending on the type of volcano, as well as the human factors that increase or decrease vulnerability. The strength of an eruption is measured on the **Volcanic Explosivity Index (VEI)** – an eight-point scale where each higher number is ten times greater than the last. A VEI of 6 occurs every 50–100 years, whereas a VEI of 8 occurs approximately every 50 000 years. When the supervolcano erupted under Yellowstone National Park in the USA 640 000 years ago, its ash spread over 1000 km from the volcano.

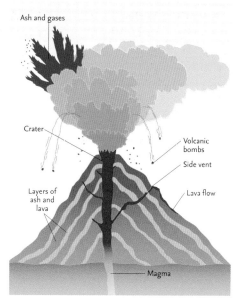

△ Fig. 6.11 The structure of a typical stratovolcano.

Generally shield volcanoes have spectacular but not dangerous eruptions, whereas stratovolcanoes are the most dangerous as they contain gases that increase the explosivity. Potential impacts from a volcanic eruption:

- Lava flows – can be fast moving down the sides of volcanoes.
- Gas clouds – **carbon dioxide** and nitrous oxide released from the volcano.
- Volcanic bombs – giant rocks thrown from the volcano.
- **Pyroclastic flows** – superheated fast moving clouds of ash and gas.
- **Lahars** – violent mudflows caused when ice/snow on volcanoes melts and mixes with ash, mud, trees.
- Loss of life and damage to property.
- Ash fall.
- Loss of farmland and destroyed **habitats**.

The impacts of both earthquakes and volcanoes are well known but vary between locations. These **natural hazards** become disasters when they interact with humans at risk. The scale of the disaster will depend upon level of vulnerability as well as the size of the eruption or earthquake.

Managing the impacts of earthquakes and volcanoes before, during and after an event

Due to the known location of plate boundaries, geologists and Earth scientists are able to determine which places are at most risk from earthquakes and volcanoes. It is not yet possible to predict exactly where and when an earthquake will occur, but we do know that the risk of an earthquake is much higher in Japan than it is Germany, for example. Equally, volcanoes are large landscape features so people know where they are. They also give off signs of an impending eruption so it is possible to give warnings to people to evacuate. With an increasing global population – particularly in lower-income countries – there are increasing numbers of vulnerable people living in high risk areas. In the past 100 years there have been an increasing number of hazards recorded that are affecting more people and causing significantly more financial impact. Trying to reduce the risk from hazards is a major environmental management challenge that requires action before, during and after the event.

One thing is clear: humans are unable to stop earthquakes or volcanic eruptions from occurring, so efforts to reduce vulnerability must focus on prediction, planning, preparation and response.

Reducing earthquake risk beforehand

In known earthquake risk areas, it is possible to reduce the impact of earthquakes by the following methods:

- Monitoring **fault lines** using lasers and satellite technology to see if there is an increase in strain.
- Mapping faults accurately and looking at evidence of historical earthquakes.
- Detecting radon gas (sometimes given off before earthquakes).
- Implementing rigorous building regulations, so new buildings are fitted with earthquake-proof designs.
- **Retrofitting** old buildings to reduce the damage caused by earthquakes.
- Educating the population about how to prepare for and act during an earthquake.
- Conducting large-scale earthquake drills with emergency services.
- Ensuring that local governments have detailed emergency management plans.

Reducing earthquake risk during the event

While predicting an earthquake is not possible, the technology does exist to give fast warning to people when one does occur. Even a 10 second warning can be enough to get under cover. In Japan, as soon as an earthquake occurs, a warning flashes on the TV screen, to smartphone apps and websites giving people precious seconds to prepare. In Los Angeles, **seismometers** send signals to medical, fire and rescue stations which automatically open the doors – ensuring emergency vehicles are not trapped. If adequate education and public awareness has occurred, people will know to drop, cover and hold on. People should also have emergency supply kits in their houses.

Reducing earthquake risk after the event

In the immediate aftermath of an earthquake there will be chaos and confusion. It is likely that people will be dead, seriously injured and trapped in buildings. Large numbers of people will be out on the streets and there will be a fear of aftershocks. The immediate responses to an earthquake are vital in reducing the impact in terms of deaths. The response phase can be broken down into several stages:

- An immediate search and rescue operation in the hours and days following the earthquake. This is a critical phase where specialist rescue teams with sniffer dogs and lifting equipment can look for trapped people. Emergency field hospitals are set up to treat injured people. Separated families can use technology like Google Person Finder to track down family and friends.
- Meeting the immediate needs of the survivors with emergency aid. There will be homeless people in need of food, clean water and shelter.
- The clear up, demolish, repair and planning phase.
- Rebuild, replace and reconstruct.

Many of the actions taken to reduce risk by decreasing vulnerability are dependent on the level of **economic development** of the country involved. High-income countries can afford to spend money, whereas poorer nations struggle to enforce building codes, to retrofit buildings and to spend enough money on emergency response. This means they are much more reliant on emergency foreign aid – which can take time to arrive. Consequently, death tolls and damage from similar size and depth earthquakes are higher in low-income countries.

△ Fig. 6.12 A disaster survival kit.

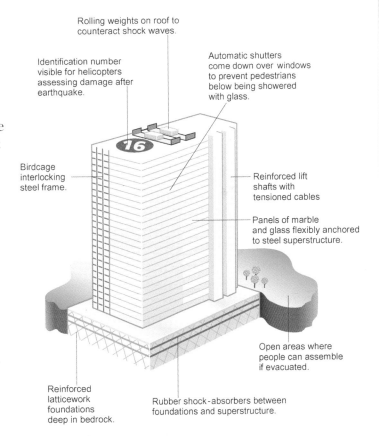

Rolling weights on roof to counteract shock waves.

Identification number visible for helicopters assessing damage after earthquake.

Automatic shutters come down over windows to prevent pedestrians below being showered with glass.

Birdcage interlocking steel frame.

Reinforced lift shafts with tensioned cables

Panels of marble and glass flexibly anchored to steel superstructure.

Open areas where people can assemble if evacuated.

Reinforced latticework foundations deep in bedrock.

Rubber shock-absorbers between foundations and superstructure.

△ Fig. 6.13 An earthquake-proof building.

Reducing the risk from volcanic eruptions
Before

- People in lower-income countries are much less likely to have the capacity to cope with volcanic eruptions than those in wealthier nations. However, volcanoes are easier to monitor and often give off clear signs of an impending eruption, meaning people can be evacuated.
- Evacuation plans can be developed based on historical ash records.
- Volcanoes can be monitored from space as well as locally using tiltmeters that look at their shape.
- Seismometers can detect movements in magma below the surface.
- Gas levels can be monitored.
- Predictions as to the likely ash fall can be made – leading to **hazard risk maps**.
- People can be evacuated from areas likely to be hit by pyroclastic flows or lahars.
- Local people can be educated about how to react if a volcano does erupt.
- Volcano shelters can be built.

△ Fig. 6.14 A volcano shelter in Indonesia.

During

Once a volcano has erupted, people need to be evacuated quickly from the area. Some people will be in shelters but will only have limited supplies. The risk from lahars might be high so ongoing monitoring is needed. Local air traffic will need to be diverted. Some eruptions can continue for weeks and months, so people will not be able to return home and will need to be resettled.

△ Fig. 6.15 An evacuation route in the USA.

After

For those caught in the immediate aftermath, there is a need for rescue. Some buildings nearby may be damaged, and the effects of a lahar can be seen miles downstream with damaged infrastructure. Ash-fall may need to be cleared from rooftops for tens or even hundreds of kilometres around. Some settlements will need to be abandoned permanently. However, the highly fertile ash will lead to people returning to farm the land in the future.

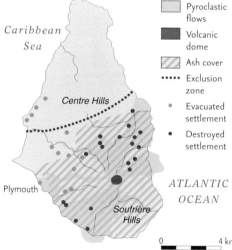

Caribbean Sea

Centre Hills

Plymouth

ATLANTIC OCEAN

Soufrière Hills

0   4 km

	Pyroclastic flows
	Volcanic dome
	Ash cover
·····	Exclusion zone
•	Evacuated settlement
•	Destroyed settlement

△ Fig. 6.16 A volcano hazard map of Montserrat in the Caribbean.

TROPICAL CYCLONES
The distribution and causes of tropical cyclones

A cyclone is a powerful **tropical** storm – an area of intense low pressure that forms over warm water. They bring strong winds,

torrential rain and **storm surges**.
Around the world they are given
different names:

- Hurricanes in the Atlantic Ocean
- Typhoons in the Pacific Ocean
- Cyclones in the Indian Ocean.

Tropical cyclones tend to form as
follows:

△ Fig. 6.17 Hurricane Katrina in the
Gulf of Mexico.

- Between 5° and 20° north and south
  of the equator. Figure 6.18 shows the
  global distribution of tropical cyclones.
- Over warm tropical water where the surface temperature is at least
  27 °C and ocean depth of at least 60 m. Figure 6.19 shows ocean
  surface temperatures. There is a clear correlation between cyclone
  distribution and ocean temperature.
- When powerful convection of warm moist air occurs, this rises, cools,
  condenses and forms storm clouds. Fuelled by the ocean temperatures,
  the storm grows and begins to rotate due to the **coriolis effect**.

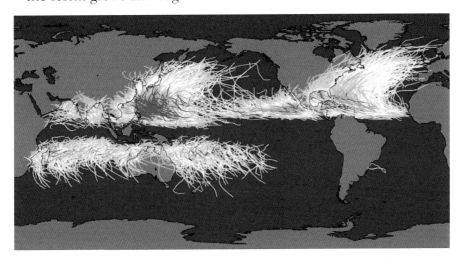

Saffir-Simpson scale

- Tropical depression
- Tropical storm
- Category 1 storm
- Category 2 storm
- Category 3 storm
- Category 4 storm
- Category 5 storm

△ Fig. 6.18 The global distribution of tropical cyclones.

Sea Surface Temperature (°C)

△ Fig. 6.19 Ocean surface temperature.   −2   35

The life cycle of a tropical cyclone

1. **Tropical Disturbance** – Thunderstorms form as warm moist air rises. These are pushed westwards by coastal winds.

2. **Tropical Depression** – Storms combine and begin to spin with a maximum wind speed of 62 km/h.

3. **Tropical Storm** – Spiralling winds churn up the sea, causing more moisture to be picked up. The storm grows in strength and begins to have a larger circular shape. The maximum wind speeds are 63–118 km/h, with heavy rainfall.

4. **Tropical cyclone** – Forms with sustained wind speed of 119 km/h or more. There is clear rotation around a central eye. The low pressure in the centre creates an area of suction that causes storm surges when reaching land.

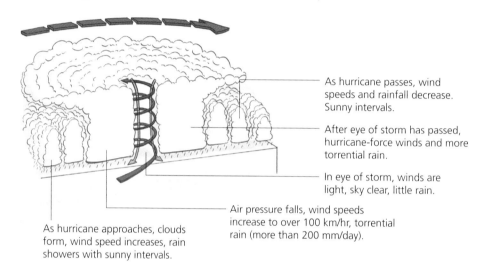

As hurricane passes, wind speeds and rainfall decrease. Sunny intervals.

After eye of storm has passed, hurricane-force winds and more torrential rain.

In eye of storm, winds are light, sky clear, little rain.

Air pressure falls, wind speeds increase to over 100 km/hr, torrential rain (more than 200 mm/day).

As hurricane approaches, clouds form, wind speed increases, rain showers with sunny intervals.

∆ Fig. 6.20 The structure of a tropical cyclone.

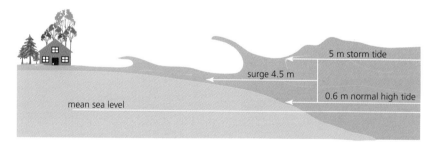

5 m storm tide

surge 4.5 m

0.6 m normal high tide

mean sea level

∆ Fig. 6.21 A storm surge.

Impacts of tropical cyclones on people and the environment

Tropical cyclones are measured on the **Saffir-Simpson hurricane wind scale**, which is based on the sustained windspeed. The scale includes an estimate for the potential damage each category will cause:

Category	Sustained winds	Storm surge	Possible damage from wind and storm surge
1	119–153 km/h	1.2–1.5 m	**Very dangerous winds will produce some damage** Damage primarily to poorly constructed houses, mobile homes and trees, along with some coastal road flooding.
2	154–177 km/h	1.8–2.4 m	**Extremely dangerous winds will cause extensive damage** Damage to roofing, doors and windows on well-built homes and buildings. Considerable damage to trees, mobile homes, power lines, poorly-constructed signs, and piers. Coastal roads flooded.
3 (major)	178–208 km/h	2.7–3.7 m	**Devastating damage will occur** Severe flooding and structural damage to homes. Poorly-built houses and mobile homes destroyed. Trees uprooted, power lines destroyed.
4 (major)	209–251 km/h	3.9–5.5 m	**Catastrophic damage will occur** Well-built structures will have significant damage. Severe flooding inland. Most trees snapped or uprooted. Area will be uninhabitable for weeks.
5 (major)	252 km/h or higher	+5.5 m	**Catastrophic damage will occur** Severe flooding reaches far inland. Wide ranging destruction to all buildings and structures. Most of the area will be uninhabitable for weeks or months.

△ Table 6.2 The Saffir-Simpson scale, showing the impact of tropical cyclones.

The impact of a tropical cyclone will vary depending on a number of factors:

- the vulnerability of the population (wealth, education, preparedness, responses)
- the category of the storm
- the size of the storm surge.

Cyclones will cause extensive damage to infrastructure as well as loss of life. Hurricane Katrina (category 5 in 2005) is estimated to have cost US$125 billion damage to the Gulf Coast of the USA. In low-income countries, damage to housing is often devastating and the saltwater flooding from the storm surge destroys crops. This presents very real issues for food supply. Furthermore, fishing fleets are often destroyed, adding to the issue and creating a need for urgent international assistance. Water supplies are often

△ Fig. 6.22 Tropical cyclone Haiyan approaches the Philippines.

contaminated, leading to the threat of water-borne diseases such as cholera. The overall effect of a tropical cyclone on a lower-income country such as the Philippines can be devastating to the area hit by the strongest winds and highest storm surge.

Managing impacts of tropical cyclones before, during and after an event

Tropical cyclones cause significant damage to all countries where they make landfall. They are intensively studied to understand their behaviour and to make predictions about how they will move and where they will affect. It is possible to reduce the impact of these hazards by taking action before, during and after the event. The extent to which these strategies is successful often depends on the level of vulnerability and the capacity of a population to cope with the effects.

△ Fig. 6.23 The devastation in Tacloban City, Philippines.

Reducing tropical cyclone risk beforehand

- Tropical cyclones are often hundreds of kilometres across and can be tracked by satellites. Predictions can be made after gathering data and using computer models to forecast the path.
- Warnings can be given hours and sometimes days in advance.
- Evacuation plans can be drawn up.
- Emergency training drills can be carried out to prepare disaster responses.
- Houses can be boarded up to reduce damage.
- Building design can provide more resistance to strong winds and they can be raised from the ground to protect against storm surges.
- Food supplies can be stored on higher ground.
- Cyclone shelters can be provided, along with warning systems.
- Education is key to reducing risk, as people will be better prepared.

Reducing tropical cyclone risk during the event

The key to reducing risk from tropical cyclones is to prepare before the event and evacuate or seek shelter. Once the high winds and storm surges hit, people need to stay inside and wait for the storm to pass. Places without evacuation plans or those people who stay behind are extremely vulnerable and will need immediate assistance to cope with the after effects.

Reducing tropical cyclone risk after the event

Once the storm has passed, it is likely that major damage will have been done to buildings and the water and power infrastructure. Those who stayed in the affected area will need assistance with food, water and shelter. It is likely that victims will be trapped amongst the debris, so there is a risk of the spread of disease. Social networking can play a role in reuniting families, and in lower-income countries, international aid will be needed to provide immediate assistance. One charity, Shelterbox, sends supplies and tents in a disaster relief box (Figure 6.26) to affected areas. Once the rescue phase has ended, plans will need to be made to reconstruct buildings and infrastructure, which can take years.

△ Fig. 6.24 A Cyclone Shelter in Bangladesh.

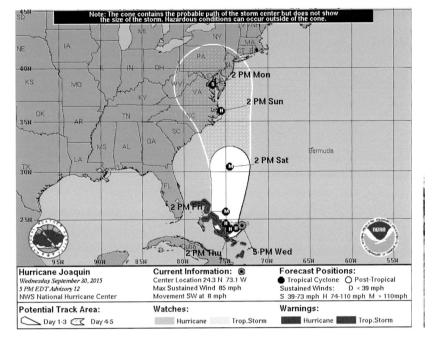

△ Fig. 6.25 A hurricane path prediction.

△ Fig. 6.26 A tent provided by Shelterbox to a family in Tacloban City.

FLOODING

The causes of flooding

Flooding occurs when an area of land is covered or submerged with water. Flooding has a range of causes that can be made worse by human activity. It is important to note that rivers have **floodplains** in the lower sections to allow the natural system to respond to a rapid increase in water, but these flat sections – known as 'floodplains' – make the land attractive to develop. A flood in an area with no human activity is unlikely to lead to a disaster, whereas a flood in an area with a heavily developed floodplain can lead to loss of life, damage to property and financial losses.

To understand river flooding, it is important to understand the **water cycle** and specifically what happens when rain reaches the ground. Some rainfall lands directly in the river channel; the vast majority will fall on the surrounding drainage basin. Some will land directly on the ground and infiltrate into the soil, with some percolating into the underlying rock. Some will flow directly over the surface as **surface run-off** and enter into rivers and streams. Some rain will be intercepted by trees, before falling to the ground. In urban areas, rain can enter rivers more rapidly due to the **impermeable** surfaces. The relative balance between all of these factors can cause water to enter rivers rapidly or slowly. If the water enters rapidly, then the discharge of the river will increase rapidly – potentially causing flooding downstream.

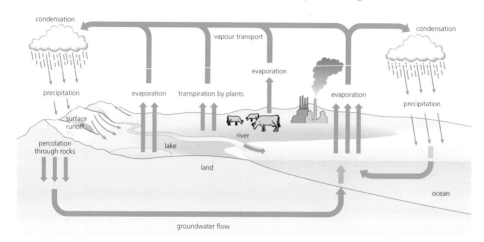

△ Fig. 6.27 The water cycle.

The main causes of flooding are shown in Figure 6.28.

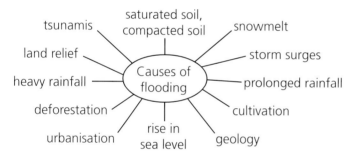

△ Fig. 6.28 Causes of flooding.

Heavy rainfall – Flooding can occur when very heavy rain falls, even in short bursts. Sometimes water will not even flow into rivers, but instead will accumulate and cause flooding away from rivers. Heavy rain can also cause rapid surface run-off, which causes rivers to burst their banks.

Prolonged rainfall – Rain that falls for a prolonged period can cause the soil to become saturated. Any further rainfall will not be absorbed into the soil and instead will run off the surface rapidly, increasing flood risk.

Snowmelt – In spring, snow and ice in mountain regions begin to melt and they are vital in feeding fresh water into rivers. However, rapid melting would cause a too-fast increase in input into river channels, causing flooding downstream.

Land relief – The height and shape of the land is an important factor in determining how water behaves when it falls as **precipitation**. Steep slopes lead to faster surface run-off, whereas gentle slopes allow water the time to infiltrate and enter rivers more slowly. However, when floods occur, flat land will then allow floodwater to spread easily from the river across the floodplain.

Geology – In some places, the underlying geology is permeable, which means water can pass through the rocks. However, in places where the underlying rock is impermeable, water cannot pass through, which leads to the soil above becoming saturated more quickly and increasing flood risk.

Saturated soil, compacted soil – When precipitation lands on saturated soil it has no way of entering into the soil, so will run off downhill, entering rivers and streams more quickly. If it has been compacted by agricultural activity, then it will act like an impermeable surface and will cause rapid surface run-off.

Deforestation – Trees intercept rainfall and slow down the speed at which water enters rivers and stream. Loss of trees through deforestation will increase surface run-off and **soil erosion**, as the roots will no longer bind the soil together. This can cause further problems as river channel capacity can be reduced as the rivers are full of sediment.

Cultivation – Poor land management can lead to an increase in surface run-off as compaction of the soil leads to impermeable surfaces. Fields of crops intercept less rainfall and removal of hedges and trees can increase surface run-off.

Urbanisation – Urban areas are full of impermeable concrete and tarmac areas. Furthermore, roofs catch rainwater and efficiently channel it to drain systems below. Growth of urban areas can also lead to river channel modification. Combined, these factors can lead to a rapid increase in the speed at which water enters rivers. Unrestricted building on floodplains will further increase the risk from flooding.

Storm surges – Tropical cyclones and large storms combined with high tides can lead to violent storm surges, which flood low lying coastal areas and river estuaries.

Tsunamis – Undersea earthquakes and landslides can cause massive displacement of water, which sends huge volumes of water heading inland. These powerful waves can travel for kilometres inland – causing devastation.

Rise in sea level – Rising global temperatures cause the thermal expansion of oceans as well as melting ice caps, leading to a rise in sea level. High tides in low-lying areas will increasingly cause flooding in the future.

Impacts of flooding on people and the environment

When floods occur, depending on the scale and location, they can cause death and widespread devastation. Flooding can be severe in both high- and low-income countries, but high-income countries tend to be better prepared and have a higher capacity to cope.

In December 2010, Queensland in Australia averaged 300 mm of rain, with some areas receiving up to 600 mm in one month – six times the average. This was then followed by tropical cyclone Tasha, which brought another 150–250 mm of rain to the east coast of Australia. After the spring rains of September to November, the soil was completely saturated, causing rivers across the state to burst their banks. The heavy rain continued into January, causing the Queensland rivers that flow into the Brisbane River to be overcome. By 11 January 2011 the Brisbane River broke its banks, flooding the centre of the city and causing substantial damage to the city's infrastructure. Across the state the floods forced the evacuation of thousands of people from towns and cities. Up to ninety towns and 200 000 people were affected:

- An area of 500 000 sq km was affected – an area larger than the size of Germany.
- 35 deaths – 21 from one town.
- 3570 businesses were completely flooded.
- US$4 billion in losses from the mining, **tourism** and farming industries:
  - 80 per cent of coal mines were affected.
  - Crops were destroyed, leading to a rise in food prices. Floods destroyed more than 75 per cent of Australia's banana crop and 30 per cent of the sugar cane.
  - Thousands of sheep and cows were killed.
- 19 000 km of roads were damaged.
- 28 per cent of the rail network was damaged.

△ Fig. 6.29 Central Brisbane, Queensland, Australia underwater in 2011.

- 28 000 homes had to be rebuilt.
- 17 bridges were damaged or destroyed.
- Drinking water supplies were contaminated as reservoirs flooded.
- Floodwater mixed with sewage leading to health concerns.
- Floodwater entering the sea leading to damage to the Great Barrier Reef.
- Repair costs were estimated to be billions of dollars, with US$2.55 billion in business and household insurance claims alone.

△ Fig. 6.30 Farmland damaged by flood waters in Queensland.

While the flooding was devastating for many communities, there was a strong response. Around 55 000 people volunteered to help with the clean-up, and insurance companies paid out to repair and rebuild houses. The government increased taxes temporarily to pay for the recovery. This was a significant event, but one that Queensland has already recovered from due to the higher capacity to cope found in higher-income countries. Lower-income countries tend to have less resilience, and a loss of food and contaminated water often leads to the spread of water-borne diseases like cholera, which can cause higher death tolls than the original floods.

Managing the impacts of flooding before, during and after an event

In the past 100 years the number of floods has increased significantly. Rising population, increasing deforestation, urbanisation and channel modification are impacting how rivers respond to inputs of rain. Increased atmospheric temperatures are leading to heavier and more prolonged periods of rainfall and rising sea levels. Flood risk has to be managed to control or reduce the impact of flooding. This can be done in lots of ways.

Reducing flood risk before the event

Evaluating flood risk and mapping: government agencies can evaluate the risk any particular area is at from flooding by studying how a river behaves with a certain input of precipitation. Computer models are built to show what will happen if 200 mm of rain falls onto a saturated area and how quickly the water will enter the river and move downstream. Factors such as the geology, slope angle, vegetation cover and land use are taken into account and are used to generate a flood risk map. These are built taking into account the **recurrence interval** of floods of certain sizes.

Smaller floods occur more frequently than larger floods, which could have a 1000-year recurrence interval. Planners have to decide what level of flood protection they will provide by risk assessing the area and looking at historical records. Scientists are also able to model how quickly a river is likely to rise by using a **storm hydrograph**. By monitoring river levels over time, it is possible to then predict the **lag time** between a rainfall event and how a river will rise and fall when surface run-off is combined with throughflow of water in the soil and **groundwater flow**.

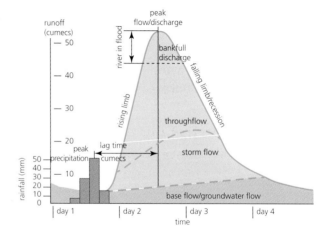

△ Fig. 6.31 A flood hydrograph.

Using these monitoring systems alongside flood risk maps allows warning systems to alert people to prepare for a flood.

This does require forward planning and infrastructure investment, so planning for floods is more effective in higher-income countries. However, despite this many floods do and will continue to occur with significant financial impacts. Governments have to undertake a cost-benefit analysis to evaluate the costs of a flood versus the cost of building **flood defences**.

Flood control is possible before a flood occurs. A combination of strategies can be highly effective:

• flood risk mapping
• monitoring
• hard engineering – building dams, levees, flood relief channels, concrete embankments, control gates

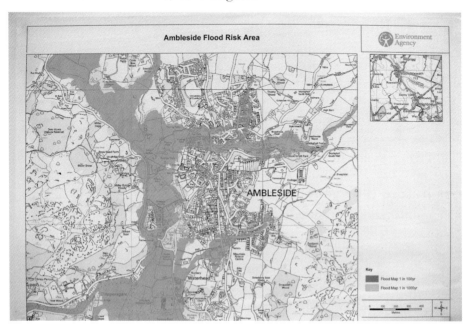

△ Fig. 6.32 A flood risk map.

- soft engineering – planting trees, preserving marshland and wetlands, controlled flooding
- flood-proofing houses
- land-use zoning to avoid construction on flood plains
- people in high risk areas should take out flood insurance.

Reducing flood risk during the event

Even with flood defences in place, flooding will still occur if the input of water into the channel is greater than the capacity of the channel, and flood defences are overwhelmed. If this does happen, then the steps taken beforehand can reduce damage to property as well as giving people a warning to evacuate. However, sudden rises in river levels often catch people unaware, or are on such a large scale that there is little that can be done. When this happens, efforts to reduce risk must be focused on search and rescue, with people being taken to shelters to wait for the flood water to recede.

Reducing flood risk after the event

Once flood waters have receded, they leave behind huge amounts of sediment, damaged infrastructure and property, destroyed belongings and even lost lives. The recovery will require clean-up and pumping of water followed by removal of destroyed furniture, demolition of properties beyond repair and full damage assessments on bridges, roads, water and power networks. People will also need to complete insurance claims.

In the longer term, the causes of the flood will need to be examined to see if steps can be taken to prevent further floods in the future. Flood management plans, using soft engineering, that are integrated and work with the river can be developed alongside levees, dams and embankments.

△ Fig. 6.33 Rescue helicopters over Boscastle in Cornwall, UK after a flash flood.

△ Fig. 6.34 Boscastle flood in the UK in 2004.

DROUGHT

The causes of drought

A **drought** is defined as a prolonged period of abnormally low rainfall, leading to a shortage of water. The exact amount of time and lack of water varies depending on location in the world. The definition varies because of the different **climate** patterns that exist globally, so what is considered a drought in one part of the world is normal in another. Many areas of the Earth have a dry or arid climate that receive less than 250 mm of rainfall, so these places are particularly vulnerable to less than average rainfall. However, droughts can also occur in countries that receive variable rainfall throughout the year. Drought can lead to a range of problems from a hosepipe ban to complete crop failure, **famine** and starvation.

△ Fig. 6.35 Dead livestock from the 2011 East Africa drought.

There are many factors that lead to a drought being declared. It is important to note that natural causes of drought cause changes in the supply of water, whereas human causes tend to be mismanagement that leads to greater demand or poor management of dwindling supplies. Droughts have a slow speed of onset so can be forecast, but are very difficult to manage due to the wide area they can cover.

Natural causes	Human causes
Weather patterns	**Poor farming practice**
High pressure anticyclone systems of dry, stable, warm, descending air can sit over a large area for long periods and lead to a lack of rainfall.	Overcultivation of crops may use up local water supplies. Growing of cash crops for export can lead to groundwater depletion.
Climate change	**Overabstraction**
Warming of the atmosphere is leading to changes in rainfall patterns, with places in already arid areas becoming drier, for example in Sub-Saharan Africa.	Removal of groundwater from wells and aquifers can reduce available water supply, which makes drought more severe.
ENSO	**Deforestation**
The fluctuation of climate patterns in the Pacific can lead to drought in Australia and much drier conditions across Southeast Asia.	This changes the local hydrological cycle and leads to an increase in surface run-off and soil erosion.
Climatic factors	**Conflict**
Distance from the sea, altitude and relief all play a part in the level of moisture an area receives.	This can cause people to migrate to marginal areas with less rainfall and less water availability.

△ Table 6.3 Causes of drought.

The impacts of drought on people and the environment

As with other natural hazards, the impact of a drought will vary significantly depending upon the level of vulnerability of the population affected, as well as the capacity of the region to cope with the effects. When a drought occurs there are many possible impacts:

- **Death of organisms** – Some plants can adapt to arid conditions, however, many cannot and will die. This causes damage to habitats and a loss of **biodiversity**.
- **Increased soil erosion** – Dry soil can be easily blown away by the wind or washed away if there is rain. Once the soil has been eroded there will be a decline in productivity of the land. This can lead to **desertification**.
- **Decline in the water supply** – A fall in water levels in rivers and lakes will cause the water supply to drop. The impact of this ranges from inconvenient (such as restrictions on use of hosepipes and sprinklers) to severe (lack of drinking water, poor nutrition, famine, **forced migration**, conflict over water and food sources).
- **Crops** – The lack of rain can result in crop loss and a decline in crop yields means a decrease in land prices, and unemployment due to declines in production.
- **Starvation** – Collapse of food supplies and drinking water sources in low-income countries can lead to mass starvation.
- **Decrease in air quality** – In dry conditions, soil loses moisture and dust is released into the **atmosphere**.
- **Increased risk of wildfires** – Lightning can ignite fires in dry trees, which spread rapidly. Drought conditions contributed to the Southeast Asian haze in 2015.
- **Desertification** – Extended drought, **overgrazing**, **overcultivation** and deforestation can lead to soil erosion, which in turn leads to originally fertile land becoming desert. Areas vulnerable to desertification can be seen in Figure 6.37. This is a significant global environmental management challenge.

△ Fig. 6.36 A nearly empty reservoir in California, USA.

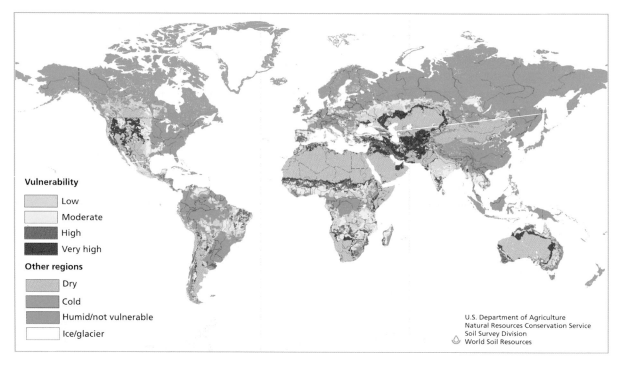

Vulnerability
- Low
- Moderate
- High
- Very high

Other regions
- Dry
- Cold
- Humid/not vulnerable
- Ice/glacier

U.S. Department of Agriculture
Natural Resources Conservation Service
Soil Survey Division
World Soil Resources

△ Fig. 6.37 Global vulnerability to desertification.

Managing the impacts of drought before, during and after an event

The ability to manage the impact of a drought will depend upon the level of development within a country, which will affect planning, action and responses.

Reducing the risk from drought beforehand

Drought-prone areas can develop infrastructure to manage the impact of a drought by ensuring that water supplies are maximised and that water supply can be increased if necessary by the following methods:

- Transferring water from other parts of a country.
- Developing **desalination**.
- Exploiting unused **groundwater** in **aquifers**.
- Working to reduce water **consumption** on an ongoing basis through education.

Having well-developed forecasting and monitoring will also assist in forward planning. Understanding of weather and climate patterns will allow governments to assess drought risk and to issue warnings: although scientists cannot predict how long and how intense a drought might be, warnings allow for prior preparation and planning to reduce the worst impacts.

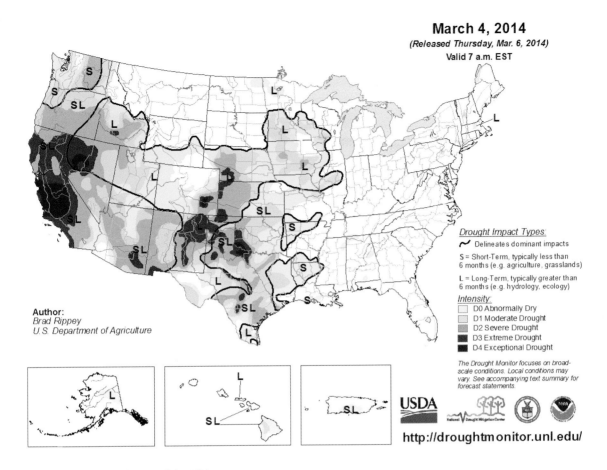

March 4, 2014
(Released Thursday, Mar. 6, 2014)
Valid 7 a.m. EST

Author:
Brad Rippey
U.S. Department of Agriculture

Drought Impact Types:
~ Delineates dominant impacts
S = Short-Term, typically less than 6 months (e.g. agriculture, grasslands)
L = Long-Term, typically greater than 6 months (e.g. hydrology, ecology)
Intensity:
D0 Abnormally Dry
D1 Moderate Drought
D2 Severe Drought
D3 Extreme Drought
D4 Exceptional Drought

The Drought Monitor focuses on broad-scale conditions. Local conditions may vary. See accompanying text summary for forecast statements.

USDA

http://droughtmonitor.unl.edu/

△ Fig. 6.38 Drought risk map of the USA.

Reducing the risks during drought

During a drought in high-income countries, restriction on water consumption can be brought in for households, businesses and farmers. In extreme cases, water rationing can be introduced where supplies are switched off and replaced with water trucks. Households will be encouraged to conserve water, **reuse** water and harvest rainwater. In low-income countries, drought increases pressure of water and food supplies and can cause famine. This can cause **migration** into refugee camps where international aid is needed to provide food, water and shelter. Emergency supplies can be sent out to rural areas in trucks to provide drinking water if wells have dried up.

△ Fig. 6.39 Emergency water supplies delivered in southern Ethiopia.

Reducing the risks after drought

Once the rains have returned and the drought is declared over, work needs to be done to develop a region's capacity to cope with future droughts:

△ Fig. 6.40 Drought relief supplies bound for Somalia.

- Developing water supplies.
- Ensuring food production sustainability through development of more drought-resistant crops.
- Combatting desertification.
- Education programmes on **water conservation**.

With a predicted increase in global temperatures and an associated rise in drought risk, building **community** resilience to drought is a vital management challenge across the world.

OPPORTUNITIES PRESENTED BY NATURAL HAZARDS
Volcanic activity

△ Fig. 6.41 Batur volcano in Bali, Indonesia provides many opportunities to generate income for local people.

Natural hazards can completely devastate landscapes and cause huge loss of life and damage to infrastructure. Living in hazard areas means you are at risk from the impacts of hazards. Despite the risk, many people choose to live in at-risk areas due to the opportunities that certain hazards bring to generate income.

Figure 6.41 shows Batur, a volcano in northern Bali, Indonesia. It contains an impressive caldera (lake in a volcanic crater), which formed over 20 000 years ago. Inside the caldera is a lake and the active stratovolcano, Batur. The most recent eruption was in 2000, but Batur has shown more recent signs of activity – although no eruptions. The original eruption that formed the 10-km wide caldera happened over 20 000 years ago and would have been catastrophic. Despite the risk that exists in this area and in other volcanic areas around the world, people continue to live and work nearby. There are fifteen villages in and around the caldera with locals relying on **agriculture** for income. The volcanic ash is highly fertile and allows a large range of crops to be grown. Furthermore, a tourism boom in Bali has lead to the development of tourist treks to the summit as well as eco-tourist bike rides. The arrival of tourists brings money to the local economy and starts a positive multiplier (where businesses expand and take on more staff, average incomes go up and this leads to more money in the local economy). The lake is the largest in Bali, so is also used to provide fresh drinking water and water for **irrigation** of the famous rice terraces. The lake also supports a local fishing **industry** and some water sports.

△ Fig. 6.42 Rice terraces on fertile volcanic soil, irrigated from Batur caldera in Bali.

Volcanic activity also creates **minerals** that can be mined. The dark area on Batur is **surface mining** of volcanic ash, which is used in industry and construction. The volcanic rock is carved into statues that are sold for export around the world. In other regions of the world, rising magma in the crust alters the surrounding rock and creates many of the minerals that are in common use today, such as bauxite, nickel, gold, diamonds, copper, zinc and lead.

Volcanic activity can also be harnessed to produce electricity. In Iceland, which sits on top of the Mid-Atlantic Ridge and is a hot spot, almost all of the heating, hot water and power generation comes from **geothermal power**. In the winter, the capital Reykjavík has its pavements heated to keep them ice free, using the abundant geothermal heat available.

△ Fig. 6.43 Geothermal power generation in Iceland.

Flooding

River flooding presents significant challenges that impact upon people and the environment. However, when a river floods it will be carrying a large volume of sediment. As the flood waters recede, the sediment – called **alluvium** – is deposited on the surrounding land. Alluvium is highly fertile as it contains sand, clay, gravel and organic matter. In some parts of the world, deposited alluvium contains gold and gemstones from eroded rock.

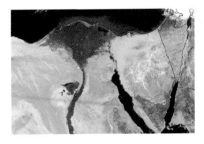

△ Fig. 6.44 Egypt from space.

Figure 6.44 show Egypt from space. Egypt is mostly covered in desert, except for a small green strip that surrounds the River Nile. Before the construction of the Aswan High Dam, the Nile would flood annually, so the floodplain and delta at the mouth of the river contain large volumes of highly fertile soil that is used for agriculture, supported by irrigation from the river. In Egypt, the Nile is known as the river of life.

Around the world, the **deposition** of fertile sediment by flooding supports agriculture. Figure 6.45 shows the Paraná River in South America. This river has a history of severe flooding, but we can clearly see the patchwork of fields that identifies intensive farming. Like volcanoes, fertile soil from flooding can lead to a positive multiplier in an area, generating income and supporting the economy.

△ Fig. 6.45 Intensive agriculture on the Paraná River floodplain, Brazil.

CASE STUDY

IMPACT OF EARTHQUAKES IN HAITI AND NEW ZEALAND

In 2010 and 2011 devastating earthquakes hit very contrasting countries. In January 2010, the city of Port-au-Prince, Haiti was decimated by a powerful earthquake that killed over 200 000 people. Just over 12 months later, Christchurch in New Zealand was hit by a strong, shallow focused earthquake that came after a stronger quake in September 2010. The impact was devastating to the **central business district (CBD)**, killing 185 people. For all people concerned in both earthquakes, the actions taken before, during and after the event had a significant impact on the damage and the death toll.

Haiti declared independence from France in 1804. Haiti has suffered from political instability and is currently the poorest country in the western hemisphere.	
Area	27 750 sq km
Population	9 996 731 (July 2014 estimate)
Population density	360 people/sq km
Population growth rate	1.08%
Infant mortality rate	49.43 deaths/1000 live births
Life expectancy at birth	63.18 years
Adult literacy rate	48.7%
Number of hospital beds	1.3 beds/1000 people (2007)
Population with access to improved drinking water	64%
Risk from major infectious diseases	High
GDP per person	US$1300 (2013 estimate)
GDP growth rate	3.4% (2013 estimate)

△ Table 6.4 Haiti fact file.

The Haiti earthquake struck on 12 January 2010 at 16:53 local time. The epicentre was just 15 km southwest of Haiti's capital, Port-au-Prince. Measuring 7 on the Richter scale and with a depth of 10 km, the earthquake had devastating consequences.

- 222 750 people died and 300 000 were injured.
- 105 000 houses were destroyed and 188 383 were damaged.
- 4000 schools were damaged or destroyed.
- The presidential palace collapsed, along with three hospitals, the main prison and the United Nations headquarters.
- The main port was so severely damaged that ships carrying aid could not dock.
- 19 million cubic metres of rubble and debris were left.

- An outbreak of cholera followed the disaster in October 2010.
- By July 2011, 5899 people had died as a result of the outbreak and 216 000 were infected.

△ Fig. 6.46 Damage to buildings after the earthquake in Haiti.

A commonwealth country that became independent from Great Britain in 1907, New Zealand is a stable, prosperous country famed for its dramatic landscapes.	
Area	268 838 sq km
Population	4 438 393 (July 2015 estimate)
Population density	17 people/sq km
Population growth rate	0.82%
Infant mortality rate	4.52 deaths/1000 live births
Life expectancy at birth	81.05 years
Adult literacy rate	99%
Number of hospital beds	2.3 beds/1000 population (2011)
Percentage of population with access to improved drinking water	100%
Risk from major infectious diseases	Extremely low
GDP per capita	US$36 200 (2015 estimate)
GDP growth rate	3.4% (2015 estimate)

△ Table 6.5 New Zealand fact file.

At 12:51 (local time) on 22 February 2011, the Christchurch earthquake began. The epicentre was just 6.7 km southeast of central Christchurch, with a depth of 5.95 km. It reached 6.3 on the Richter scale and, like the 2010 Haiti earthquake, it caused huge damage to the city and surrounding area.

- The Canterbury TV building suffered a catastrophic collapse and fire, causing 115 of the 185 deaths.
- Large rockfalls caused further damage in the hills around the city.
- East Christchurch suffered very badly from liquefaction as it was built on a swamp. Large parts of the city suffered as a consequence, and water and silt were squeezed upwards through the soil. Roads and parks were flooded, houses sunk and sewage pipes cracked.

△ Fig. 6.47 Damage after the Christchurch earthquake.

- Urban search and rescue teams were rescuing people within one hour of the earthquake, and international teams arrived within twenty-four hours.

Comparing responses

	Haiti 2010	Christchurch 2011
Before the earthquake	<ul><li>Haiti was very poorly prepared for an earthquake. Scientists had predicted the area was overdue for a quake – it was over 200 years since the last big earthquake.</li><li>The city of 2 million people was built on unstable soil, prone to intense shaking and liquefaction. Infrastructure and buildings were often poorly constructed and not built to any recognised earthquake-proofing standards, meaning they would 'pancake' in an earthquake.</li><li>Haiti was politically unstable and was the poorest country in the western hemisphere, with low literacy and life expectancy. The capital had 500 000 people living in slum conditions without running water and adequate sanitation. Consequently, the capacity to cope was very low.</li></ul>	<ul><li>Christchurch is the largest city on the South Island of New Zealand. The country has a very dynamic landscape and a history of tectonic activity. Prior to 2010 Christchurch had not experienced a major earthquake for over 100 years. However, in September 2010, the city was shaken by a 7.3 magnitude earthquake with an epicentre nearly 40 km from the city. This caused widespread damage and disruption with minor injuries. There was no loss of life.</li><li>This earthquake reminded many people of the need to plan for a major earthquake and to prepare homes and business. It also enabled urban search and rescue teams to practice drills in a real-life situation. New Zealand has stringent earthquake-proof building regulations, which are inspected regularly, disaster management plans, education in schools and regular drills, so has a high capacity to cope.</li></ul>
During the earthquake	<ul><li>The shallow focus and nearby epicentre meant there was intense shaking. The lack of preparedness was devastating.</li><li>The port and airport were severely damaged, the phone system was destroyed, the prison, hospitals, UN and aid agency headquarters and presidential palace collapsed. 50 per cent of buildings collapsed, killing over a hundred thousand people immediately and trapping tens of thousands more. People, buildings, government and infrastructure were not adequate to manage the impact of the earthquake.</li></ul>	<ul><li>The February 2011 quake came as a shock: less powerful, but much closer to the city and a much shallower focus that directed energy at the city centre.</li><li>Between 7–25 seconds of shaking damaged 100 000 buildings and caused the iconic cathedral to collapse. The Canterbury TV building collapsed completely.</li><li>While there was large-scale damage and panic, many people had known they should drop, cover and hold on. Most damaged buildings did not completely collapse, meaning people inside could escape.</li><li>Intense liquefaction meant some areas flooded and were more seriously damaged by the magnified shaking, but did not collapse completely.</li></ul>
After the earthquake	<ul><li>The response from the Haitian government was very slow as it too had been severely damaged.</li><li>Search and rescue was limited by resources, so survivors searched rubble with bare hands. International relief was slow to arrive due to the damaged port and airport. There was limited coordination on the ground. Bodies were piled up in the streets as morgues were overwhelmed. Foreign aid began to arrive, with rescue workers and doctors first to arrive to treat the 300 000 injured people and search for others.</li><li>While many countries around the world sent aid, the USA led the efforts, sending seventeen US Navy ships with hospital facilities, twelve aircraft, forty-eight helicopters and tonnes of food and medical equipment.</li><li>Once the rescue phase ended, efforts moved to providing food, water and shelter for the 1.5 million homeless people.</li><li>Long-term recovery progress has been very slow but the city was so badly damaged it is difficult to recover quickly, although over US$3.5 billion was donated.</li><li>Many individual citizens have had to work to rebuild their own homes. The World Bank and other agencies are working to build some houses and government buildings. There is now a nationwide building code, brought up to earthquake-proof standards. Privately built homes do not have to follow this however. Scientists are working on cheap earthquake-proof housing solutions to increase the capacity of places like Haiti to cope with earthquakes in the future.</li></ul>	<ul><li>Well-trained and equipped search and rescue teams were searching buildings in less than one hour, with international help arriving within 24 hours.</li><li>Many people were trapped in the Canterbury TV building (which had been illegally and unknowingly built to a lower standard).</li><li>Of the total death toll of 185 people, 115 died here. Large numbers of people were at work so were long distances from their homes. Power, water and sewage systems were not functioning. Many people were made homeless.</li><li>Once the rescue effort had ended, the city centre was sealed off and engineers moved in to assess buildings for demolition or repair. Government efforts focused on restoring infrastructure to residential areas. The national government set up an earthquake commission to support the recovery and aid people with insurance claims and rebuilding. Furthermore, they designated large areas as vulnerable to future earthquakes due to the liquefaction, paid off house owners, banned future housing and are currently consulting the public on how best to use the land.</li><li>Five years on there are still signs of the earthquake in the city centre, but much of Christchurch is back to normal or on the road to recovery. The New Zealand government has further strengthened earthquake building codes – particularly the retrofitting of old buildings that were more severely affected.</li><li>The earthquake, while traumatic and tragic, has increased the capacity of the area to cope with future quakes due to the increased resilience and disaster preparedness lessons learned.</li></ul>

△ Table 6.6 Managing impacts and reducing risk – comparing the Haiti and Christchurch earthquakes.

IMPACT OF TYPHOON HAIYAN 2013

The Philippines is a hazard hotspot that is at risk from typhoons, volcanic eruptions, earthquakes and tsunami, flooding and landslides. The high and growing population are living in a country that is showing real signs of economic progress, but also one that is struggling to cope with population growth and urbanisation. Many people live in slum conditions in the capital Manila, while other cities in outlying islands are also struggling to develop the infrastructure to support the population. Many people live in self-built homes, made out of wood or concrete and corrugated iron. The sheer number of hazards faced by the Philippines leads to constant setbacks for parts of the country, which in turn causes more internal migration to big cities like Manila that are unable to keep pace with the expansion needed. Consequently, the Philippines has a large number of people who are highly vulnerable to natural hazards. The economic development has increased the capacity of the government and military to cope with the impact after a typhoon, but this capacity is not evenly distributed or building codes, for example, adequately enforced.

The Philippines is a former Spanish colony that came under US control after a war in 1898. In 1935 it became a self-governing commonwealth, but it was invaded by Japan in 1942. After World War 2, the country declared independence. The USA closed its last military base in 1992.	
Area	300 000 sq km
Population	107 668 231
Population density	359 people/sq km
Population growth rate	1.81% (2014 estimate)
Infant mortality rate	17.64 deaths/1000 live births
Life expectancy at birth	72.48 years
Adult literacy rate	95.4%
Number of hospital beds	1 bed/1000 people (2011)
Percentage of population with access to improved drinking water	92.4%
Risk from major infectious diseases	High
GDP per person	US$4700 (2013 estimate)
GDP growth rate	6.8% (2013 estimate)

△ Table 6.7 Fact file on the Philippines.

Date	Disaster type	Persons affected
November 2013	Storm (Tropical Cyclone Haiyan)	16 106 807
December 2012	Storm (Tropical Cyclone Bopha)	6 246 664
November 1990	Storm (Tropical Cyclone Mike)	6 159 569
September 2009	Storm (Tropical Cyclone Ondoy)	4 901 763
June 2008	Storm (Tropical Cyclone Fengsheng)	4 785 460

△ Table 6.8 Recent significant natural disasters in the Philippines.

Source: EM-DAT: The OFDA/CRED International Disaster Database

www.emdat.be – Université Catholique de Louvain – Brussels, Belgium.

Typhoon Haiyan struck on 8 November 2013 at 4:40 local time. Gusts of wind of 275 km per hour, and sustained winds of 237 km per hour caused a 7.6 metre-high storm surge. The consequences were shocking and the city of Tacloban suffered catastrophic damage:

- The death toll reached over 6000.

- 4.1 million people were displaced and 1.1 million homes were damaged or destroyed.

- 5.6 million people were in need of food aid and over 14.1 million people across 46 provinces were affected by the typhoon.

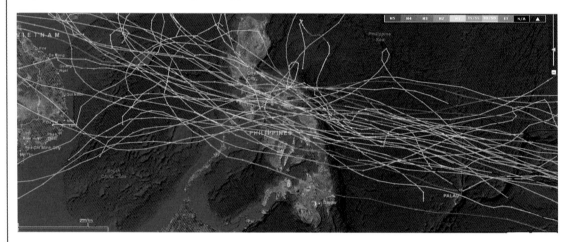

△ Fig. 6.48 Storm track map of the Philippines.

△ Fig. 6.49 Flooding and destruction after Typhoon Haiyan.

△ Fig. 6.50 Slums were damaged and destroyed after Typhoon Haiyan.

Managing impacts and reducing risk from Typhoon Haiyan

Typhoon Haiyan was the twenty-fifth tropical storm to track over the Philippines in 2013. The category 5 typhoon was the most powerful storm to hit land since records began. It had winds gusting up to 275 km/h and a storm surge 8 metres high. The flimsy wooden structures of Tacloban and the surrounding area were ripped apart. Thousands died. The disaster affected over 14 million people – the highest number in the region's history.

Typhoon Haiyan was clearly visible on satellite imagery and the government issued warnings to people across the regions likely to be affected. Despite a well-designed and well-practised disaster management system, the country was not fully prepared for Typhoon Haiyan. Hazard maps that identified areas at risk from storm surges were not available for Tacloban. These are critical in educating people to move out of harm's way. A tsunami risk map of the area did exist, but this was not used to evacuate people away from the storm surge. A lack of joined-up planning between agencies led to more people being at risk. In Tacloban, evacuation centres were often one-storey buildings that were destroyed by the massive storm surge. Many local people did not understand the seriousness of the warnings, highlighting a lack of effective education. Government warnings to evacuate were often ignored as residents did not understand what a storm surge was or feared their homes would be looted.

Once the storm surge had receded and winds died down, the vast impact simply overwhelmed the local government. Survivors struggled to find food and water and an immediate aid effort was launched. Within 4 days nearly 20 000 personnel from the Philippines had been deployed. There was also a massive international response, which lacked coordination to start with. Aid distribution was challenging as Tacloban airport was too small to accommodate the number of planes being sent to the area, forcing some to be turned back. On the ground, desperate people began looting homes and food storage depots until more law enforcement officials arrived as well as food aid. It took up to a week for officials to reach some remote areas to assess damage and provide aid. A global crowdsourcing campaign was launched to allow people around the world to assess before and after satellite imagery for evidence of damaged structures. This information was fed to officials on the ground to direct the aid effort.

In the aftermath, the government of the Philippines was criticised for a slow response, but the scale of the disaster was overwhelming. Today, many areas are recovering with new wooden buildings being constructed on the coast and infrastructure back online. People are traumatised by the events of 2013 and would prefer to live on high ground, but need to make a living from fishing. Areas classified as no-build zones to avoid future storm surges have been covered with new flimsy buildings. However, mangrove swamps, which absorb storm waves, have been replanted to reduce risk. Disaster analysis experts have advised that along the Pacific Coast of the Philippines there are new evacuation centres built that are properly located, designed and built. Furthermore, new hazard risk maps and better warning systems are being developed. These valuable lessons should begin to reduce risk in the future – vital in a world where, due to climate change, typhoon intensity is increasing.

End of topic checklist

Key terms

abstraction, active, agriculture, aid, alluvium, aquifer, CBD, channel flow, collision plate boundaries, conservative/transform plate boundaries, constructive/divergent plate boundaries, convection currents, core, coriolis effect, cost-benefit analysis, crop yields, crust, cultivation, deforestation, desalination, desertification, destructive/convergent plate boundaries, dormant, drought, earthquake, epicentre, evaporation, extinct, famine, fault line, fertile, flood defence, floodplain, focus, forced migration, geothermal power, groundwater flow, hazard risk map, impermeable, infiltration, infrastructure, interception, irrigation, lag time, lahar, lava, liquefaction, lithosphere, magma, magnitude, mantle, mid-ocean ridge, migration, minerals, mining, natural disaster, natural hazard, ocean trench, overgrazing, percolation, permeable, plate boundary, precipitation, pyroclastic flow, recurrence interval, relief, retrofitting, Richter scale, rift valley, risk, river channel, Saffir-Simpson scale, saturated soil, seismic waves, seismometer, shield volcano, soil erosion, storm hydrograph, storm surge, storm track, stratovolcano, subduction, surface run-off, tectonic plate, topography, tourism, tropical cyclone, tsunami, urban, urbanisation, VEI, volcano, vulnerability, water-borne disease, water conservation, water cycle, water transfer, wildfire

Important vocabulary

aftermath, building codes, capacity to cope, colony, communities, crowdsourcing, disease, distribution, drill, engineering, eruption, evacuation, expanding, explosive, fertile, financial, food storage, fractured, friction, impact, insurance claim, intensity, intensive, interaction, landscape, magnitude, management plan, monitoring, multiplier, observation, planning, predict, prediction, preparation, pressure, properties, reconstruction, rehabilitation, relationship, resilience, response, risk assessment, scale, search and rescue, shelter, shockwave, strain, structure, submerged, temperature, warning system

During your study of this topic you should have learned:

○ How the Earth is structured and the different properties of the crust, mantle and core.

○ Where earthquakes and volcanoes occur around the world.

○ Why tectonic plates move and what happens at plate boundaries.

End of topic checklist continued

◯ How volcanoes are formed.

◯ That the impact of tectonic activity can be devastating and that the magnitude of the event does not always mean a worse impact.

◯ That different nations have different levels of vulnerability to natural hazards because of their capacity to cope with them.

◯ How tropical cyclones form, their impact and how this can be managed.

◯ How and why flooding occurs.

◯ How floods affect people and how they are managed.

◯ How drought affects people and the environment.

◯ How hazards can be managed to reduce risk.

◯ How natural hazards can benefit people.

◯ How the impact and response to an earthquake will vary between high and low-income countries and the effect this has on the scale of the disaster.

◯ How the impact of Typhoon Haiyan was managed in the Philippines.

The questions for Section 6 start on page 254.

Relative to the size of the Earth, the atmosphere – upon which we all depend – is incredibly small. Around 75 per cent of the mass of the atmosphere is found within the first 14 km, in a layer called the troposphere, which is where all weather occurs. The atmosphere is composed mainly of nitrogen and oxygen with smaller concentrations of water vapour, argon and carbon dioxide. Carbon dioxide is a vital greenhouse gas that keeps the temperature on the planet liveable for humans. Atmospheric processes are responsible for weather and climate, for example, driving monsoon rain patterns that provide water for millions of people. However, in the past 200 years, human activity has changed the composition of the atmosphere. Due to the burning of fossil fuels, there is now more carbon dioxide in the atmosphere than at any point in recorded human history; in fact it is higher than any point in the last 650 000 years. This is having a significant impact on global temperatures and weather patterns. Furthermore, atmospheric pollution in the form of carbon monoxide and sulfur dioxide from vehicles and burning of coal is having a significant impact on the environment and human health. The challenge of managing the impact of atmospheric pollution sustainably is vital on a planet with an increasing and energy-hungry population.

CONTENTS

LEARNING OBJECTIVES

Describe the structure and composition of the atmosphere.

Describe the natural greenhouse effect.

Describe and explain the causes of atmospheric pollution, with reference to:

- smog

- acid rain

- ozone layer depletion

- enhanced greenhouse effect

Describe and explain the impact of atmospheric pollution.

Describe and explain the strategies used by individuals, governments and the international community to reduce the effects of atmospheric pollution.

Study the causes, impact and management of a specific example of atmospheric pollution.

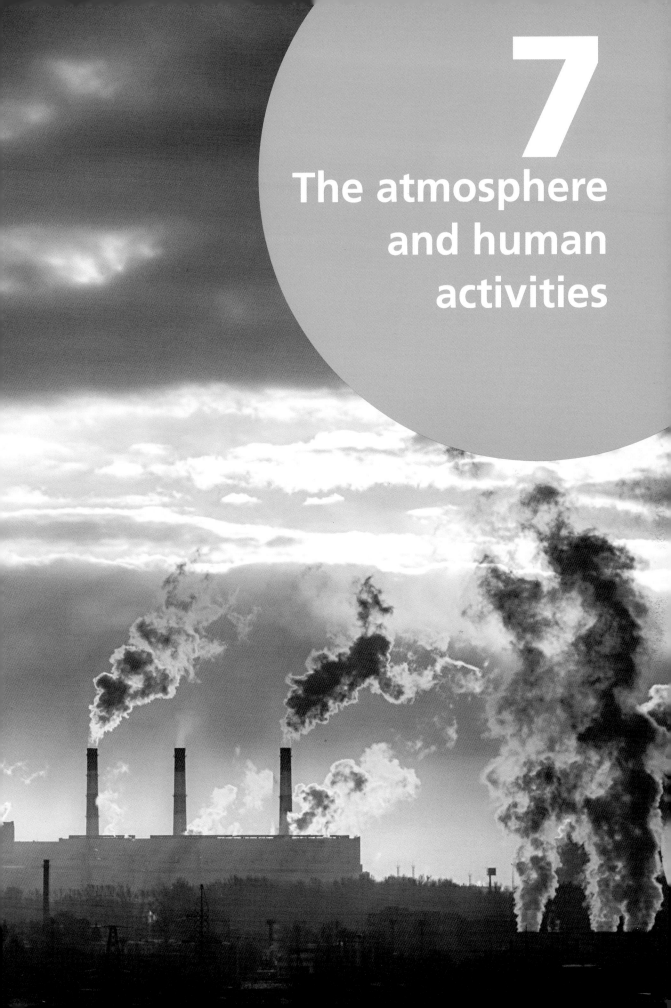

7

The atmosphere and human activities

THE ATMOSPHERE

The structure of the atmosphere

Exosphere
Height: 600 – 10 000 km
Temperature: Highly variable; too little air to measure accurately.
Features: This is the uppermost part of our atmosphere which merges into space. This is where many satellites orbit the Earth.

Thermosphere
Height: 85 – 600 km
Temperature: Rises continually up to 1000 °C due to the absorbing of solar energy by relatively few molecules and atoms.
Features: This layer is so thin, that although the air molecules are hot, to us it would be freezing. The International Space Station orbits in this layer. The lower part is where highly energy -charged particles from the sun strike the atmosphere and form the beautiful aurora seen in polar regions.

Mesosphere
Height: 50 – 85 km
Temperature: Decreases with altitude to about –100 °C.
Features: The coldest layer of the atmosphere. Ice clouds form here that are visible at sunset. Meteors burn up in this layer.

Stratosphere
Height: 14.5 – 50 km
Temperature: Stable, then increases with altitude due to the ozone layer. From –50 °C to 0 °C.
Features: A zone of dry, thin air that is cold and clear. It contains the ozone layer (19–48 km) which absorbs and scatters incoming solar radiation and protecting us from harmful UV radiation.

Troposphere
Height: From the surface to 8 to 14.5 km
Temperature: Decreases with height at 6.5 °C/km.
Features: The most dense part of our atmosphere contains almost all atmospheric water vapour and most of our weather.

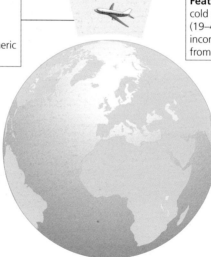

The composition of the atmosphere

The **atmosphere** is made up mainly of nitrogen and oxygen, with smaller proportions of gases like argon and traces of **carbon dioxide**, neon, helium, methane, nitrous oxide and ozone. The relative proportion is shown in Figure 7.1.

The main components – nitrogen, oxygen and argon – remain relatively constant, whereas the trace gases vary over time and by location. Human activity is modifying the proportions of these gases, which play a vital role in regulating the Earth's **climate**. **Greenhouse gases** such as **water vapour**, carbon dioxide, methane and ozone, interact with incoming and outgoing **solar radiation** and warm the atmosphere. Ozone in the atmosphere filters out parts of the incoming ultraviolet radiation from sunlight and protects plants, animals and humans from the damaging effects of the sun. The ultraviolet radiation that does reach Earth causes sunburn in humans – illustrating the importance of the **ozone layer** in protecting life on Earth.

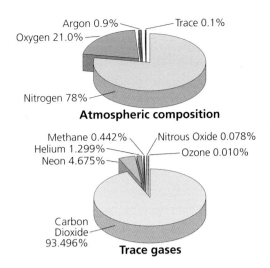

△ Fig. 7.1 The composition of the atmosphere.

The natural greenhouse effect

The greenhouse gases absorb energy from the sun, creating a natural greenhouse effect that warms the Earth's surface. This makes Planet Earth habitable for life. Without these gases the average temperature of the Earth's surface would be –18 °C, instead of today's average of –15 °C.

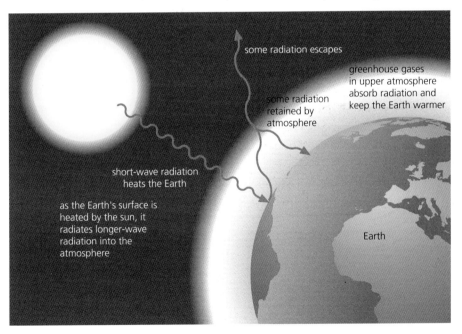

△ Fig. 7.2 The natural greenhouse effect.

ATMOSPHERIC POLLUTION – CAUSES AND IMPACTS

Relative to the mass of the Earth, the atmosphere is very small. Since the beginning of the industrial revolution, human activity has been impacting the atmosphere. Burning of **fossil fuels**, vehicle **emissions** and industrial processes are changing the composition of the atmosphere and impacting human health and the **environment**. Atmospheric **pollution** is having a detrimental effect on air quality in our cities, as well as leading to **acid rain**, depletion of the vital ozone layer and **climate change**.

△ Fig. 7.3 Congested city streets in Bangkok lead to increases in vehicle emissions.

Causes of smog

Smog is a term for visible air pollution that was first used in the early 20th century to describe a mixture of smoke from burning coal and fog. In 1952, over 12 000 people died in a great smog event in London, when the city was enveloped for four days in smog caused by a combination of stable air conditions, low winds and excessive burning of coal. Many major cities experience smog today, although with a greater range of causes:

- coal emissions
- industrial emissions of volatile organic compounds (VOCs)
- vehicle emissions
- forest fires
- **photochemical reactions**
- **temperature inversions**.

Much of the smog that affects cities like Beijing, Shanghai, Los Angeles and Mexico City is caused by photochemical reactions between sunlight, nitrogen oxides and VOCs. The nitrogen oxide is emitted from vehicle exhausts, burning coal and from industrial processes in factories. VOCs are organic chemicals that easily enter the surrounding air, for example, from petrol, paints and cleaning products. The sunlight causes a reaction and the creation of ground level ozone, which at this level is harmful to humans.

△ Fig. 7.4 Smog over Shanghai, China.

Photochemical smog can become a significant threat to human health when it accumulates due to temperature inversions. These occur when the air next to the surface is colder than the air above – trapping the colder, dense air in place and preventing it from blowing away and dispersing.

A further cause of smog can be smoke from uncontrolled burning of forests. The smoke reduces air quality and in cities, reacts with other pollutants to create a haze. This has been a significant problem in Southeast Asia.

△ Fig. 7.5 Pedestrians walking through smog.

Impact of smog

Smog is clearly visible and has a significant impact on human health. Although many cities monitor air

quality levels, issue masks and in extreme cases close schools, the smog can still enter buildings and affect people. Common effects are:

- burning eyes and throat
- shortness of breath, wheezing and coughing
- chest pain when inhaling
- asthma attacks
- risk of **respiratory diseases**
- pulmonary inflammation
- increased risk of heart attack.

These effects will vary depending on a range of factors, such as the length of time the smog lasts and the level of pollution. There are groups of people who are more sensitive: children, adults who are active outdoors, people with breathing diseases like asthma, and elderly people. Globally, air pollution is a significant health risk, and the World Health Organization has described it as the single biggest environmental health risk. Outdoor air pollution kills over 3 million people each year and is rising.

Impact of acid rain

When atmospheric water mixes with sulfur dioxide and nitrogen oxide – emitted from **thermal power** stations, vehicle pollution and **industry** – they are converted into sulfuric and nitric acid, which can fall as rain. **Prevailing winds** mean that the acid rain often falls in other countries away from the source of the pollution. This causes conflict between countries and needs careful management.

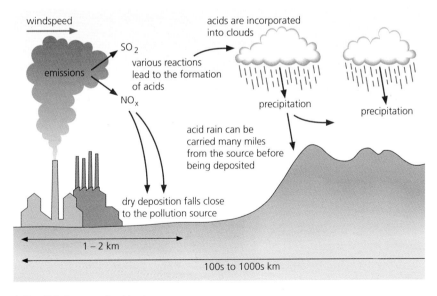

windspeed

acids are incorporated into clouds

SO$_2$

various reactions lead to the formation of acids

emissions

NO$_x$

precipitation

precipitation

acid rain can be carried many miles from the source before being deposited

dry deposition falls close to the pollution source

1 – 2 km

100s to 1000s km

△ Fig. 7.6 Causes of acid rain.

Figure 7.7 Shows the extent of sulfur dioxide emissions globally. The dry sulfur and nitrogen oxides cause damage to buildings when they corrode metal and paint and cause damage to stone. This is particularly visible on old monuments such as the lion in Figure 7.8.

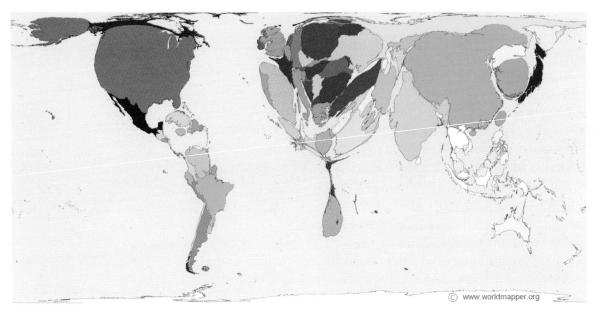

△ Fig. 7.7 Proportional map showing sulfur dioxide emissions.

When combined with water vapour, the wet **deposition** of acidic material causes significant damage to the environment:

- Acidification of bodies of water. When acidic rainwater enters streams, lakes and marshes it often carries aluminium that it has leached from the soil. This, along with sulfuric and nitric acid, damages **ecosystems** by harming the most sensitive **species** and destroying **food chains**. For example, frogs can survive a more acidic environment than their sources of food, so a mildly acidic environment will still harm them. The acidic water has a significant impact on aquatic plants and fish **populations**, as well as the non-aquatic species that rely upon them in the ecosystem.

△ Fig. 7.8 The impact of acid rain on a stone monument in the UK.

- Effect on fish populations. Acid rain will cause fish eggs not to hatch and with increasing acidity will kill adult fish or their sources of food. The net result is a reduction in fish population numbers and a loss of some species, reducing **biodiversity**. Those that are sensitive but not killed might suffer from lower body weight and smaller size. Nitrogen pollution from acid rain and other agricultural sources is impacting fish in coastal waters.

△ Fig. 7.9 Fish killed by acidic water.

- Damage to crops and vegetation. Forests can be destroyed when the acidic water destroys soil nutrients and damages roots. This leads to loss of leaves and needles. The acidic rainwater reduces soil fertility by increasing the acidity. This lowers agricultural productivity by reducing the types of crop that can grow.

Ozone layer depletion

The layer of ozone in the **stratosphere** shields the Earth from harmful ultraviolet B radiation. Ozone is highly reactive and is constantly being formed and broken down, which leads to global variation each year in the amount of ozone present in the atmosphere due to natural factors such as the Earth's orbit. Ozone reacts and is broken down by chemicals such as chlorine, which has been released into the atmosphere in large quantities over time. One atom of chlorine can break down more than 1 000 000 ozone molecules.

There is significant concern over the impact that atmospheric pollution is having on the ozone layer. One major cause of ozone depletion is the use of chemicals called **chlorofluorocarbons (CFCs)**. These were commonly found in aerosol cans and refrigerators used in high-income countries in the past century. High in the atmosphere, the CFCs react with sunlight and form chlorine, which destroys ozone. The greatest depletion of ozone can be found in the polar regions, due to the seasonal impact of prolonged darkness in winter followed by constant sunlight in summer, with Antarctica having the greatest losses. This varies seasonally, but at its greatest extent in 2006 the depletion covered 27.5 million sq km. From the 1980s onwards, global levels of ozone were in decline, but a ban on CFCs in 1996 led to the start of a recovery, with rates of depletion slowing.

△ Fig. 7.10 Trees killed by acid rain.

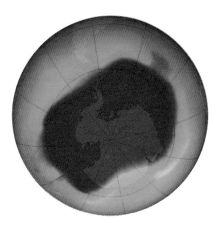

△ Fig. 7.11 A false colour image showing the extent of the 'hole' in the ozone layer over Antarctica in 2006.

Impact of ozone depletion

Although there has been a global reduction in the quantity of ozone, the depletion is uneven. This means that the impact is uneven. An increase in the amount of ultraviolet B radiation reaching Earth has been shown to have the following impacts on people and the environment:

- Increase in the number of skin cancer cases in affected regions.
- Increase in the reported cases of cataracts in eyes (a clouding of the eye lens).
- Damage to plant tissues and reduction in plant growth.
- Damage to ecosystems and **food webs** due to changed insect behaviour.

The enhanced greenhouse effect and its impact

The burning of fossil fuels, intensive **agriculture** and vehicle emissions have led to a significant increase in levels of greenhouse gases in the atmosphere. These in turn absorb more of the outgoing solar radiation and lead to a warming of the atmosphere. Human activity is enhancing the natural greenhouse effect and making it more effective at trapping heat. This is known as the **enhanced greenhouse effect**. Figure 7.12 shows how observed CO_2 levels in the atmosphere have increased over the past 100 years.

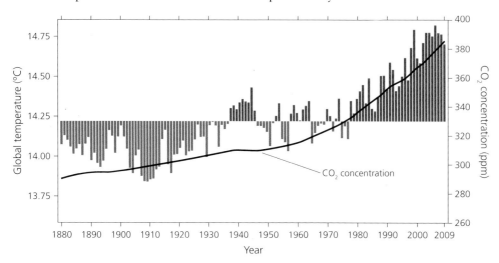

△ Fig. 7.12 Graph showing increase in atmospheric carbon dioxide levels and temperatures from 1880 to the present time.

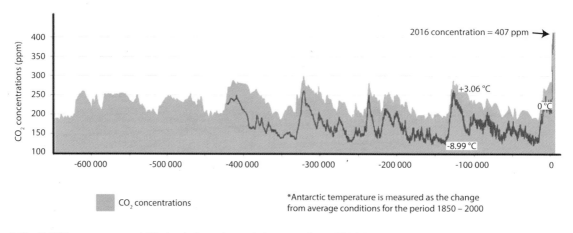

△ Fig. 7.13 Temperature and CO_2 levels from Antarctic ice cores from 650 000 years ago to 2006.

Using ice cores from Antarctica, it is possible to reconstruct 650 000 years of temperature and atmospheric CO_2 levels. Figure 7.13 shows the relationship between CO_2 levels and atmospheric temperature – higher CO_2 leads to higher temperatures. 650 000 years before Common Era the level of CO_2 had never gone above 300 parts per million (ppm). Today it is 407 ppm. Clearly there are fluctuations in the global temperature that are caused by complex orbital cycles and variations in solar output. However, human activity and agriculture are releasing high levels of the greenhouse gases CO_2 and methane to create an enhanced greenhouse effect, which is changing global surface temperatures.

The expected increase in global temperatures is hard to predict exactly, as attempts are being made to reduce greenhouse gas emissions and to slow the enhanced greenhouse effect. However, using sophisticated climate models and supercomputers, climatologists have been able to predict the likely impact of different levels of warming throughout the 21st century, as seen in Figure 7.14.

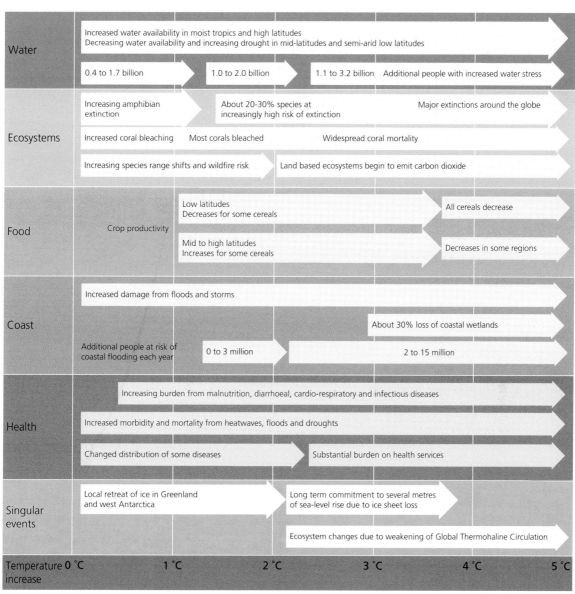

△ Fig. 7.14 Global impacts projected for changes in climate associated with different amounts of increase in global average surface temperature in the 21st century.

MANAGING ATMOSPHERIC POLLUTION

The impact of atmospheric pollution globally – whether directly on human health and ecosystems or indirectly through climate change – is a significant environmental management challenge. It is vital that individuals, governments and the international **community** act to reduce the impact of smog, acid rain, ozone depletion and climate change. There are a vast range of strategies that can be used to reduce the effects of atmospheric pollution.

Reducing your carbon footprint

Individuals can calculate the amount of CO_2 they are responsible for emitting into the atmosphere each year, then work on reducing their **carbon footprint** by the following methods:

- using public transport
- flying less
- using less energy and switching sources (for example, installing solar panels)
- eating more locally produced food
- driving less, walking more
- repairing not replacing, reducing waste, reusing materials, recycling.

Reduced use of fossil fuels

Burning fossil fuels increases greenhouse gas emissions, creates smog and leads to acid rain. Working to reduce the use of these by replacing them with **renewable energy** sources is vital. Development of solar, HEP, wind, wave and tidal power all have the potential over time to reduce our use of fossil fuels.

Energy efficiency

Wasting energy leads to greater demand and therefore greater use of fossil fuels. It is possible for individuals to become significantly more energy-efficient at home by installing smart meters, new boilers, and insulation or cooling building design. There are lots of strategies summarised in Section 2 (see pages 38–42).

Carbon capture and storage

As we transition to a lower carbon world, there will still be fossil fuels being burned. One solution to this is to capture and store the carbon as it is released from large sources, such as coal-fired power stations. The most common process is to separate the carbon from the air in the waste gas produced from burning coal. The captured carbon can then be transported by pipeline to suitable storage sites in geological formation. In addition, carbon can be captured by planting forests or by injecting it into lakes with bacteria present that break down the carbon dioxide. This is a developing technology that has not yet been built on a large enough scale.

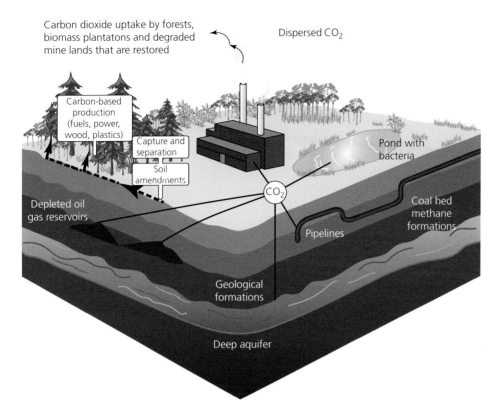

Carbon dioxide uptake by forests, biomass plantatons and degraded mine lands that are restored

Dispersed CO_2

Carbon-based production (fuels, power, wood, plastics)

Capture and separation

Soil amendments

Pond with bacteria

Depleted oil gas reservoirs

CO_2

Coal hed methane formations

Pipelines

Geological formations

Deep aquifer

△ Fig. 7.15 Carbon capture and storage.

Flue-gas desulfurisation

It is possible to develop technologies that remove sulfur dioxide from the gases released from fossil fuel power stations. There has been a significant reduction in the amount of sulfur dioxide emissions in many countries due to the impact of acid rain leading to action. Sulfur has been removed from petrol prior to **consumption** and is collected by scrubbing the gas in alkaline mixtures as it is being released. This has reduced the amount of acid rain that is falling.

Reforestation and afforestation

Replanting of forests and planting new forest areas are effective strategies to reduce atmospheric pollution, as trees take in carbon dioxide and produce oxygen. They also increase biodiversity, provide **habitats** and slow water down – reducing the risk of floods.

Taxation

Governments are able to introduce green taxes that encourage people to change behaviours. For example, taxing older, more polluting cars while reducing tax on newer efficient cars will encourage a shift to newer cars. Equally, reducing tax on public transport keeps prices lower and should encourage greater use and an associated reduction in vehicle emissions. Furthermore, taxing emissions of carbon forces polluting industries to develop methods of carbon capture or to shift to renewable energy sources.

Transport policies

As seen in Section 2 (see page 41), governments are able to introduce transport policies to reduce vehicle emissions and reduce smog. This has been particularly effective in Singapore where a combination of higher vehicle tax, electronic road pricing (ERP) and an efficient, cheap **mass rapid transit (MRT)** system has reduced cars on the road.

Catalytic converters

Cars are now fitted with catalytic converters, which convert toxic pollutants from petrol engines into less toxic pollutants such as CO_2 and water vapour. They do not remove CO_2, which is released into the atmosphere. They are effective at reducing carbon monoxide and nitrogen oxides released, but do not eliminate them entirely.

△ Fig. 7.16 Car exhaust gases are reduced by catalytic converters.

International agreement and policies

While individuals and governments can take action to reduce atmospheric pollution, many of the impacts occur in countries that are not responsible for the main sources of pollution. Therefore, this requires large-scale international agreement and the development of effective policies. There have been a number of attempts to reach global agreement to reduce greenhouse gases, with variable success. The most recent agreement provides great hope that it will be the strongest international agreement to date on limiting greenhouse gas emissions. In the 2016 Paris Agreement, 177 countries have committed to the following:

• Limit global temperature increase to below 2 °C above pre-industrial levels.
• Increase global **adaptation** to a changing climate and to lower greenhouse gas emissions.
• Finance low greenhouse gas development.
• Cap greenhouse gas emissions as soon as possible.

CFC replacement

Another example of international agreement was the 1989 Montreal Protocol on substances that deplete the ozone layer. This highly successful agreement led to the phasing out then eventual ban of CFCs. The ban has meant that there has been a reduction in ozone depletion. However, the replacement gases are strong greenhouse gases that are now contributing to the enhanced greenhouse effect.

CASE STUDY

SOUTHEAST ASIAN HAZE, 2015/2016

In September 2015, huge areas of Southeast Asia were covered in smoke, which had a significant impact on air quality across the region. Fires on the Indonesian islands of Sumatra and Kalimantan in Borneo led to cross-boundary air pollution in Brunei, Cambodia, Malaysia, The Philippines, Singapore, Thailand and Vietnam. In Indonesia a state of emergency was declared in six states.

△ Fig. 7.17 Satellite image showing fires and smoke haze across Southeast Asia in 2015.

△ Fig. 7.18 Locations of the Indonesian fires in September 2015.

Causes

This air pollution crisis was caused by uncontrolled burning of forests in Indonesia. The forest fires begin when slash and burn forest clearance was used to remove the trees to clear the way for planting palm oil, which is used globally to produce cheap vegetable oil. Much of the soil contained flammable and high carbon peat, which will burn uncontrollably and even burn underground. 2015 is the latest in a long line of haze events caused by burning in Indonesia. In 2015, the dry season was much drier than usual due to the El Niño climate phenomenon. Prevailing winds carried the smoke from the source to countries across the region. Some of the burning is illegal and on protected land. However, many of the fires are on land owned by palm oil plantations and pulpwood companies meaning the fires are the responsibility of large businesses.

Impact

The impact was greatest in Indonesia itself, where air quality over Sumatra was classified as four times higher than the hazardous level. Helicopters trying to put the fires out were unable to fly due to the low visibility. In some states, children were evacuated to safer zones. Regional impacts included the following:

△ Fig. 7.19 Tackling the fires.

- Nineteen deaths were directly caused by the fires.
- There were an estimated 500 000 cases of respiratory infections.
- There were an estimated 100 000 premature deaths in the region.
- Thousands suffered skin and eye irritations.
- The financial impact on Indonesia was estimated at US$47 billion.
- Unhealthy air quality was recorded across Malaysia.
- Over 4700 schools closed across Malaysia, affecting nearly 3 million students.
- The Kuala Lumpur Marathon was cancelled.
- Outdoor play was cancelled at schools in Singapore.
- The World Swimming Championship was disrupted in Singapore.
- Poor air quality was recorded in Thailand, Vietnam, Cambodia, The Philippines and Brunei.

Management

Management of the issue is complex. Once heavy rains returned in late October 2015, many of the fires were put out and air quality improved. Prior to this, the Indonesian and Malaysian governments tried to tackle the fires by using planes, helicopters and cloud seeding. Across the region, people were issued with free face masks and some local authorities chose to close schools.

Once the fires have begun, management of the problem is about dealing with current crisis and reducing the impact. However, management of this issue requires efforts to reduce the number of fires starting in the first place. This can be achieved by the following measures:

- Closer international cooperation and signing agreements.
- Ending the process of slash and burn by making it illegal and prosecuting guilty people and companies.
- Educating smallholders to use more sustainable forest management techniques.
- Reducing consumption of palm oil that is not certified as sustainable.
- Reducing corruption that protects companies guilty of starting fires.
- Monitoring of land ownership with the use of GIS systems.

Unless there is focused effort to reduce the causes of the problem, it is likely that another air pollution crisis will occur in the region.

End of topic checklist

Key terms

acid rain, afforestation, atmosphere, carbon capture and storage, carbon dioxide, carbon footprint, CFC, deposition, desulfurisation, El Niño, emissions, enhanced greenhouse effect, GIS, mesosphere, natural greenhouse effect, ozone layer, peat, photochemical reactions, prevailing wind, respiratory disease, slash and burn, solar radiation, stratosphere, temperature inversion, thermosphere, troposphere, vegetation, VOCs, water vapour

Important vocabulary

absorb, agreement, agriculture, aluminium, Asia, asthma, cataracts, climate, climatologist, composition, concentrations, conflict, crops, detrimental, emitted, environment, factors, fertility, flue, geological formation, habitable, haze, human health, impact, industrial revolution, industry, insulation, leach, management, models, observed, palm oil, pedestrian, plantation, pollution, population, process, productivity, protocol, radiation, react, recovery, seasonally, sensitive, skin cancer, supercomputer, sustainable, taxation, temperature, water bodies, weather

During your study of this topic you should have learned:

○ To describe the structure and composition of the atmosphere.

○ How the atmosphere is structured into different layers that have different properties.

○ The gases that form the atmosphere.

○ How the planet is kept habitable by the natural greenhouse effect.

○ How to explain the causes and impact of smog.

○ How to explain the causes and impact of acid rain.

○ How to explain the causes and impact of ozone depletion.

○ How to explain the causes and impact of the enhanced greenhouse effect.

○ How to describe and explain a range of different strategies used by individuals, governments and the international community to reduce the effects of atmospheric pollution.

○ That the Southeast Asian Haze of 2015 was a complex air pollution crisis that might happen again.

The questions for Section 7 start on page 257.

The number of people living on Earth is increasingly rapidly. This, combined with a very uneven distribution and density of population across the Earth's surface, presents one of the greatest challenges of the twenty-first century.

Whilst some areas of the world still contain very few people, many other locations are endeavouring to cope with a mass of humanity. As the carrying capacity of some of these areas is put under acute pressure, supporting ecosystems can experience very serious and long-term environmental changes.

Although the net growth in world population is around 80 million per year, this figure hides important differences between regions and countries. Many low-income countries with less advanced economies have a very young population structure. As a consequence, population growth rates can be rapid. Some governments faced with this situation have responded by introducing anti-natalist policies designed to reduce the rate of population increase. In contrast, some high-income countries with advanced economies now have an ageing population structure. This presents problems of a different, but equally serious, nature, and it is not uncommon to find these countries implementing pro-natalist policies to boost population growth rates.

CONTENTS

LEARNING OBJECTIVES

Identify where people live in the world.

Describe and explain the growth curve of populations.

Describe and explain the changes in human populations.

Describe population structure in MEDCs and LEDCs.

Evaluate strategies for managing human population size.

Describe and explain the strategies a named country or region has used to manage population size.

8

Human population

HUMAN POPULATION DISTRIBUTION AND DENSITY

Population distribution means the pattern of where people live on Earth. **Population density** is the average number of people living in a square kilometre and is used to estimate whether an area is **sparsely** or **densely populated**. Global population is not evenly distributed. Some areas are crowded, whilst others have few or no people.

Where do people live in the world?

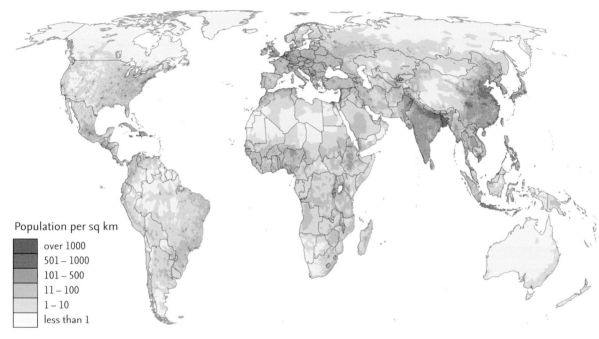

Population per sq km

- over 1000
- 501 – 1000
- 101 – 500
- 11 – 100
- 1 – 10
- less than 1

△ Fig 8.1 World population map.

Some areas of the world have more advantages as places to live than others, and have higher population densities as a result. Population pressure in these areas can build up on resources, such as land, water and food. These areas become overpopulated if population density exceeds the **carrying capacity** of the **environment** to maintain a decent **quality of life** for people. This can cause disasters such as **famine**, war and the spread of disease.

Physical factors that influence the distribution and density of population include the following:

- **Climate** – People are attracted to temperate areas with mild temperatures and evenly distributed rainfall, which offers greater opportunities for farming than areas with more extreme weather patterns.
- **Relief** – Flat, lower lying and gently undulating landscapes are attractive because they are easier to settle, farm and to construct transport links. Higher, steeper, colder more rugged land with thin acidic soils is generally avoided.

- Soils – Places with deeper more fertile soils often have higher population densities because farming is more productive than locations with shallow and infertile soils where fewer people can be supported.
- **Natural resources** – Locations with rich naturally occurring materials, for example, **minerals**, forests and water, which boost economic activity, attract people, whilst places with little to exploit commercially tend to be less populated.
- **Accessibility** – Areas that are easily reached, such as river valleys or coastal locations, tend to have higher concentrations of people than more remote and inaccessible inland areas.
- Vegetation – Regions with dense or potentially hazardous vegetation, for example, forest or swamps, generally have fewer people than more open grassland areas where the environment is more easily managed.

Human factors that influence the distribution and density of population include the following:

- Political – Generally people are attracted more to places with stable, peaceful and democratic governments than politically volatile regions where conflict is common.
- Economic – High income and economically developed nations, where living standards and job opportunities are greater than less economically advanced regions, attract high population numbers.
- Communications – Businesses are drawn to places with good transport networks and trading links. Migrants move in to fill the jobs created which in turn attracts other industries and services and more people seeking employment.
- Social – Governments can influence population distribution through policies encouraging or restricting **immigration** or selecting locations for new towns, industrial expansion or routes for transport links.

It is rare for just one of these factors to be responsible for determining population distribution and density, as illustrated by the following example from Japan.

Average population density in Japan is 349 per sq km, but this figure hides huge differences between one part of the country and another. In the mountains of Honshu Island, population density is less than 1 per sq km, whilst in the centre of Tokyo-Yokohama, just 100 km away, it exceeds 2600 per sq km. One in three Japanese people live along the Pacific coast of the main island Honshu, and over 90 per cent of the population squeeze onto the flat land of the coastal plains of the four main islands.

- 75 per cent of Japan is made up of mountains divided by deep narrow valleys. The climate can be extreme, with average temperatures of 1 °C in winter and a cool 10 °C in summer. **Precipitation** of both rain and snow is heavy – sometimes exceeding 5000 mm annually. Slopes are steep and soils shallow and acidic; the mountains are covered with

△ Fig 8.2 A remote valley in the mountains of Honshu Island.

Sea of Okhotsk

Asahikawa

Kitami

▲ *Asahi-dake 2290*

Hokkaidō

Otaru

Sapporo

Tomakomai

Obihiro Kushiro

Muroran

Hakodate

Tsugaru-kaikyō

Hirosaki

Aomori

Hachinohe

Akita

Morioka

Sakata

Ishinomaki

Sea of Japan (East Sea)

Sadoga-shima

Niigata

Yamagata

Sendai

Nagaoka

Aizu-wakamatsu

Kōriyama

Jōetsu

Iwaki

Toyama

Nagano

Utsunomiya

Hitachi

Kanazawā

Yariga-take 3180 ▲

Maebashi

Mito

Komatsu

Matsumoto

Ueda

Ōyama

Tsuchiura

Fukui

Saitama

Tōkyō

3192 ▲

Chiba

Matsue

Tottori

Shirane-san ▲ 3776

Kōfu

Kawasaki

Fuji-san

Yokohama

Ōgaki

Gifu

Numazu

Kyōto

Nagoya

Shizuoka

Ōsaka

Tsu

Toyota

Okayama

Kōbe

Suzuka

Hamamatsu

Oki-shotō

Hiroshima

Sakai

Matsusaka Ise

Tsushima

Higashi-suidō

Shimonoseki

Takamatsu

Wakayama

Kita-Kyūshū

Seto-naikai

Matsuyama

Iki

Tokushima

Kii-suidō

Fukuoka

Kurume

Kōchi

Sasebo

Kuju-san 1788 ▲

Shikoku

Nagasaki

Kumamoto

Kyūshū

Miyazaki

Kagoshima

PACIFIC OCEAN

Relief in metres

5000
3000
2000
1000
500
200
sea level

△ Fig 8.3 Relief map of Japan.

Sapporo

Sendai

Tōkyō

Kyōto

Nagoya

Yokohama

Hiroshima

Kōbe

Ōsaka

Kawasaki

Fukuoka

Persons per sq km

over 250
100 – 250
10 – 100
0 – 10

Cities

⬤ over 25 000 000

● 10 000 000 – 25 000 000

• 1 000 000 – 10 000 000

△ Fig 8.4 Population density and urban areas of Japan.

△ Fig 8.5 Tokyo cityscape.

dense forest and there is very little flat land. Many areas are remote and isolated, and constructing transport links and settlements is very challenging and expensive. Consequently the mountains are very difficult places to live: there are few job opportunities, farming is very hard and few industries choose to locate here.

- Almost all flat land in Japan occurs along the coastal plains. With a milder climate and more regular rainfall, this is where most of the farming **industry** is located. Gentler relief makes it easier to construct roads, railways, and large ports. Excellent communications and port facilities have attracted industries such as steel mills and oil refineries, supported by thousands of smaller companies including banks and insurance companies. The need for workers has led to the growth of huge cities, where people live mostly in high rise multi-storey apartments, which maximise the use of small plots of expensive land.

CHANGES IN POPULATION SIZE

What is the growth curve of populations?

The **growth curve of populations** is a theory that attempts to describe and explain how and why the number of living things in a given area or **habitat** changes over time. It is an **ecological** theory based on how organisms such as bacteria behave in the animal kingdom. The theory is based on the assumption that limited resources will always control the growth and continued existence of living things. According to the theory, all populations of living things follow a sigmoid- or 'S'-shaped graph curve, which consists of five stages:

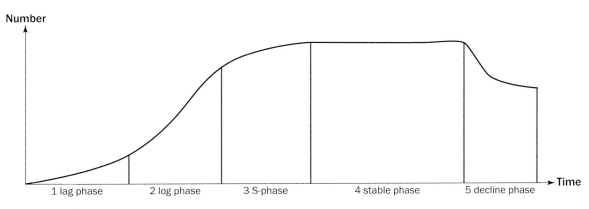

△ Fig 8.6 Population growth curve.

1. **Lag phase** – Population growth is slow as organisms adjust to the environment.

2. **Log phase** – Exponential growth occurs as the number of living things increases at a constantly growing rate because available resources such as food and water are unlimited.

3. **S-phase** – The population growth rate begins to slow down as the availability of resources to support living things becomes restricted and finite.

4. Stable phase – The carrying capacity for the population has been reached and the population number becomes stable. The carrying capacity is the maximum population size that can be supported by the resources available in a particular environment.

5. Decline phase – The population exceeds the carrying capacity of the environment, leading to overpopulation and a crash in numbers. This may be triggered by a sudden change meaning that the environment can no longer support the population, such as a drought causing food shortages.

Many environmentalists argue that the theory is not relevant to human beings and how world population has changed over the past 2 million years. Its main failing, they say, is that it does not take into account the effect of human intelligence and ingenuity. Unlike bacteria or other animals, human beings have been able to increase the carrying capacity of environments by, for example, developing intensive **agriculture** through the domestication of animals and wild grains and creating sophisticated **irrigation** schemes. In addition, humans have been able to combat disease through increased medical care and improved sanitary conditions, antibiotics, surgical procedures, vaccines and health education. This has allowed ever greater populations to live in finite environments without catastrophic crashes in numbers.

Even when natural or man-made disasters occur that could drastically reduce population numbers in different places, the theory does not take into account the effect of human emotion and solidarity, such as the donation of emergency and development aid, which reduces their effects.

How and why do human populations change?

The world's population is growing by 1.13 per cent a year – the equivalent of about 2.37 people per second or 83 million annually – and now stands at 7.349 billion. It is predicted to reach 11.2 billion by 2100. World population grows because

△ Fig 8.7 Automatic irrigation system.

△ Fig 8.8 Food aid distribution.

each year more people are being born than dying. The average number of live births in the world per 1000 people was 19.4 in 2015; this figure is called the **birth rate**. In 2015, the **death rate** – the average number of deaths in the world per 1000 population – was 7.89. As a result, that year, the world's population increased by 11.51 per 1000 population. This figure is known as the **natural increase**. The greater the difference between birth rate and death rate, the faster the population grows.

The two most important factors determining the level of birth rate in a country are **infant mortality** (the number of deaths of children aged less than 1 year per 1000 live births) and **life expectancy** (the average number of years that a person is expected to live). The greatest influences on infant mortality and life expectancy, and therefore birth rate, are as follows:

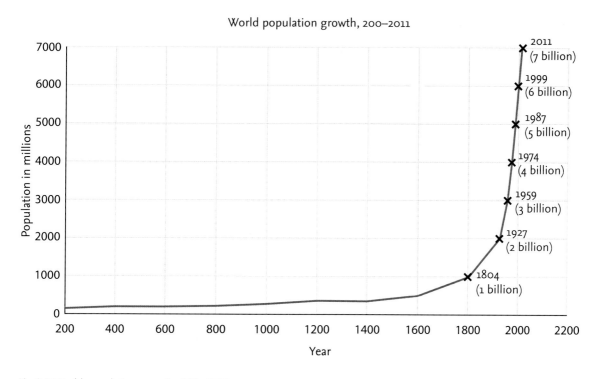

Fig 8.9 World population growth, 200–2011.

- **Age–sex structure** and **sex ratio** – whether the population has a large or small proportion of young people and more or fewer women than men.
- The quality of childbirth and post-natal health care programmes available.
- The availability of family planning services and contraception.
- The level of education and particularly literacy rates amongst women.
- The average age at which women marry and have their first child.
- The influence of religion and social customs, for example, the use of artificial contraception is forbidden in both Islamic and Roman Catholic teachings except under exceptional circumstances.
- The effect of any government policies to boost or reduce population growth.
- Economic influences – rising costs of bringing up children can contribute to lowering birth rates in **MEDCs**, whilst poverty in **LEDCs** tends to increase birth rates.

Death rates are particularly influenced by the following:

- Standard and availability of medical facilities and health care services.
- Diet and levels of nutrition particularly amongst children and young women.

- Availability of clean drinking water.
- Quality of sanitation and hygiene services, especially sewage disposal.
- Presence and severity of infectious diseases.
- Social and political issues such as conflict and war or high levels of violent crime.
- Age–sex structure and sex ratio – whether the population has a large or small proportion of older people and more or fewer men than women.
- Living standards – death rates are higher in regions where living standards are poor.

A third factor has to be considered when explaining changes in populations of individual countries – **migration**. This refers to the movement of people from one place to another, and in particular, immigration (people moving into the country) and **emigration** (people moving out). At the end of a year, the following calculation is made to see whether the number of people in a country has increased or fallen:

Birth rate – death rate ± **net migration** (difference between immigrants and emigrants) = population change

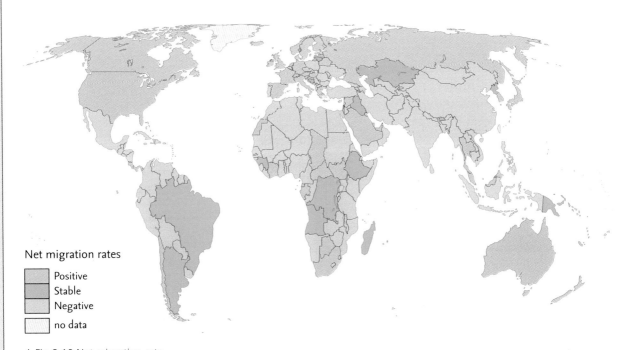

Net migration rates

Positive
Stable
Negative
no data

△ Fig 8.10 Net migration rate.

POPULATION STRUCTURE

The population structure in MEDCs and LEDCs

Population structure refers to the composition or make up of the people living in a place like a town or city, or in a larger area such as a country or continent. A graph called a population pyramid is often used to show the gender and age structure of a population. Of particular significance are the proportions of people in the 0–14 years (called 'younger dependents' because they are not yet in employment), 15–64 years (referred to as 'economically active' because they are of working age) and 65+ years ('older dependents', who have mostly retired) cohorts. Knowing the numbers in these three cohorts enables the **dependency ratio** of a population to be calculated. This is the ratio between those of working age (the economically active) who are paying taxes, and those of non-working age (the dependents), who rely on the taxes to support them, for example, to fund government pensions and the costs of public services such as education and medical care. For example:

- A country of 40 million people, with 20 million dependents, would have a dependency ratio of 1:1.
- A country of 60 million people, with 20 million dependents, would have a dependency ratio of 2:1.
- A country of 90 million people, with 60 million dependents, would have a dependency ratio of 1:2.

Having more than one tax paying worker for each dependent person (a low dependency ratio) is seen as positive thing, as this spreads the burden of tax and funding public services, such as schools, across many employed people. In countries with a high dependency ratio, where there may be several dependents for each tax payer, governments may have to raise tax levels and cut expenditure on public services in order to meet costs.

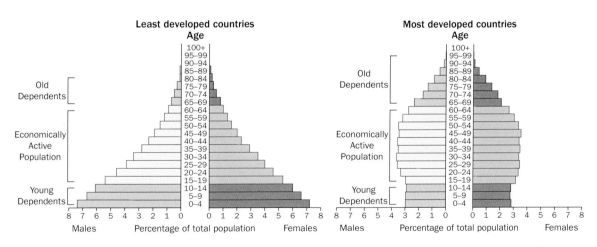

△ Fig 8.11 Typical population structure of LEDCs.

△ Fig 8.12 Typical population structure of MEDCs.

The population pyramids of the poorest countries of the world tend to show:

- A wide base because of a high birth rate and many children being born each year.
- A large proportion of young dependents aged 0–5 years as a result of the high birth rate.
- An even decline in shape up the age groups as the death rate is high at all ages.
- A narrow, short, top with few people living into old age because life expectancy is low.

In contrast, the population pyramids of the wealthiest countries of the world tend to show.

- A narrow base because of a low birth rate and few children being born each year.
- A low proportion of young dependents aged 0–5 years as a result of the low birth rate.
- A shape of straight sides up the age groups as the death rate is low at all ages.
- A tall, wide, top with many living to old age because life expectancy is high.

MANAGING HUMAN POPULATION SIZE

How do countries manage human population size?

Although the world's population is increasing by 1.13 per cent or 83 million people annually, these average figures hide very important differences between countries. Each year, 97 per cent of all babies are born in LEDCs, and in the poorest 48 countries of the world, the average annual population change is 2.4 per cent. These countries alone will have 2 billion inhabitants (22 per cent of the world total) by 2050. Many see environmental degradation, the depletion of **natural resources**, mass poverty and political instability in some low income countries as evidence of overpopulation – more people than the carrying capacity of the environment can support.

In response, a number of governments have introduced **anti-natalist** population policies designed to reduce birth rates and stabilise numbers. These are aimed at encouraging fewer births and often involve incentives or inducements. Most of these policies, such as those in South Korea and Kenya, have been voluntary. Both countries have focused on improved health and education, and the provision of free family planning supplies, information and services. Sex and reproductive health programmes were introduced in schools, and promotional literature and advertising emphasised the benefits to mother and child of spacing children and of 'a small and prosperous family'. At the same time, efforts were made to raise the health education levels and general status of girls and women in society. This had the effect of increasing the average age at which women married and reducing the number of children they had during their lifetime. South Korea introduced its **anti-natalist policy** in 1962, when the total **fertility rate** of the population was 6.2 children per woman. By 1984, that figure had reduced to 1.74.

Other countries have imposed compulsory measures for managing population size, such as the forced sterilisation of 11 million men and women in the 1970s as part of India's population control programme, and China's One Child Policy.

In contrast, the birth rates in many high income MEDCs such as Germany, Japan, and Italy have dropped to a level at, or even below, the death rate, for example, the death rate in Japan is 10/1000 compared with a birth rate of 8/1000. The average number of children born per woman of reproductive age in France in 2010 was 2.03. By 2014 this had dropped to 1.99, but to keep population numbers stable this figure needs to be 2.1. In response, the French government introduced a **pro-natalist** policy to boost the birth rate by offering couples incentives to have a third child:

- Free pre- and post-natal care for mothers and babies.
- Subsidised day care nurseries, crèches and childminders to reduce the cost of child care.
- Generous tax allowances for each parent until the child is 18.
- Improved pensions and child benefit allowances.
- Full pay maternity leave of 40 weeks (usually 20 weeks) for either parent.
- Priority to families for the allocation of state housing, and 100 per cent mortgages.

△ Fig 8.13 Family planning clinic in Uganda.

△ Fig 8.14 Family planning poster.

△ Fig 8.15 Three child family in France.

CASE STUDY

MANAGING POPULATION GROWTH IN CHINA

In 1949, the government of the new People's Republic of China saw its already large and rapidly growing population as an important means of helping the country become a strong economic power. Couples were encouraged to have as many children as they liked to increase the workforce. However, by the 1960s it was clear that the country was facing a crisis, with the population increasing at an average of 18 million per decade. Population growth was clearly outstripping the government's

△ Fig 8.16 One child family in China.

capacity to provide additional food and public services such as health care, education and housing at the same rate. Living standards dropped and there was social unrest and widespread famine, during which tens of millions died.

As China's population approached 1 billion in 1979, the government acted, and a programme of measures, commonly known as the One Child Policy, were introduced, with the objectives of reducing the birth rate's natural increase and fertility to levels that would be sustainable in the long term. The government made it clear that from then on, couples should have only one child. Minimum ages for marriage of 22 years for men and 20 years for women were introduced. Deviation from this policy would only be allowed under exceptional circumstances, such as the birth of twins, stillbirths or subsequent accidental deaths of single children.

The government sought to persuade couples through propaganda to do their voluntary and patriotic duty for their motherland to ensure the strength and security of their young country. This was backed up by a range of economic incentives. Couples with one child who made a public pledge to have no more children received rewards and benefits, including longer paid maternity leave, free child care, priority for housing and government pensions.

Together with offering inducements, the government also set up hundreds of thousands of family planning teams for women's affairs. Members made weekly visits to couples in their allocated area or commune to ensure women were using their contraceptive effectively and were not attempting to conceal an unapproved pregnancy. For couples with a child, the team endeavoured to persuade the woman to undergo sterilisation and to assess whether grandparents might be applying pressure on the couple to have a second baby. Each commune set a quota or limit to the number of pregnancies it would approve in any one year and couples applied in writing to be placed on the 'waiting their turn' list.

Achievements

According to government officials, their policy has succeeded in preventing over 400 million births since 1979 and has achieved significant reductions in key indicators of population growth:

Year	Birth rate	Natural increase	Fertility	Annual growth rate %	Total population (millions)
1979	18.21	16.61	5.01	1.9	975
2015	12.08	4.92	1.56	0.5	1357

△ Table 8.1 Population growth in China.

Issues

- During the past 35 years, China's population policy has been very heavily criticised by human rights organisations. They highlight frequent reports of unacceptable coercive methods being used by government officials to persuade women to undergo forced abortions and sterilisation.

- Many serious social and cultural changes have occurred as a result of the policy. In China, like many other Asian countries, family lineage is traced through sons. Sons are not only responsible for maintaining the family name but also for providing practical support for their parents when they are elderly. Girl children traditionally leave their family home on marriage and assume responsibility for their husband's parents. Single children now grow up without brothers and sisters or aunts and uncles – traditional extended family structures have all but disappeared.

- The policy has been much more successful in urban rather than rural areas. In cities, couples are generally more inclined to have just one child as he or she will have to be financially supported until the child finds work (at least 16 years). In countryside areas, children become an economic asset much earlier, undertaking farming work when they are not at school from perhaps as young as 7 or 8 years. There is more incentive therefore in the countryside to have more than one child. In addition, many more urban dwellers are employed in state-run enterprises that offer pensions, than their rural counterparts. The guarantee of a pension means there is less pressure in urban areas to have children to provide practical support in old age.

- China is now the most gender-imbalanced country in the world. There are 118 boys for every 100 girls born and it is estimated that there will be 60 million more men than women by 2020. One cause of this is women undergoing abortions after couples have determined that they are expecting a girl child. Female infanticide (deliberately abandoning girl children at birth) also occurs. Consequently, today there is a shortage of young women of marriageable age and millions of men who will forever be bachelors.

- China's population is ageing rapidly. By 2030, 25 per cent of the population will be over 60. In the future, single children will be bearing the cost of looking after elderly parents (and in many cases their grandparents) on their own. Significant numbers will have to give up work to do this, which will have a serious impact on the economy. This situation is made worse because China now has a shrinking workforce, which fell by 2.4 million in 2013 alone because of the lack of young people.

- Faced with the implications of these issues, the government relaxed the One Child Policy in 2013. This adjustment allows couples to have a second child if either their first child is a girl or if both parents are single children themselves.

End of topic checklist

Key terms

age–sex structure, anti-natalist policy, birth rate, carrying capacity, death rate, dependency ratio, ecological, economically active, exponential growth, family planning, growth curve of populations, health care programme, human factors, infant mortality, life expectancy, living standards, migration, natural increase, natural resources, net migration, older dependents, overpopulation, physical factors, population density, population distribution, population pyramid, population structure, pro-natalist policy, reproductive age, sex ratio, young dependents

Important vocabulary

accessibility, aid, climate, constraint, contraception, culture, dense, development, disaster, disease, economic, education, emigration, famine, fertility, forest, habitat, immigration, island, literate, management, medicine, mountains, opportunity, patriotic, pattern, plain, political, port, precipitation, propaganda, relief, religion, rural settlement, social, soil, sparse, sterilisation, sustainability, tax, temperate, tropical, urban, valley, vegetation, war

During your study of this topic you should have learned that:

○ The population of the world is unevenly distributed across its surface resulting in some areas being densely populated whilst others remain almost empty.

○ Areas of the world with physical and human advantages for life attract people whilst areas with physical and human constraints or challenges will generally be avoided.

○ Areas with dense populations can become overpopulated if the pressure of people exceeds the carrying capacity of the environment to support them.

○ Japan is a very good example of a country with an uneven population distribution caused by a combination of physical and human factors.

○ The growth curve of populations attempts to explain how and why the number of living things changes over time as they pass through five stages.

○ The growth in human populations does not tend to fit the growth curve too closely as people are capable of increasing the carrying capacity of the environments in which they live.

○ The population of the Earth is rising each year because average birth rates are greater than average death rates, leading to an annual natural increase.

End of topic checklist continued

○ Birth and death rates will rise or fall as a result of many social, cultural and political factors.

○ Whether the population of a specific country rises or falls depends on the level of the birth and death rate and also on net migration.

○ Population structure describes the composition or make up of people living in a place or area and population pyramids are used to show this graphically.

○ There are several important differences between the population structure of LEDCs and MEDCs.

○ Although overall the world's population is increasing, some of the lowest income countries are experiencing very rapid growth whilst numbers are declining in other high income countries.

○ Some countries such as China are adopting anti-natalist policies to reduce population growth whilst others such as France are following pro-natalist programmes to increase the birth rate.

The questions for Section 8 start on page 260.

Human life depends on the healthy functioning of ecosystems and the diversity of organisms that live in the countless habitats they contain. However, the number and variety of living things is declining rapidly as a consequence of natural habitat loss resulting from human activities. Serious consequences already include the extinction of many species and drastic reductions in gene pools.

Deforestation to make way for farming is a major cause of biodiversity loss and the decline in genetic diversity. It also contributes to global warming, climate change and soil erosion, which can lead to desertification. If managed sustainably, forests have the potential to be a renewable natural resource capable of providing many economic, environmental, social and cultural benefits while at the same time conserving their biodiversity for future generations.

Sustainable management requires ecologists to understand as fully as possible how ecosystems operate and particularly the numbers, distribution and variation of species that interact within them. This requires the skilled application of a variety of quantitative sampling methods. Such information is crucial if conservation programmes based on the principles of sustainable development are to be successful in the long term.

CONTENTS

LEARNING OBJECTIVES

Define the terms *ecosystem, population, community, habitat* and *niche*.

Describe the biotic (living) and abiotic (non-living) components of an ecosystem.

Describe biotic interactions.

Describe the process of photosynthesis.

Describe energy flow using food chains, food webs and trophic levels.

Describe and explain ecological pyramids based on numbers and energy.

Describe the process of respiration.

Describe the carbon cycle.

Describe and explain causes and impacts of habitat loss.

Describe and explain the causes and impacts of deforestation.

Describe and explain the need for sustainable management of forests.

Describe and evaluate methods of estimating biodiversity.

Apply sampling techniques to unfamiliar situations.

Evaluate national and international strategies for conserving the biodiversity and genetic resources of natural ecosystems.

Study the causes and impacts of deforestation in a named area.

Study the conservation of a named species.

Study a named biosphere reserve.

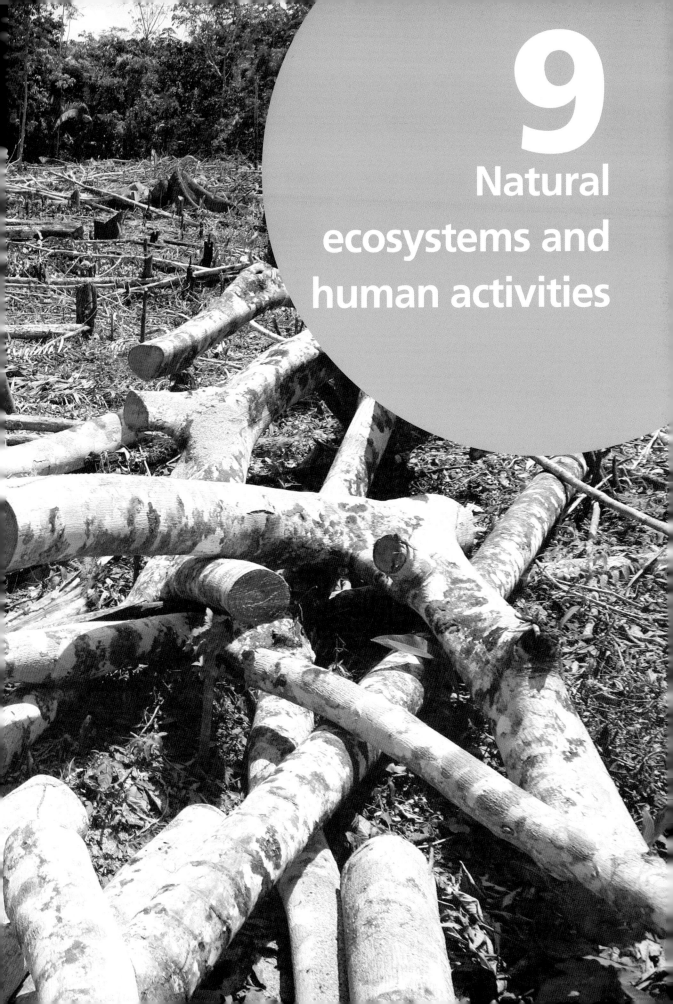

9
Natural ecosystems and human activities

ECOSYSTEMS

An **ecosystem** is the **community** of living plant, animal and micro-organism **species** in an area (the biotic community) and how they interact with each other and with non-living (abiotic) elements of the **environment**, such as **rocks**, soil and water.

An ecosystem includes different **habitats** and the larger the ecosystem, the greater their number. A habitat is the location within an ecosystem that meets the living needs of particular plant or animal species – the shelter, water, food and space they require to survive. A leaf may provide just one habitat but a forest will contain many thousands. Most habitats will be shared by different species forming a community of living things that interact with each other. Within the community, competition arises for resources and so every living thing evolves to inhabit its own **ecological niche** within it. This refers to the unique way in which it is adapted to living in the habitat, for example, the type of food it eats, its shelter requirements and behaviour patterns. The habitat of the Australian desert death adder (Figure 9.2) is porcupine grass and rock outcrops. Its ecological niche is highly specialised. It is only active by night and can remain motionless for days with only the tip of its tail twitching to mimic a worm or caterpillar to which its prey such as lizards are attracted.

△ Fig. 9.1 A rock pool is a small ecosystem.

△ Fig. 9.2 Australian desert death adder.

Every organism occupies one of five trophic or feeding levels within a **food chain**. A food chain represents a succession of organisms that eat another organism and are, in turn, eaten themselves.

1. **Producers:** These are plants or algae that can manufacture their own food from nutrients in soil or water such as nitrates or through **photosynthesis**. During photosynthesis, radiant energy from the sun (sunlight) is absorbed by the green pigment called **chlorophyll** in plant leaves. The energy is used to convert CO_2, water and **minerals** absorbed from the soil into glucose (sugar) and oxygen. Plants use some of this glucose to keep them alive through aerobic **respiration** and some is converted into proteins and carbohydrates and stored. Producers at the first **trophic level** produce the food on which all other living things depend. The word equation for photosynthesis is:

$$\text{carbon dioxide + water} \xrightarrow{\text{SUNLIGHT}} \text{sugar + oxygen}$$

$$\downarrow$$

2. **Primary consumers:** Animals are unable to manufacture their own food and need to eat other organisms. Primary **consumers** are **herbivores** that feed on primary producers. They also use aerobic respiration to release energy from food they consume. Aerobic respiration occurs in mitochondria cells where enzymes control the release of energy when glucose reacts chemically with oxygen. The process is expressed like this:

glucose + oxygen $\longrightarrow$ carbon dioxide + water (+ **ENERGY**)

$$\downarrow$$

3. **Secondary consumers:** These are animals that eat other animals (carnivores) or both plants and animals (omnivores) and obtain their energy from food by way of aerobic respiration.

$$\downarrow$$

4. **Tertiary or apex consumers:** These are organisms at the top of the food chain with no predators (other than humans), and that are capable of feeding on both primary and secondary consumers.

$$\downarrow$$

5. **Decomposers:** Include worms, fungi and micro-organisms such as bacteria that feed on dead matter and waste. They break down complex substances into simpler inorganic chemicals that return to the abiotic environment as recycled mineral nutrients for producers to use again.

A food chain describes in simple terms what occurs when individual living things at different trophic levels eat each other to obtain the food they require. In nature it is very rare for an organism to be eaten by just one other predator as the food chain in Figure 9.3 suggests. The feeding patterns of most living things are more complex than this. An omnivore such as a grizzly bear is a primary consumer when feeding on plants and a secondary or tertiary consumer when eating other animals. A **food web** (Figure 9.4) is a better representation of the feeding relationships in an ecosystem as it shows how living things are both interconnected and interdependent.

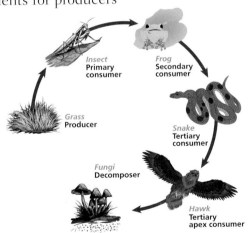

△ Fig. 9.3 Example of a simple food chain.

Food chains and food webs also help in understanding energy flow through the trophic levels. Producers store the sun's energy in chemical compounds such as proteins and carbohydrates. Herbivores gain this store of energy when they eat plants. They use some of this energy in respiration and store the remainder. In turn their energy store is ingested by primary and tertiary consumers when they eat herbivores who consume some and store the rest. At each trophic level, some energy is lost and the remainder passed on. At the final trophic level, remaining chemical stores of energy are recycled through decomposition and return to the abiotic environment (soil) as mineral nutrients. Stores of energy are greatest at the first trophic level and diminish steadily through the food chain. This can be shown graphically by a **pyramid of energy**.

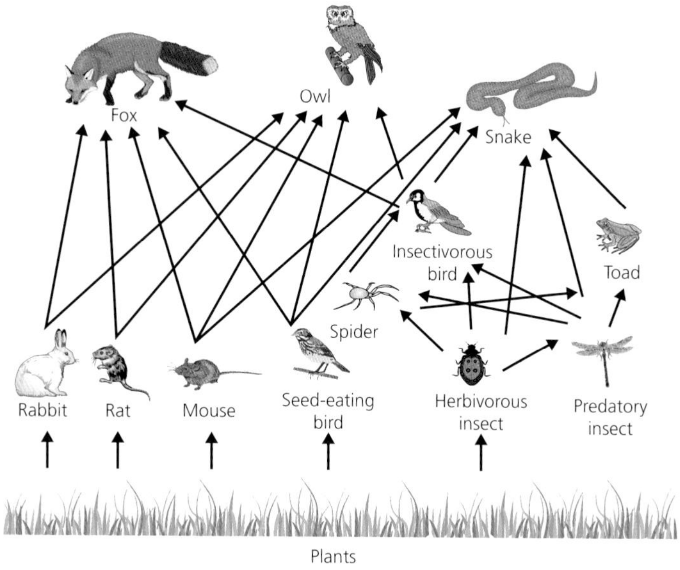

△ Fig. 9.4 A simplified food web.

Nutrients and chemical elements are continually transferred or 'cycled' between the biotic and abiotic parts of an ecosystem. In the **carbon cycle**, **carbon dioxide** in the **atmosphere** is converted to compounds such as carbohydrates in 'producer' plants during photosynthesis. This process is often referred to as the 'fixing' of carbon. Respiration in plants returns some of this fixed carbon back to the atmosphere as carbon dioxide. At each stage of the food chain, further carbon dioxide is released to the atmosphere by consumers at different levels through respiration of compounds such as glucose. When organisms die their bodies decay as they are digested by composers. The complex carbon compounds remaining are taken into the bodies of the **decomposers**, where some may be converted to carbon dioxide during respiration.

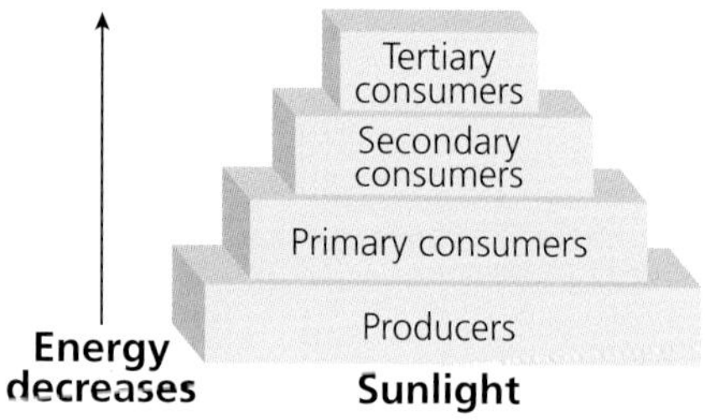

Energy decreases **Sunlight**

△ Fig. 9.5 Pyramid of energy.

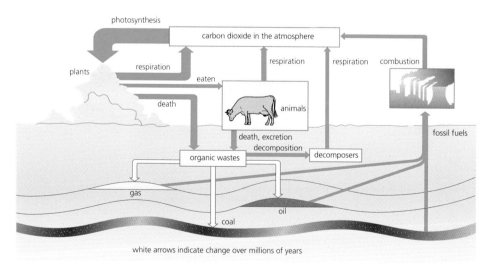

△ Fig. 9.6 A summary of the carbon cycle.

In many food chains there are far more producers than primary consumers and far more primary consumers than secondary and apex consumers and this can be shown in an ecological **pyramid of numbers** (Figure 9.7). Each bar in the pyramid represents a different feeding level, starting with the producers at the bottom and ending with the apex consumer at the top. The width of each bar is drawn to scale representing the numbers of individuals in the level.

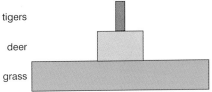

△ Fig. 9.7 A typical pyramid of numbers.

Abiotic components of an ecosystem are all of the non-living, chemical and physical things with which animals, plants and microorganisms interact and depend upon. Chemical factors will include the pH level and mineral content of the soil together with the geology of the underlying rock. Physical elements encompass **climate** (particularly its seasonal pattern of temperature, **precipitation** and humidity), the **relief** of the land, the availability and quality of water, oxygen and ambient light levels, and the strength and direction of **prevailing winds**. All of these will affect the number and diversity of living things found in an ecosystem. If the abiotic factors are very challenging then organisms will adapt to cope, for example polar bears have thick layers of greasy fur that sheds water in extreme Arctic conditions.

No living thing within a community exists in isolation. Every organism interacts on a regular basis with others. Examples are given below.

Competition

This occurs when there is a shortage of one or more resources required by a number of living things such as territory, water and food supplies. It can be the cause of aggression both within and between species.

Predation

This interaction involves one organism preying on another as a source of food (Figure 9.8).

△ Fig. 9.8 A cheetah feeding on a Thomson gazelle.

Pollination

During the pollination season pollen containing male gametes or sperm cells is transported to the female reproductive organs of seed plants (Figure 9.9).

Mutualism

This interaction involves both individuals benefitting from the activity of another through a symbiotic relationship (Figure 9.10). Oxpeckers extract parasitic insects and ticks for food from the hide of buffaloes, which benefits both creatures.

△ Fig. 9.9 Japanese cedar tree pollen dispersed in the wind.

△ Fig. 9.10 Red billed oxpeckers feeding on a buffalo.

ECOSYSTEMS UNDER THREAT

Between 1970 and 2014, the planet lost 52 per cent of its **biodiversity** (number and variety of living things) including 76 per cent of **freshwater** life and 39 per cent of marine life. A total of 16 928 species are currently facing extinction – one in four animals, one in three amphibians and one in eight birds. The consequences of these losses on the **gene pools** of individual species has been serious. Genes are found in the nucleus of cells and provide the instructions for what the plant or animal will look like, how it will survive and how it will interact

△ Fig. 9.11 Endangered species such as the giant panda have reduced gene pools.

with its environment. Through inheritance, this genetic material is passed from one generation to the next. A gene pool is the set of all the genes or genetic information of a particular species. As a species declines in number so does its gene pool or genetic diversity, making inbreeding and problems adapting to new environments more likely.

The decline in biodiversity and gene pool diversity is being caused mostly by natural habitat loss. Increasing **natural resource** exploitation is putting unsustainable pressure on many of the ecosystems upon which all life depends. Habitats may be destroyed entirely, such as by filling in a marsh, degraded (reduced in quality) or fragmented (divided up into sections). Habitats are lost through human actions, the most important of which is the conversion of land to farming.

DEFORESTATION

Deforestation is the clear-cutting or permanent destruction of forests and woodlands. Over 30 per cent of the world's land surface is covered in forest, which is rapidly being cleared. The United Nations (UN) estimates that 73 000 sq km of forest is destroyed each year, equivalent to an area the size of the country of Panama.

Causes of deforestation

Clearing woodland so that the land can be farmed is the most important reason for forest loss and setting up beef cattle ranches causes more deforestation than any other type of farming.

△ Fig. 9.12 Cattle ranch on newly cleared rainforest in the Amazon Basin, Brazil.

Wood is a very important natural resource in the construction, furniture and paper **manufacturing** industries. Timber extraction and logging accounts for the felling of 10 billion trees a year and 35 per cent of these are processed into paper-based products. Demand for paper globally has quadrupled in the last 40 years. Swedish company IKEA (Figure 9.13) is the world's largest single consumer of wood. It manufactures 100 million pieces of wood-based furniture a year, which are sold in 300 stores globally.

△ Fig. 9.13 IKEA outlet in Adelaide, Australia.

Removing forest to extract valuable rocks and minerals occurs throughout the world. In the Amazon rainforest, the greatest impact is from the exploitation of alluvial gold deposits mined by large commercial companies and local people. Huge areas of forest have been cleared along river channels and across former river **floodplains** to access gold deposits.

△ Fig. 9.14 Gold panning on the River Mapiri, Bolivia.

The rapid growth of cities (Figure 9.15) leading to urban sprawl is another important cause of deforestation. In 1950 only 30 per cent of the world's **population** lived in urban areas. By 2014 this figure had reached 54 per cent and is projected to be 66 per cent by 2050.

The construction of new transport links leads to tree loss but the number of trees removed to create the actual route of the road is often insignificant compared with other secondary effects. Roads and the fences and culverts that run alongside forests fragment them into smaller and smaller parcels of land. The new road can also quickly become a route for settlers, farmers and mining companies who are now able to reach and exploit remoter

△ Fig. 9.15 Urban growth encroaching on forest, Barcelona, Spain.

areas of the forest that previously were inaccessible. The Belem to Brasília highway was the first to be constructed across the Amazon Basin rainforest in 1958 and by 1978 over 2 million settlers had travelled down it to open up the forest. Construction of the 4000 km Trans-Amazonian Highway began in 1972.

△ Fig. 9.16 An unpaved section of the Trans-Amazonian Highway.

Impacts of deforestation

Habitat loss and depletion of biodiversity and gene pool diversity

Impacts are greatest in the **tropical** rainforest, which is the most productive and diverse ecosystem found on land and habitat for over half of the world's plant, animal and micro-organism species. Loss of just one plant or tree species can be catastrophic for many other species in the same community whose existence may be dependent upon it. The parasitic rafflesia plant (Figure 9.17), found mainly in the rainforest of Indonesia, demonstrates how fragile this ecosystem can be. It is one of the rarest and most endangered plants. Rootless, leafless and stemless, its survival depends entirely on the nourishment and physical support it gains from just one vine called Tetastigma.

△ Fig. 9.17 Rafflesia flower growing on its host in the Sabah area of Borneo.

Global warming and climate change

Forests are huge **carbon stores** because carbon dioxide is taken up from the atmosphere during photosynthesis and used to produce the chemical compounds that make up the trees. As much as 300 billion tonnes of carbon worldwide may be stored in forest biomass. When trees are burned or left to rot, the stored carbon is released as carbon dioxide and this currently amounts to 1 billion tonnes a year. Carbon dioxide is a potent **greenhouse gas** contributing to **global warming**, which will see average planetary temperatures rise 2–3 °C by 2100.

Soil erosion and desertification

Removing the protective cover of trees and their roots often causes erosion when soil is washed or blown away by heavy rain or strong winds. Top layers of the soil contain most nutrients, from the decay of dead vegetation, so soil erosion quickly removes essential nutrients from the land. Soil nutrients are also lost through **leaching**, which is the soaking away of soluble nutrients in soils because after deforestation there are few plant roots in the soil to absorb the nutrients and lock them away in plant tissue. Land degraded by soil erosion can become desert through a process known as **desertification**. As much as 24 billion tonnes of fertile topsoil disappears from around the world every year as a result of desertification. This soil could support the growing of 20 million tonnes of food grain. **Overgrazing** of animals in deforested areas is the main cause of desertification. Because of increasing numbers of farmers in dry regions, cattle herds now tend to be fenced into confined areas and no longer allowed to roam in search of fresh pasture and water. The situation is made worse by the construction of boreholes at specific locations to bring underground water to the surface and create waterholes. This allows animals to stay all year in places that previously they may have only grazed for a few months, leading to the overgrazing of the surrounding area and making it very vulnerable to soil erosion and desertification.

△ Fig. 9.18 Cattle at a waterhole in Botswana.

MANAGING FORESTS

Forests are a potentially **sustainable** and renewable natural resource that with careful **stewardship** by forest managers could continue to exist indefinitely to meet the needs of future generations. This means increasing their economic benefits, including timber and food, to meet society's needs in a way that conserves and maintains the environmental, social, cultural and spiritual value of forest ecosystems. Achieving this balance will be critical to the survival of forests and the communities that depend upon them in the future. The multiple functions of forests are discussed below.

Carbon sinks, stores and offset programmes

Growing forests remove carbon dioxide from the atmosphere during photosynthesis, and mature forests and the soils in which they grow act as huge carbon stores. Asian forests alone absorb about five tonnes of carbon dioxide per 0.01 sq km per year. Healthy forests are one way of mitigating or reducing the severity or seriousness of global warming as they can 'fix' or sequestrate carbon dioxide from the atmosphere. Tropical forests currently absorb about 18 per cent of all the carbon dioxide released from the burning of **fossil fuels** each year.

Maintaining the water cycle

Forests are a critical component of the water or hydrological cycle (see Figure 4.3 in Section 4), which describes the constant circulation and recycling of the world's water. Most of the world's water is in the oceans. Energy from the sun heats the surface of the oceans, and water evaporates as **water vapour** into the atmosphere. The warm moist air rises because it is less dense. As the water vapour rises, it cools down and condenses back into water droplets. Clouds form and precipitation occurs as the water droplets get bigger and heavier and eventually fall as rain or snow. Trees take up water through their roots from the soil to deliver nutrients to their leaves. During photosynthesis, water also evaporates into the atmosphere as water vapour from small pores called stomata in leaves through the process of **transpiration**. This moisture contributes to the formation of rain clouds. Transpiration accounts for at least 10 per cent of the entire world's evaporating water. A mature oak tree can transpire 40 000 litres of water vapour a year. Moisture generated by forests circulates in the atmosphere and can affect the amount of rainfall a place receives thousands of miles from where it originated. When forests are cut down, less moisture is released into the atmosphere, rainfall declines and this can be a cause of **drought** and desertification.

Prevention of soil erosion

Forest cover helps to prevent soil erosion in two ways. Firstly, tree roots grow into the soil, creating a strong stabilising network which binds it in place and prevents compaction. Rainwater then soaks into the air pockets between the soil grains rather than running off over its surface and causing erosion. Secondly, tree foliage protects the soil from the erosive impact of heavy rain drops. Leaves and branches intercept falling rainwater and lessen its energy when it eventually hits the soil below. Rainwater

△ Fig. 9.19 Litter layer on forest floor.

drips from the foliage or flows slowly down stems and trunks until it soaks into the soil. Ground cover and the litter layer on forest floors also protects the soil from heavy rainfall (Figure 9.19).

Biodiversity and genetic gene pools

Forests are the most biodiversity-rich habitats on land. Over two-thirds of known land-based species live in forests and 60 per cent of all higher plant species are located in rainforests. Conserving this rich biodiversity is essential for the **sustainable development** of human populations. People use over 40 000 species of plants and animals on a daily basis for building materials, fodder, clothing, energy and as a source of medicines, and the majority of these originated in forests. In the Amazon Basin alone, the genes of 1300 species of wild forest plants are used to manufacture modern medicines and 40 per cent of the pharmaceuticals used in the United States are either based on, or synthesised from, natural components found in forest plants, animals and microorganisms. Less than 1 per cent of known forest species have

△ Fig. 9.20 A periwinkle flower.

been examined so far for their potential medicinal, agricultural or industrial value and new species are being discovered all the time. Laboratory-based **genetic engineering** of medicines, food crops and **pesticides** depends on the harvesting of naturally occurring genetic material from forest species. Vincristine, extracted from the rainforest plant, periwinkle (Figure 9.20), is one of the world's most powerful anti-cancer drugs.

Food and industrial raw materials

For thousands of years, people relied on meat, fish, fruits, nuts, seeds, parts of foliage and pods from trees, shrubs and animals in the world's forests to feed themselves and their livestock as part of a subsistence hunter-gatherer existence. Today many **indigenous** forest peoples such as the Efe pygmies of central Africa continue to survive through **subsistence farming** of manioc, beans and rice crops using **slash and burn** techniques or a combination of farming and other activities including fishing or timber extraction or small scale mining such as gold

△ Fig. 9.21 A pygmy hunter-gatherer of the Central African Republic.

panning. In modern times, many forest-based plant species have been selected for intensive commercial growing. Today 80 per cent of all commercially produced food crops originated from plant species discovered in forests.

Over 1.6 billion people rely on forests for their livelihoods which, in addition to farming, includes the extraction of industrial raw materials

△ Fig. 9.22 Forest cover being burned off to allow oil tar mining in northern Alberta, Canada.

△ Fig. 9.23 Woman panning for gold in a Madagascan forest river.

and **tourism**. Globally, wood is by far the most important commercial forest raw material. Tropical, temperate and boreal forests are the location of mining and quarrying operations to extract rock, minerals and hydrocarbons such as crude oil or natural gas required by power generation and manufacturing industries. Large-scale commercial mines such as those extracting oil from **tar sands** found beneath the forests of northern Canada employ 133 000 people in Alberta alone. Small-scale mining carried out by nomadic men and women in forests also involves many people worldwide. They travel together and look for alluvial sites that might contain gold or diamonds and extract the minerals before moving on to new locations.

Ecotourism

Ecotourism is defined as 'responsible travel to natural areas that conserves the environment, sustains the wellbeing of the local people, and involves interpretation and education'. Ecotourists seek locations with authentic local cultural experiences and natural environments, with activities such as wildlife watching, hiking and volunteering on community projects. They minimise their ecological impact on places and ensure local people receive a fair income for hosting them. They choose to camp or stay in locally owned accommodation rather than foreign-owned hotels and buy produce from and eat in local communities rather than supermarkets and chain restaurants. Ecotourism accounts for 7 per cent of all spending on annual holidays (over US$1 billion) and the number of people taking ecotourism trips is currently increasing by 20 per cent a year. Forests with their rich biodiversity and cultural and historic heritage are particularly favoured by ecotourists. For local people, ecotourists bring income and create employment opportunities that improve their livelihood and also encourage them to conserve the forest ecosystem. Forest-based ecotourism companies that hire and obtain their goods and services locally can return as much as 95 per cent of what they earn back into the local economy compared with an average of just 20 per cent from typical all inclusive package holidays operated by foreign companies.

MEASURING AND MANAGING BIODIVERSITY

It is often very important to ecologists and environmental managers to measure how diverse a habitat or community of living things is, for example, when they are asked to assess the likely impact of opening a mine or giving permission for a new housing estate to be built. In most situations, both the size of the habitat and lack of time mean that the entire habitat cannot be studied in minute detail to identify every living thing. Biodiversity is estimated through sampling several small locations to represent the whole community and the data obtained is extrapolated. This means making an assumption or judgement about the whole area based on the information collected in the sample areas. For example, if one pair of a bird species was

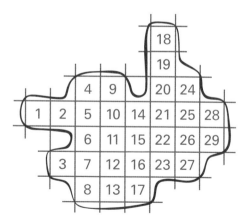

Δ Fig. 9.24 A numbered grid map of a habitat identified for biodiversity sampling.

found in 1000 sq m of forest then the assumption would be that ten pairs would exist in an entire forest of 10 000 sq m.

When estimating biodiversity it is very important to use methods that ensure the sample areas selected represent the entire habitat as closely as possible and that each individual in a population, for example, of birds, has an equal chance of being selected. Achieving this requires the design of random sampling methods in which the observer does not decide when or where to take measurements to remove human error or bias. For example, a numbered 10 sq m grid might be laid over a map of the habitat to be surveyed. The number of the square to be sampled will then be selected from a computer generated random number. Systematic sampling is a form of random sampling where samples are only taken at fixed intervals, for example, every 50 metres, usually along a line or transect across the habitat.

Ecologists use a variety of sampling methods to discover the following:

- The richness or total number of different species found in a community.
- The diversity or variation between and within different species that make up this number.
- The distribution and density of different species across the habitat.

Quadrats

Quadrats consist of a square frame that may be subdivided into smaller squares and are used to identify the number, variety and spread of living things (usually plants and slow moving animals such as slugs) within the frame. A commonly used quadrat is one square metre. While this size may be ideal for smaller or more open and accessible habitats such as low growing heathland, larger quadrats are often required for sampling bigger, taller and denser communities such as woodlands. Similarly a much smaller quadrat may be appropriate for sampling a microhabitat such as a rock pool.

△ Fig. 9.25 Underwater research on a coral reef using digital photography to do transect species counts in Abrolhos, Brazil.

Line transect

This involves laying a measuring tape or rope with marked points across the habitat to be sampled. Continuous sampling is then carried out, involving the identification and recording of all the species touching the line along its entire length, or systematic sampling where only the presence or absence of species at intervals is recorded.

△ Fig. 9.26 A transect line laid out across grassland in Wyoming, United States.

△ Fig. 9.27 Arachnologist catching spiders with pooter, Italy.

Pooters

Pooters are small jars used for collecting insect species with two long tubes. One tube goes into the ecologist's mouth and the other goes over the insect. The insect or small organism is sucked into the jar and a fine mesh over the end of the suction tube prevents the collector swallowing it.

Pitfall traps

Pitfall traps usually consist of a buried and covered container, the rim of which is level with the ground surface. Insects and ground crawling animals such as beetles reaching the lip of the container fall in and are unable to climb back out. The collector then returns after a fixed time period to identify what has been caught. Pitfall traps are particularly useful in habitats such as dense woodland where it may be difficult to catch creatures by other means such as a sweep net.

△ Fig. 9.28 Pitfall trap.

Evaluating the limitations, validity and reliability of sampling methods

Considerable caution has to be used when samples obtained using these techniques are extrapolated in order to make estimates about the number, variety and distribution of living things within an entire habitat. The validity of such estimates will be limited by the following:

• The sample size. For example, the reliability of any results will be greater if fifty rather than just ten pooters were used within a habitat and during night time as well as the day.

- Sampling frequency. For example, data from quadrat sampling would be more trustworthy if surveys were carried out at a location six times during the year rather than just once.
- Human error. For example, while it may be easier to place a transect line along or close to an existing path through a wood, the data generated is unlikely to be very representative of the wood as a whole. It may also be tempting for ecologists to use just small quadrats when sampling because they are easier to use but the data gained will be less reliable than that generated from using larger quadrats requiring more effort and time to analyse the data.

Conserving biodiversity and genetic resources

Increasing awareness of how the sustainability of human life depends on healthy functioning ecosystems and the biodiversity and genetic reservoirs they contain has highlighted the importance of conserving these precious natural resources. Ecotourism with its emphasis on the sustainability of biodiversity, landscapes and local communities is a good example of one approach that aims to enable people to 'consume' a resource but also have minimal impact on the ecosystems and biodiversity which underpins it.

Sustainable harvesting of wild plant and animal species

This approach to **conservation** involves the carefully regulated collection of leaves, plants, trees and animals in a manner that ensures the long-term viability of the ecosystem by leaving the resources or 'ecological capital' in place from which it will continually regenerate. Not uprooting plants, taking only a limited number of leaves and fruit from a tree and hunting outside of the breeding season and over as wide an area as possible are examples of this approach. For example, thousands of sustainable natural rubber tappers and Brazil nut and palm hearts collectors in Brazil can earn four times as much sustainably harvesting their forests than as factory workers in urban areas. Harvesting forest products in this way also creates a vested interest amongst local people to maintain and protect the biodiversity and genetic diversity of the forest.

△ Fig. 9.29 Rubber tapping is an example of sustainably harvesting forest resources.

The Campfire programme began in Zimbabwe in the 1980s and is a good example of the harvesting of wildlife resources at the same time as conserving fragile ecosystems. Many communities now actively protect local wildlife, recognising it as a valuable economic asset. They can generate income by selling hunting concessions to professional hunters and safari operators. Prices as high as US$25 000 can be paid to a single elephant or lion. Hunting is strictly controlled and monitored so that younger breeding animals are never taken. Communities may also gain income from providing a mounting and taxidermy service, selling surplus animals to other **national parks** or game reserves, sustainably harvesting crocodile eggs and timber and selling the meat from trophy hunted animals.

△ Fig. 9.30 A trophy hunter with a blesbok antelope in Namibia, Africa.

Sustainable forestry

A sustainable forest is one in which careful management and stewardship ensures that as trees are felled they are replaced with seedlings that in time replace the harvested trees. Forests continue as fully functioning ecosystems with conserved biodiversity as well as providing livelihoods for local people and recreational facilities for visitors and tourists. Under the Sustainable Forest Initiative (SFI), forest managers can apply for SFI certification if they meet strict standards such as ensuring that endangered species and water supplies are protected. Making an effort to obtain certification is worthwhile as wood with an SFI kite mark will often sell at higher prices than non-certified timber.

Designating protected areas

Establishing national parks and wildlife reserves to conserve biodiversity, protect landscapes and enhance the economic and social conditions of local communities is a conservation policy adopted by over one hundred countries. In 1911, Canada set up the world's first national park service and today protects more sq kilometres of national park land than any other country. National parks are often designated in order to protect rare plants or animals, fragile ecosystems, distinctive landscapes, geologic features or combinations of any of these.

△ Fig. 9.31 Northeast Greenland National Park is the largest of the world's 6000 national parks.

△ Fig. 9.32a and 9.32b Sagarmatha National Park in Nepal contains Mount Everest and also a number of endangered species including the snow leopard.

UNESCO biosphere reserves seek to demonstrate how a balance can be achieved in designated areas between the conservation of biodiversity and improving the wellbeing of people through sustainable development. There are currently 669 biosphere reserves in 120 countries. Biosphere reserves have a core area in which ecosystems are strictly protected to ensure the conservation of landscapes, biodiversity and genetic variation. Surrounding the core area is a buffer zone where activities that support ecological research, monitoring, training and education are supported. Beyond is a transition area where environmentally sustainable activity is encouraged that improves economic and human wellbeing.

Extractive reserves

Over 30 000 sq km of Brazilian rainforest are now part of extractive reserves. Land is owned by the government but responsibility for its use is allocated only to local indigenous peoples. Forest managers ensure that a balance is maintained between conserving biodiversity, exploiting resources such as timber, fish, minerals, fruit and nuts and rubber, and maintaining family based **agriculture**. In many reserves this strategy has succeeded in increasing economic prosperity and independence for local communities while conserving huge areas of the Amazon rainforest.

Seed banks

Seed banks protect biodiversity in case natural reserves of seeds elsewhere in the world are destroyed or reduced by catastrophic events such as **natural disasters**, disease and wars. The seeds include those of existing food crops or plants that possess genes that have already been used as the basis of modern synthetically produced medicines. Seeds of endangered plant species are also collected. Although about 10 million seed samples are held in 1300 banks around the world, this figure represents a very small fraction of the world's biodiversity. The Millennium Seed Bank in the UK is the largest in the world and aims ultimately to store the seeds of every plant.

△ Fig. 9.33 Technician sorting rare seeds at the Millennium Seed Bank.

CASE STUDY: DEFORESTATION IN BORNEO

The Borneo rainforest is 140 million years old. Worldwide, there are over 15 000 species of plants and 5000 of these can only be found in Borneo. Three thousand species of trees, 221 species of mammals, 420 species of birds and over 440 different species of freshwater fish are found on the island. There are carnivorous plants, the world's largest flower and trees that reach up to 60 m in height.

Location	Southeast Asia (south of the South China Sea). Borneo is shared by three countries – Indonesia (Kalimantan) 73%, Malaysia (Sabah and Sarawak) 26% and Brunei 1%.
Area	743 330 sq km – the world's third-largest island
Population	19 804 064 (as of 2010)
Population density	21.52 people per sq km
Highest point	Mount Kinabalu – 4095 m
Longest river	Kapuas in West Kalimantan – 1143 km
Climate	Equatorial

△ Table 9.1 Borneo fact file.

Borneo is the world's third largest island and governed by three countries – Malaysia, Indonesia and Brunei. Almost the entire island was originally covered by rainforest but this dropped to 76 per cent by 1973 and is now less than 50 per cent. Since 1973 an area of forest the size of Switzerland has been cleared and the annual rate of deforestation is over 20 000 sq km.

This means that Borneo could lose all of its forest outside protected areas by 2020. The main causes of deforestation are outlined on the next page.

1950
1985
2000
2005
2010
2020

△ Fig. 9.34 Forest cover on Borneo.

△ Fig. 9.35 Forest in Borneo being cleared for oil palm plantations.

Commercial and illegal logging

Half the world's tropical timber is sourced from Borneo and used in the manufacture of furniture, building construction and the plywood industry. Logging is poorly regulated, which means that small-scale illegal logging by local people is common. It is estimated that half of all logged wood in Borneo (valued at US$500 million) is obtained illegally because new logging roads built by commercial operators have opened up previously inaccessible areas of forest to illegal traders.

Food production

With 261 million people, Indonesia has the fourth largest population in the world and an average annual increase of 1.17 per cent means there are an extra 3 million mouths

△ Fig. 9.36 A satellite image of Borneo taken in 2002 showing the smoke haze from burning forest.

to feed each year. As a result, large areas of forest have been cleared as part of government food farming programmes such as the Mega Rice Project which converted 10 000 sq km of primary forest to rice paddies. In addition, hundreds of sq km of forest are cleared by commercial farming companies and subsistence farmers each year, usually by burning. When conditions are very dry these fires can spread out of control and ignite huge areas of forest that may burn unchecked for years.

Agro-industrial crops

Agro-industrial crops are non-food crops or products. Over 10 per cent of Borneo's forest has already been cleared and replaced with rubber trees, fast growing acacia trees used for the pulp and paper industry and oil palm. Global demand for palm oil (oil produced from the fruit of the oil palm tree) is the single most important cause of deforestation in Borneo. Palm oil is used in an astonishing range of products such as margarine, crisps, soaps, fish fingers and chewing gum. Because palm oil is used in the manufacture of so many products, it is a valuable commodity. Around 50 million tonnes of palm oil is produced in Borneo annually on 120 000 sq km of previously forested land.

△ Fig. 9.37 Newly planted and established palm oil.

△ Fig. 9.38 The fruit of oil palm trees which is heated and squeezed to extract vegetable oil.

Borneo is one of the most biodiverse places on the planet and deforestation is now endangering the existence of many of its unique species, including the orang-utan. As the area of forest continues to be reduced and fragmented, hundreds of species will approach extinction within a decade. The largest mammals such as the pygmy elephant that require huge and continuous areas of forest in order to feed and breed are at greatest risk. New roads through the forest provide easy access for poachers and traders seeking endangered animals, including the clouded leopard and sun bear for skins, body parts or to capture and sell as pets.

△ Fig. 9.39 The clouded leopard is officially 'vulnerable to extinction' in Borneo.

As species become extinct, genetic diversity is reduced, and this is no better illustrated than in the plight of orang-utans, which share 96.4 per cent of human genes. By 2020 only a few completely separate populations of orang-utans will exist, meaning that inbreeding will become more common. Inbred offspring will find it increasingly difficult to adapt to environmental change and population numbers will drop below a level from which they can return or face statistically irrecoverable extinction.

Deforestation is also releasing vast quantities of stored carbon both directly from the burning of trees and indirectly through soil disturbance. Cleared areas that are drained to prepare them for food crops become very dry and the risk of fire is then great. Fires such as those in 1997 and 1998 resulted in serious pollution levels and risks to health as a haze of smoke and carbon dioxide spread west from Borneo as far as Singapore.

Forest removal has also seriously affected many of Borneo's rivers and water supplies, which has impacted on the lives of the indigenous Penan people who are one of the last subsistence hunter-gather communities in the world. A healthy forest soaks up heavy rainfall brought by tropical storms to the island and then releases it gradually into rivers, ensuring that communities have a regular and even supply of water. Once forests are removed, rainfall quickly erodes the exposed topsoil. Rivers then become blocked with sediment and flood. As trees disappear there is also less transpiration, which affects rainfall patterns leading to highly destructive flood and drought cycles.

CONSERVING THE MOUNTAIN GORILLA

The mountain gorilla inhabits dense high altitude forest in the Virunga Mountains in the Democratic Republic of the Congo, Rwanda and Uganda and the Bwindi National Park in Uganda. Mountain gorillas typically live in social groups made up of a dominant male, three adult females and four to five offspring. They are not particularly territorial and so regularly interact with other social groups. During the past century, numbers of mountain gorillas have been decimated and today the species of just 620 is designated as 'critically endangered'. Several factors are responsible for this: hunting and collecting, habitat loss, disease and conflict.

Hunting and collecting

Gorillas are frequently killed for body parts, especially their heads, hands and feet, which are sold as ornaments. Infants are caught alive and sold illegally to zoos and as pets. Although not usually hunted for their meat, gorillas are often critically injured by traps and snares set for other animals.

Habitat loss

Deforestation is occurring as a result of human population pressure on gorilla habitat. Through the expansion of subsistence farming, commercial cattle farming and logging, the forest is both reducing in size and becoming fragmented. Gorillas are increasingly confined to isolated pockets of forest and unable to interact with other social groups. This is leading to a reduction in the genetic diversity of gorilla groups and evidence of inbreeding such as webbed hands and feet is now identifiable. As the number of people in the forest increases, so do incidents of gorillas being killed or maimed as they encroach onto surrounding farmland in search of food.

Disease

Human genes and those of the mountain gorilla are 98 per cent identical, which means that gorillas are at serious risk of cross contamination of disease from humans to which they possess no natural immunity. Some researchers suggest that infectious respiratory diseases spread by humans may be responsible for 20 per cent of all sudden deaths in mountain gorilla populations.

Conflict

During the past 30 years, Rwanda, the Democratic Republic of the Congo and Uganda have experienced wars and civil conflict, which impacted badly on gorilla numbers. Direct effects include animals being killed by mines placed along forest trails and being shot or captured to be sold to raise funds for weapons. Habitat loss caused by the forest being felled for fuel and farming by refugees escaping the conflicts has been equally serious.

Despite these threats the number of wild mountain gorillas has increased over the past 20 years and now stands at 880 individuals. This is the result of the success of the International Gorilla Conservation Programme (IGCP), which has been working since 1991 to ensure its long-term survival. Particularly effective conservation measures include:

- Providing funding to increase both the number and improve the equipment of anti-poaching patrols in protected forest areas. This has increased the coverage and duration of patrols and reduced significantly the number of animals being poached.

- Organising and funding teams to collect hunting snares and bush meat traps from the forest.

- Setting up rehabilitation centres where orphaned or rescued young gorillas can be prepared for a return to the wild.

- Increasing the area of national parks to protect more forest and undertaking afforestation work in cleared areas to allow lost habitat to regenerate.

- Better management of visitors and tourists to minimise the likelihood of disease transmission by ensuring that they are always more than seven metres from gorillas.

- Working with local communities to increase understanding of gorillas and support for their protection and conservation. Teachers and pupils have been given information books about gorillas, and rangers run awareness and conservation programmes in local schools.

- Encouraging ecotourism and investing profits from visitors viewing gorillas back into the local community, for example, building new schools and clinics. As a result, people have come to see the monetary value of conserving the forest habitat and actively protecting gorillas.

△ Fig. 9.40 Rangers at Volcanoes National Park, Rwanda, which has the largest population of wild mountain gorillas in the world.

△ Fig. 9.41 Cleared forest now used as farmland adjacent to Volcanoes National Park, Rwanda.

△ Fig. 9.42 Male 'silverback' mountain gorilla in the forest of the Virunga mountains.

△ Fig. 9.43 Developing ecotourism is an important aspect of mountain gorilla conservation programmes.

UNESCO BIOSPHERE RESERVE, NORTH DEVON, UK

North Devon's biosphere reserve covers much of the ecosystem created by the catchment areas of the Rivers Taw and Torridge and the offshore marine areas stretching out to Lundy Island in the Bristol Channel. Located in the county of Devon in the UK, it is home to about 150 000 people and includes protected landscapes of great ecological and landscape value. However, the majority of the area is where people live and work. Lowland farmland is the most important land use.

△ Fig. 9.44 North Devon Biosphere logo.

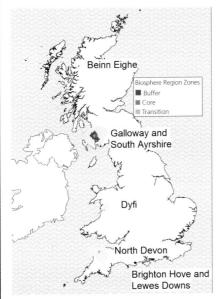

△ Fig. 9.45a The UNESCO Biosphere Reserves of the United Kingdom.

△ Fig. 9.45b North Devon biosphere reserve.

The North Devon Biosphere Partnership is the body responsible for coordinating the management of the reserve in line with the vision and objectives of an agreed strategy for the years 2014–2024. The partnership works closely with willing local communities to manage the environment sustainably in ways that will conserve unique habitats, generate income, reduce poverty and improve the health and wellbeing of people.

The core area consists of Braunton Burrows, which is a unique sand dune system habitat of hundreds of flowering plants designated as both a Special Area of Conservation and a Site of Special Scientific Interest. Management of this area focuses on ensuring the protection and enhancement of the sand dunes and its adjacent coastal habitat, which includes a coral reef with a diversity of coral and marine life seen nowhere else in the UK and the Taw and Torridge estuary, which is an important feeding ground for long distance migratory birds.

△ Fig. 9.46 Marram grass on the sand dunes of Braunton Burrows.

△ Fig. 9.47 Designated as the first Marine Conservation Area, Lundy Island forms part of the North Devon Biosphere Reserve.

The reserve's buffer zone covers the Taw and Torridge estuary as far as the towns of Barnstaple and Bideford. In this area the focus for management is on ensuring that local people can access and enjoy the special natural and cultural environment, for example, through the provision of cycleways or interpretation panels and guided walks. In the outer transition zone (which includes a large area of sea and Lundy Island) the emphasis is on encouraging sustainable employment and lifestyle projects that enhance the environment in which people live and work, for example providing high sustainable catches of fish for the local fishing industry or setting up renewable energy or forestry programmes.

△ Fig. 9.48 Unloading a catch of fish from a small fishing boat in the harbour, Ilfracombe, north Devon.

One example of how the biosphere has brought about positive change has been its work in coordinating the government funded North Devon Nature Improvement Area, which covers an area of 720 sq km and was set up in 2012. Devon Wildlife Trust is the lead partner in this project alongside sixteen other organisations. The objective is to restore large areas of culm grassland, which will act as sponges for rainfall (it is five times more effective than intensive grassland at holding water), reducing flooding and ensuring an improved summer flow of water down the rivers. This will help to make the whole of the biosphere more resilient to the effects of climate change. By 2015 progress was already clear; working with local landowners and communities, over 15 sq km of grassland had been restored and 0.8 sq km of new habitat had been created. Through the project local farmers have been provided free of charge with appropriate grazing animals or specialist machinery that will enable them to maintain the culm grassland sustainably. Over 150 community events demonstrating the importance of the culm grassland have been attended by thousands of local people. In addition fifty-two school habitat visits have provided young children with direct experience of the value of the environment and the challenges of managing it in an environmentally sustainable way. Fifty volunteers have been recruited and trained to take part in a project called Riverfly, which uses monthly samples of invertebrates to monitor water quality.

Another environmental management project within the North Devon Nature Improvement Area is focusing on improving conditions in the River Torridge for the globally endangered freshwater pearl mussel. These organisms require fast flowing streams and rivers, which are low in nutrients and have clean sandy and stony bottoms and can live up to one hundred years. In recent years, eutrophication caused by sewage and chemical fertiliser pollution together with the build-up of sediments on the bed

△ Fig. 9.49 Devon Wildlife Trust adviser talking to a farmer about Culm grassland restoration on his farm, north Devon, UK.

of the river from the run-off of eroded soil has meant that most pearl mussels are no longer breeding. Improving water quality by preventing pollution and siltation will not only benefit the pearl mussel. It will also improve conditions for salmon and sea trout, which will be an advantage for local fisheries and increase the quality of local drinking water. As the river water will be much less polluted when it eventually enters the sea, the quality of bathing water along the coast will improve, which will be a boost to local tourism businesses as more people will be attracted to the area.

△ Fig. 9.50 Orchids and spiders' webs, at Dunsdon Nature Reserve Culm grassland site in north Devon, UK.

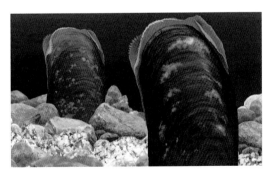

△ Fig. 9.51 Freshwater pearl mussels.

End of topic checklist

Key terms

adaptation, biodiversity, carbon cycle, carbon fixing, carbon offset, carbon store, climate change, conservation, consumers, decomposers, desertification, ecological niche, ecosystem, ecotourism, energy flow, food chain, food web, fossil fuel, gene pool, genetic diversity, global warming, habitat, harvesting, management, mitigation, natural resource, non-renewable, producers, pyramid of energy, pyramid of numbers, raw material, renewable, respiration, seed bank, sequestration, stewardship, subsistence, sustainable development, trophic level, water cycle

Important vocabulary

abiotic, aerobic, apex, biosphere, biotic, carnivore, chlorophyll, city, climate, community, competition, deforestation, designation, endangered, energy, environment, enzyme, erosion, evolution, extinct, extrapolation, glucose, herbivore, inbreeding, indigenous, limitation, migration, mitochondria, mutualism, omnivore, oxygen, photosynthesis, pollination, predation, primary, random, regenerate, relief, reproduce, reserve, secondary, species, symbiosis, systematic, tertiary, trustworthiness, urban, validity

During your study of this topic you should have learned:

- ○ Ecosystems comprise living and non-living elements and numerous habitats within which organisms adapt to their own ecological niche.

- ○ All living things occupy one of five trophic or feeding levels within a food chain or food web.

- ○ A pyramid of energy describes how energy flows through the five trophic levels of food chains and webs.

- ○ The carbon cycle identifies how nutrients and chemical elements are constantly transferred between the biotic and abiotic parts of an ecosystem.

- ○ An ecological pyramid of numbers represents the different numbers of organisms at different trophic levels within an ecosystem.

- ○ Every living thing within a community interacts with both the members of their own species and organisms belonging to other species in a variety of ways.

- ○ Biodiversity and gene pool diversity is declining globally as a result of the destruction of habitats, particularly for farming.

End of topic checklist continued

○ The cheetah is a good example of how living things are being impacted upon negatively by habitat loss.

○ Deforestation has many causes and the most important is clear felling for farming.

○ Deforestation contributes not only to biodiversity and gene pool loss but also to global warming, soil erosion and desertification.

○ The island of Borneo has been impacted by deforestation particularly seriously.

○ Forests are potentially sustainable and renewable natural resources that with careful stewardship could continue to exist indefinitely to meet the needs of future generations.

○ Ecologists use a variety of statistical sampling techniques to estimate how rich and diverse habitats are, but all are limited in their validity and reliability to some extent.

○ Many different types of conservation programmes have been set up around the world to manage ecosystems sustainably.

○ Numbers of mountain gorillas are increasing as a result of a particularly effective conservation programme.

○ The North Devon World Biosphere Reserve shows how people working in partnership with nature can bring about important environmental, economic and social progress.

The questions for Section 9 start on page 263.

End of topic questions

Note: Answers to these questions can be found at the back of the Teacher Guide.

1. Rocks and minerals and their exploitation questions

1. What is rock?

2. Describe and explain the difference between how igneous, sedimentary and metamorphic rock form and give an example of each type.

3. Using the diagram below to help, describe what happens during the rock cycle.

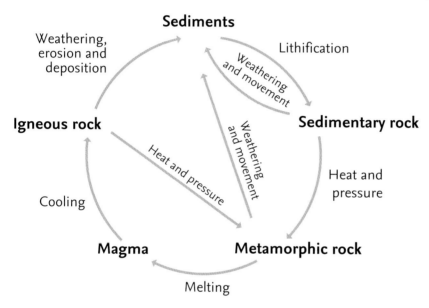

Sediments

Weathering, erosion and deposition

Lithification

Weathering and movement

Igneous rock

Sedimentary rock

Heat and pressure

Weathering and movement

Heat and pressure

Cooling

Magma

Metamorphic rock

Melting

4. Describe three examples of how rocks and minerals are vital necessities of modern life.

5. Name and describe three techniques geologists use when they are searching for underground mineral resources.

6. The photographs below show the two main methods of extracting rocks and minerals. Name the two methods and describe the main difference between them.

7. Describe in your own words four important economic factors that have to be taken into account before a new mine or quarry is likely to be opened.

8. In what ways can a new mine bring economic benefits to the area where it is opened? Give examples.

9. On a copy of the table below, summarise in your own words four examples of possible social benefits and four examples of possible social problems that might result from a mining development.

Possible social benefits	Possible social problems

10. The photograph on the right shows a woodland habitat being cleared to make way for a mine. Habitat loss is one type of environmental impact a new mine can have. Describe three other possible environmental effects of a new mine.

11. At the end of its working life a mine may undergo *remediation, restoration* and *reuse*. Summarise on a copy of the table below what each process involves and give an example to support your answer.

	What it involves	Example
Remediation		
Restoration		
Reuse		

12. In 2014, Jeff Desjardins produced the following forecast in the *Visual Capitalist* http://www.visualcapitalist.com/forecast-when-well-run-out-of-each-metal/ of when the world will run out of a range of important metals/energy sources.

Metal/energy source	Date of depletion at present rate of exploitation
Oil	2051
Antimony	2024
Indium	2035
Zinc	2031
Silver	2033
Rare Earth metals	2856
Copper	2049
Lead	2032
Gas	2073
Gold	2030
Coal	2136

a) Draw a horizontal bar graph to show this date for each metal/energy source.

b) Using the current year as the baseline, reorder this table with the list of metals and energy sources in rank order according to their number of years remaining before depletion – lowest to highest.

c) Which three of the sources in the table could be referred to as 'energy metals'?

d) Outline some of the ways in which the lifespan of precious and finite metals and energy sources such as those shown in the table could be extended in the future.

Answers to these questions can be found at the back of the Teacher Guide.

2. Energy and the environment questions

1. Define the following key terms:

   a) fossil fuel

   b) non-renewable energy source

   c) renewable energy source

2. Categorise the following energy sources into 'renewable' or 'non-renewable':
   coal, gas, nuclear, solar, hydroelectric, biomass, geothermal, tidal, oil, wind.

3. Why are fossil fuels important to humans?

4. Describe how coal is formed.

5. Describe how oil and natural gas are formed.

6. Global demand for fossil fuels has increased over time. What impact has this had on people and the environment?

7. How is electricity produced in thermal power stations?

8. Why is energy security important?

9. Draw and complete the following table:

Energy source	Renewable or non-renewable	Advantages	Disadvantages

10. Using the map below to help you, describe and explain the global distribution of energy use.

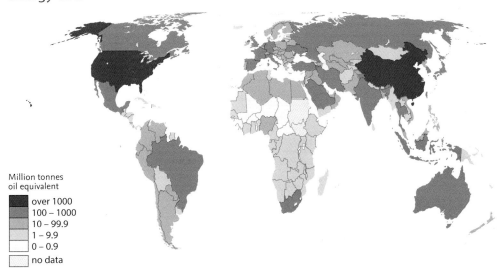

Million tonnes oil equivalent
- over 1000
- 100 – 1000
- 10 – 99.9
- 1 – 9.9
- 0 – 0.9
- no data

11. Explain how the following factors contribute to rising energy demand:

   a) domestic demand

   b) industrial demand

   c) transport

   d) wealth and development

   e) climate

12. Investigate the energy mix of the country you live in. Has it changed over time?

13. Why is it important for countries to plan for changes in the energy mix?

14. Rather than increasing supply, it is possible to reduce demand for energy. Outline how households can reduce energy consumption.

15. Why does educating people play a vital role in reducing consumption of energy?

16. Using the information in Section 2 and your own research, investigate the following developments in vehicle technology that reduce fossil fuel consumption:

   a) electric cars

   b) hybrid cars

   c) hydrogen fuel cells

   d) energy recovery systems

17. Compare and contrast the approaches taken to reduce vehicle use and energy demand, and to increase public transport use in Singapore and London. How successful has each scheme been?

18. Unconventional fossil fuel based energy sources, such as fracking and tar sands, are controversial. Outline the arguments for and against developing these sources of energy.

19. Using the image below, suggest how oil extraction from tar sands in Canada has impacted on the environment.

20. Using examples, explain how the following can be sources of oil pollution:

   a) offshore extraction

   b) pipelines

   c) marine transport

21. Oil spills are devastating to the environment. Outline the possible impacts on the following:

   a) birds   **c)** beaches

   b) marine mammals   **d)** coral reefs

22. Why has MARPOL been an important development in reducing the frequency of oil spills?

23. Evaluate the following strategies used to reduce and manage oil spills:

   a) double hulled tankers   **e)** skimmers

   b) GPS monitoring   **f)** sorbents

   c) booms   **g)** burning

   d) chemical dispersants   **h)** vacuum trucks

24. Using the information in Section 2 and your own research, produce a presentation on the Deepwater Horizon disaster in the Gulf of Mexico. Ensure it covers the following:

   a) background information

   b) causes

   c) effects (social, economic, environmental)

   d) responses (immediate, short term, long term)

Answers to these questions can be found at the back of the Teacher Guide.

3. Agriculture and the environment questions

1. Name and describe the four main constituents of soil.

2. Make a copy of the table below and then fill in the missing sections.

Mineral ion	Mineral element	How it is used in plants
Nitrate NO_3^-		Combines with glucose to form amino acids which in turn bond together to create proteins required for cell growth
	Phosphorous (P)	
		Must be present for the enzymes required for photosynthesis and respiration to function effectively
Magnesium Mg^{2+}		

3. In your own words describe why the organic content of soil is very important.

4. The two photographs below show a sandy soil and a clay soil. Describe the advantages and disadvantages of each of these soils for farmers.

Sandy soil

Clay soil

5. How is subsistence farming different from commercial farming? Give examples to support your answer.

6. Explain what the term *agricultural yield* means.

7. In farming what is rotation and how does it help to increase a farmer's yield?

8. What is a fertiliser and why do farmers use them?

9. The photograph below shows an environmental problem along a river caused by fertilisers. What is the problem and how is it caused?

10. Explain what irrigation is and describe three different ways in which farmers go about irrigating the land.

11. Outline the difference between a fungicide, herbicide and insecticide.

12. The peregrine falcon (right) is an example of a bird that in the past has been affected by *bioaccumulation* of pesticides. Explain what *bioaccumulation* is and why the peregrine falcon has suffered so badly from it.

13. How is organic farming different from intensive farming?

14. What is selective breeding and how does it help a farmer increase yields?

15. How is genetic modification or engineering different from selective breeding?

16. Outline three causes of the overproduction of food on farms in MEDCs.

17. Many subsistence farmers in LEDCs have become producers of cash crops such as coffee growing in Laos. What is a cash crop and describe why converting to cash crops might have serious long-term consequences for this farmer.

18. What is soil erosion? Explain how soil erosion can lead to desertification in places such as Senegal in the Sahel region of Africa (right).

19. Draw a labelled diagram to show three different ways in which soil erosion can be controlled and reduced by farmers.

20. Define what is meant by *sustainable agriculture*.

21. What does the *biocontrol* of pests and diseases mean? Describe an example of one kind of biocontrol used on sustainable farms.

22. In 2012, three researchers (Gaybullaev B, Chen and Gaybullaev D) published their results of fifty years of hydrological measurements of the volume of water in the Aral Sea.

Date	Water volume in cubic kilometres
1960	1093
1965	1007
1970	925
1975	786
1980	664
1985	502
1990	327
1995	239
2000	149
2005	112
2010	98

Citation: Gaybullaev, B., Chen, S. & Gaybullaev, D. Appl Water Sci (2012) 2: 285. doi:10.1007/s13201-012-0048-z

a) Draw a simple line graph, bar graph or histogram to show the changes which occurred between 1960 and 2010.

b) By what proportion did the volume of water shrink in the Aral Sea between 1960 and 2010?

c) Which five year period saw the greatest absolute decrease in the volume of water?

d) Which five year period saw the single greatest proportionate loss of water?

e) Explain the main causes of the depletion of water in the Aral Sea over this time period.

Answers to these questions can be found at the back of the Teacher Guide.

4. Water and its management questions

1. Name four stores of surface water on Earth.

2. What important natural process does the water cycle describe?

3. On a copy of the summary diagram of the water cycle below, write in the following missing labels in their correct position: *precipitation* (used twice), *vapour transport*, *transpiration by plants*, *percolation through rocks* and *groundwater flow*

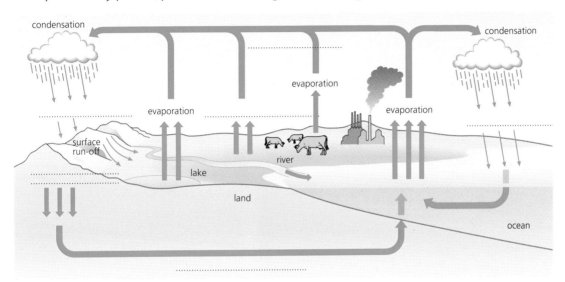

4. In your own words, and using a diagram to help, explain how water is extracted from underground aquifers.

5. Explain why groundwater reserves in some part of the world are being depleted. Describe with an example some of the effects of groundwater depletion.

6. Las Vegas in Nevada in the United States is facing a water crisis. What has caused this crisis and what is the city trying to do to solve it?

7. What does desalination involve? Why is desalination not more widely used around the world at present?

8. Outline the reasons why most water in LEDCs such as Zambia tends to be consumed by agriculture whilst most water in MEDCs like Belgium is used in industry and homes.

9. Some countries such as Egypt suffer from a physical shortage of water whilst others like Peru have economic shortages of water. Explain how these two things are different.

Egypt

Peru

10. The two Ethiopian women in the photograph are being treated for trachoma water-borne disease. Explain why people contract trachoma and other water-borne diseases such as bilharzia and typhoid.

11. The schematic diagram below shows a dam generating hydroelectricity for homes and industry. Describe three other important reasons why dams are built around the world.

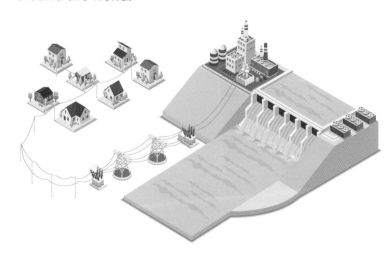

12. Multipurpose dams can bring economic benefits but also cause social and environmental problems. On a copy of the table below, fill in three more examples of economic benefits and possible costs.

Economic benefits	Social and environmental costs
Jobs are created both to construct the dam and to operate it once it is complete	Homes and livelihoods are lost when land is flooded to create reservoirs

13. On a large piece of plain paper draw an annotated diagram to show how a river might become polluted with waste from domestic, industrial and agricultural sources.

14. Approximately 2.5 billion people do not have access to improved sanitation. What does *improved sanitation* mean? Give two examples of things that could be done in the poorest countries of the world to improve sanitation and water supply for people.

15. The poster on the right is one used to draw attention to World Malaria Awareness day and the 200 million cases of the disease each year. Describe how malaria is caused and spread.

16. In your own words, describe some of the reasons why malaria is proving to be a difficult disease to eradicate.

17. Why is the risk of cholera so high in emergency camps set up after natural disasters such as the Nepal earthquake of 2015?

18. The table below shows changes in the concentration levels of selected substances in the River Rhine 1980 – 2000 reported by Villamayor-Tomas et al. www.thecommonsjournal.org/articles/10.18352/ijc.411/

Substance	1978 Base Year	1980	1984	1988	1992	1996	2000
Cadmium %	100	60	20	5	4	4	3
Zinc	100	78	43	21	20	18	10
Oxygen	100	110	120	122	125	134	136
Nitrogen	100	100	115	118	100	85	70
Phosphorous	100	78	80	43	33	25	23

a) Draw a compound line graph to show this data graphically.

b) Which chemical showed the smallest proportionate fall in concentration levels?

c) Describe what this chemical is commonly used for in agriculture and how it may inadvertently pollute rivers such as the Rhine.

d) Explain, with reference to the Sandoz chemical spill of 1986, why the concentrations of the substances in the River Rhine in the table have shown such positive trends in recent years.

Answers to these questions can be found at the back of the Teacher Guide.

5. Oceans and fisheries questions

1. Using a blank world map, produce your own annotated map that contains:

   a) the names of the major oceans

   b) the location of major warm and cold ocean currents

   c) a factfile on each of the main oceans

2. Identify why the oceans are valuable as a resource.

3. Describe the resource potential of the oceans for transport and drinking water.

4. What is an ocean current?

5. Define the following key terms:

   a) gyre

   b) thermohaline circulation

   c) upwelling

6. Why is upwelling important for biodiversity in the oceans?

7. Describe the movement of the ocean conveyor belt.

8. Describe the global distribution of marine species.

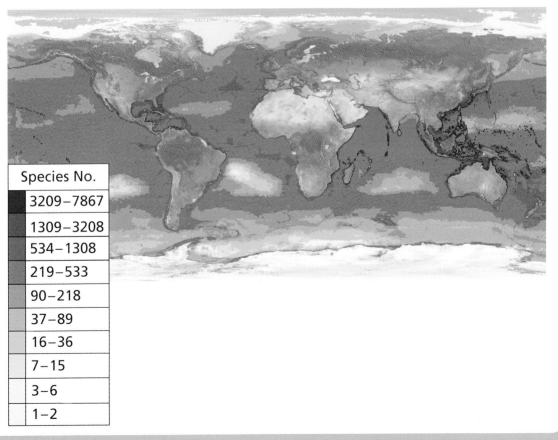

Species No.
3209–7867
1309–3208
534–1308
219–533
90–218
37–89
16–36
7–15
3–6
1–2

9. Explain why most of the world's major fisheries are found where ocean currents are present:

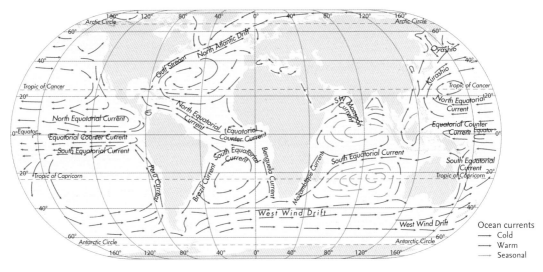

10. Using the maps on this page, outline any patterns and relationships that you observe.

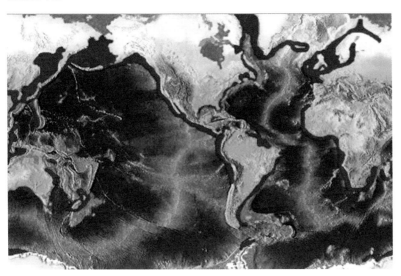

Major upwelling areas around the world

11. In your own words and using diagrams, describe the El Niño Southern Oscillation (ENSO) phenomenon.

12. Why does ENSO reduce upwelling on the Pacific coast of South America?

13. Outline the social, economic and environmental impact of ENSO on the west coast of South America.

14. Why are overfishing and bycatch significant environmental management challenges?

15. Outline the causes of overfishing.

16. How has overfishing impacted global fish stocks?

17. How can fishing net technology reduce the impact of fishing on non-target species?

18. Using examples, compare the successes of quotas and closed seasons as strategies to reduce overfishing.

19. Evaluate the success of marine protected areas, such as PIPA, in reducing pressure on fish stocks.

20. Outline the advantages and disadvantages of farming of salmon in Scotland.

21. Design and plan an investigation into the awareness of issues facing the oceans. You will need to collect data, present and analyse it, and make judgments based on your analysis. Suggest an action plan to raise awareness of all, or specific, ocean issues. Your investigation should include the following:

    - an introduction that outlines the purpose of the investigation

    - an outline of your methods, including any limitations and improvements (think about your questionnaire design and sampling strategy (Which people will you ask? Peers? Age? Gender?)

    - presentation of your results graphically

    - analysis of the data to identify patterns and trends

    - a reasoned conclusion that includes a suggested action plan to raise awareness at targeted groups.

    You can follow this up by putting your evidenced-based action plan into action with your peers.

Answers to these questions can be found at the back of the Teacher Guide.

6. Managing natural hazards questions

1. Describe and explain the differences between each layer of the Earth.

2. Describe the global distribution of earthquakes.

3. Describe the global distribution of volcanoes.

4. Describe and explain the relationship between tectonic plates and volcanic activity.

5. Draw a labelled diagram of each type of plate boundary.

6. Why are volcanoes not found on all plate boundaries?

7. Research how the tectonic plates have moved over time and how they are predicted to move in the future.

8. What is an earthquake?

9. Define the following key terms:

   a) focus

   b) epicentre

   c) magnitude

10. List the factors that determine how damaging an earthquake is.

11. How are earthquakes measured?

12. Explain why similar sized earthquakes could result in very different outcomes.

13. Research the March 2011 Tohoku earthquake in Japan. What were the primary and secondary effects?

14. How are volcanoes classified?

15. What factors affect the size and shape of volcanoes?

16. Draw a labelled diagram showing the key features of a stratovolcano.

17. Distinguish between a shield and a stratovolcano.

18. How are volcanic eruptions measured?

19. Identify, using named examples, how volcanoes can affect people and the environment.

20. Describe how the risk from earthquakes can be reduced before they occur.

21. Why do lower income countries struggle to cope after an earthquake?

22. Can the risk from volcanoes be managed? Outline the steps that can be taken.

23. Research the eruptions of Mt Merapi in Indonesia. What steps have been taken to reduce risk to local people?

24. Evaluate the effectiveness of the management of the volcanic eruption in Montserrat between 1995 and 1997.

25. Define the following key terms:

  a) tropical cyclone

  b) storm surge

  c) coriolis effect

26. Describe the global distribution of tropical cyclones.

27. Outline the conditions needed and the stages of formation of a tropical cyclone.

28. How are tropical cyclones measured?

29. Identify the key differences between a category 1 and a category 5 tropical cyclone.

30. With reference to a named example, describe and explain how tropical cyclones impact people and the environment. Include causes, effects and responses.

31. Define the following key terms:

  a) precipitation   **c)** interception

  b) infiltration   **d)** surface run-off

32. Draw a labelled diagram of the hydrological cycle.

33. Describe and explain how the following factors can lead to flooding:

  a) weather   **c)** relief

  b) geology   **d)** urbanisation

34. Using the information in Section 6 and your own research, investigate the causes, effects and responses to the 2011 Brisbane flooding.

35. How can flood risk be reduced before flooding occurs?

36. Some places are defended from flooding, others are not. What factors are taken into account when making these decisions?

37. Evaluate the following methods of flood defence:

  a) dams   **d)** flood relief channels

  b) afforestation (tree planting)   **e)** controlled flooding

  c) levees

38. Draw and complete the following table:

Physical causes of drought	Human causes of drought

39. How and why does the impact of drought vary between regions affected?

40. What is desertification?

41. Can the risk from drought be managed?

42. Describe three opportunities presented by natural hazards.

43. Why do people choose to live nearby the active volcano Batur in Bali, Indonesia?

44. Compare and contrast the impact and management of the Haiti and Christchurch earthquakes.

45. Using the information in Section 6 and your own research, investigate the impact and response to Typhoon Haiyan in the Philippines.

46. Design and plan an investigation into the relationship between either earthquake magnitude and death toll from the disasters, or tropical cyclone intensity and death toll from the disasters. You will need to collect data, present and analyse it, and reach conclusions based on your analysis. A useful research question might be: 'Is Earthquake or tropical cyclone strength the most important factor in determining death toll?'

Your investigation should include the following:

- an introduction that outlines the purpose of the investigation and your research question

- an outline of your methods, including any limitations and improvements

- presentation of your results graphically using scatter graphs

- analysis of the data to identify patterns and trends, and an explanation of anomalies

- a reasoned conclusion that includes an answer to your research question

Answers to these questions can be found at the back of the Teacher Guide.

7. The atmosphere and human activities questions

1. Complete the following table to identify the key features of Earth's atmosphere:

Name	Height	Temperature	Features
Troposphere			
Stratosphere			
Mesosphere			
Thermosphere			
Exosphere			

2. Why is the troposphere important to humans?

3. Describe the pattern of temperature change shown in the graph below:

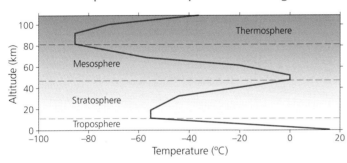

4. Describe the composition of gases that make up the atmosphere.

5. What are greenhouse gases?

6. Why is the ozone layer important?

7. Describe the function of the natural greenhouse effect.

8. Describe the main types of atmospheric pollution.

9. Using an example, describe and explain the causes, effects and management of smog.

10. Describe how the following physical characteristics can lead to a build up of atmospheric pollution on cities:

  a) calm conditions

  b) high air pressure

  c) city in a valley surrounded by steep hills

11. What causes acid rain?

12. Describe and suggest reasons for the pattern of sulfur dioxide emissions shown in the map below:

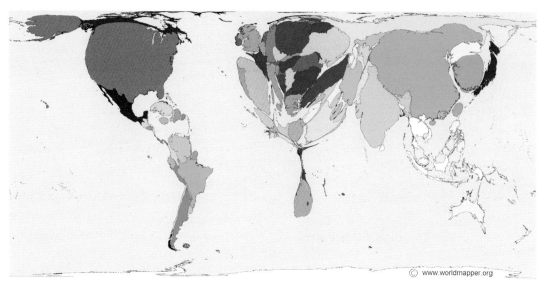

© www.worldmapper.org

13. How does acid rain impact the environment?

14. Investigate the causes, effects and management of ozone layer depletion.

15. Why do governments find it difficult to manage the causes of atmospheric pollution that lead to smog, acid rain and ozone depletion?

16. Describe the difference between the natural and enhanced greenhouse effect.

17. Describe and suggest reasons for the trend in CO_2 emissions from 1880 to the present day:

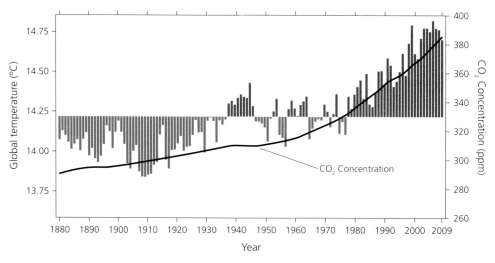

18. In your own words, describe how the enhanced greenhouse effect impacts global temperatures.

19. Using Figure 7.14 on page 187, outline the predicted impact of a 1, 3 and 5 °C rise in global temperatures.

20. Explain why some countries are more worried about the effects of global warming than others.

21. Using the information in Section 7 and your own research, describe and explain three methods of managing atmospheric pollution in cities.

22. Produce an annotated map that outlines the causes and regional impact of the 2015 Southeast Asian haze.

23. How does global demand for palm oil lead to forest fires?

24. 'Consumers of products containing palm oil are responsible for the Southeast Asian haze'. To what extent do you agree or disagree with this statement?

25. Your school will have a number of buildings and classrooms which need lighting and heating and cooling throughout the year. This will have a cost both in terms of carbon emission and the unit cost of energy. Design and plan an investigation into the energy use in your school, developing an action plan to reduce energy consumption and the carbon footprint of your school. You will need to collect data, present and analyse it, and reach conclusions based on your analysis.

Your investigation should include:

- an introduction that outlines the purpose of the investigation – 'To investigate the consumption of energy at school x'

- an energy audit of the school that includes the sources of energy used, the cost to the school and the use per room – a useful grid for this can be found in Section 7 of the Teacher Guide

- an outline of your methods, including any limitations and improvements (think about your team, who you need to speak to, when you will collect room information, the impact of factors like weather and time of day on the results)

- presentation of your results graphically – this is an excellent opportunity to use maps of the school to draw choropleth maps

- analysis of the data to identify patterns and trends and an explanation of anomalies

- reasoned conclusions that relate to the data and a clearly identified action plan to reduce energy consumption in school.

Answers to these questions can be found at the back of the Teacher Guide.

8. Human population questions

1. Define the terms *population distribution* and *population density*.

2. What does it mean if an area of the world becomes overpopulated? Give an example of one problem that overpopulation can cause.

3. Describe how each of the physical factors in the table below can affect population distribution and density in a country.

Factor	Influence on distribution and density
Climate	
Relief	
Soils	
Natural resources	
Accessibility	
Vegetation	

4. The photograph below shows one important human factor that can influence population distribution and density. Describe what this factor is and how it can affect where people live.

5. The map below shows that the population distribution and density of Japan is very uneven. Describe the pattern you can see and suggest two reasons that help to explain why this is.

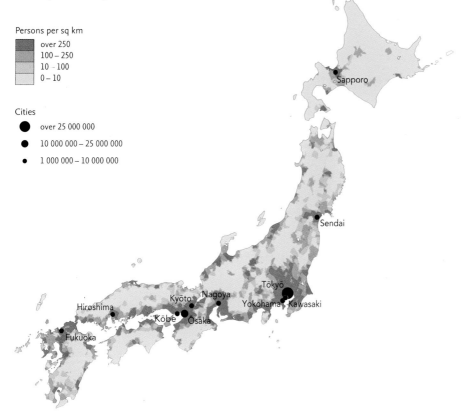

6. The graph below shows what is called the *growth curve of populations*. Describe what is happening to the population in each of the five stages shown in the graph.

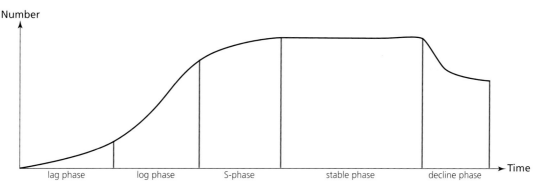

7. Define the term *population carrying capacity*.

8. Define the following terms:

   a) population   **c)** death rate

   b) birth rate   **d)** natural increase

9. If the birth rate of a country is 13.4 and the death rate 5.6 then what will its natural increase be?

10. If the death rate of a country is 8.9 and the birth rate 7.4 then what will its natural decrease be?

11. The two most important factors affecting the birth rate in a country are *infant mortality* and *life expectancy*. What do these two things measure?

12. The photograph (right) shows one important factor that will influence the birth rate in any country. Explain what this factor is and the effect it will have on the birth rate.

13. Explain the effect that each of the following factors can have on the death rate in any country:

    a) diets and levels of nutrition

    b) the availability of clean drinking water

    c) the quality of sanitation and hygiene

    d) age-sex structure and sex ratio

14. Define the following terms:

    a) migration

    b) immigration

    c) emigration

15. What is the difference between an anti-natalist and a pro-natalist population policy?

16. Why did the government of China feel it necessary to introduce its *One Child Policy* in 1979?

17. How did the *One Child Policy* persuade couples to have only one child?

18. China's *One Child Policy* succeeded in slowing population growth but created some serious issues. One of these is *gender imbalance*. What does this mean and what problems is it creating in China?

19. Study the population pyramid of France (right). France is a country pursuing a pro-natalist policy. Referring to the data in the population pyramid, explain the kind of problems which will arise in France over the next forty years if it is not successful in increasing the birth rate.

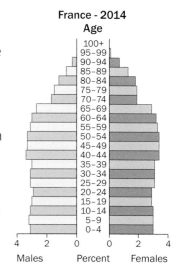

France - 2014
Age

100+
95–99
90–94
85–89
80–84
75–79
70–74
65–69
60–64
55–59
50–54
45–49
40–44
35–39
30–34
25–29
20–24
15–19
10–14
5–9
0–4

4   2   0   0   2   4
Males   Percent   Females

Answers to these questions can be found at the back of the Teacher Guide.

9. Natural ecosystems and human activities

1. Describe the difference between biotic and abiotic elements of an ecosystem.

2. Draw a simple table such as the one below and then place the different elements of an ecosystem listed here in the correct column: *plant, rainfall, bird, rock, temperature, snake, light, wind, insect, fungus*.

Biotic	Abiotic

3. Explain, with an example to help, what an ecological niche is.

4. Describe and explain using a simple diagram what occurs in a food chain using the following key terms: *trophic level, producer, photosynthesis, glucose, respiration, primary consumer, secondary consumer, tertiary consumer* and *decomposers*.

5. What does a food web show that makes it different from a food chain?

6. In a large Indian forest there will be millions of plants grazed by several thousand antelopes that will be preyed upon by a handful of tigers. What is the name of the graph that ecologists draw to show these differences?

7. Outline how carbon is continually cycled through the living and non-living parts of ecosystems.

8. In which of the two ecosystems below are the abiotic elements likely to be most challenging for living things? Explain why you feel this is.

North Island, New Zealand

Atacama Desert, Chile

END OF TOPIC QUESTIONS

9. What is adaptation in living things? Suggest how and why the living organisms below might be adapted to the environments in which they live?

Atlantic walrus

Forest tree, Ecuador

Saguaro cactus, United States

Fennec fox

10. The picture below shows one way in which living things commonly interact with each other. What is this type of interaction called? Describe and explain three other ways in which organisms commonly interact.

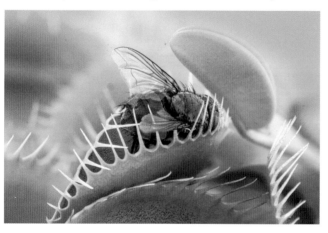

11. In your own words, explain what the terms *biodiversity* and *gene pool* mean?

12. Define the term *deforestation* and outline the main reasons for why it is happening.

13. What happens to the carbon stored in trees when they are felled and burnt? Describe and explain, using the diagram below to help, how deforestation contributes to global warming and climate change.

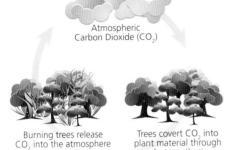

Atmospheric
Carbon Dioxide (CO_2)

Burning trees release
CO_2 into the atmosphere

Trees covert CO_2 into
plant material through
photosynthesis

14. Millions of tonnes of fertile topsoil are lost around the world each year through erosion. Write a definition of soil erosion and explain its main causes.

15. Identify different ways in which people can contribute to desertification.

16. The photograph below shows trees about to be planted in new woodland. How will they help to control soil erosion and prevent desertification?

17. Give reasons why it is important to human beings that the genes of all living things are conserved for the future.

18. These people are ecotourists enjoying a trekking holiday in the Andes Mountains of Peru. Explain how ecotourism helps to conserve ecosystems and improve the lives of local people at the same time.

19. Describe how each of the following is used to help an ecologist sample the biodiversity of a habitat:

a) quadrat

c) pooters

b) line transect

d) pitfall traps

20. Describe in your own words what you understand by the term *sustainable development*. Give some examples of how forests can be used sustainably.

21. What is the water cycle and what contribution do trees make to it?

22. Describe and explain the causes and some of the environmental and human effects of deforestation in Borneo.

23. The table below shows changes in estimated numbers of mountain gorillas in Virunga National Park which straddles the border of the Democratic Republic of the Congo, Rwanda and Uganda in central Africa.

Year	Estimated number of gorillas
1958	450
1973	271
1981	259
1984	355
1989	610
2000	601
2002	635
2004	700

a) Draw a simple line graph, bar graph or histogram to present this data.

b) By what proportion did the mountain gorilla population decline between 1958 and 1981?

c) Summarise the main reasons for this drastic drop in numbers.

d) By what proportion has the number of gorillas risen in the park since 1981?

e) Provide an overview of the conservation measures responsible for achieving this increase.

Answers to these questions can be found at the back of the Teacher Guide.

Glossary

absolute poverty Severe deprivation of human basic needs including food, water, sanitation, health, education and shelter.

abstraction The removal of water from a river or from groundwater using wells and boreholes.

accessibility How easily a place can be reached.

acid rain Rainfall that damages the environment because it has been made acidic by dissolved acid gases such as sulfur dioxide in the atmosphere.

adaptation The way in which plants and animals change to survive the environmental conditions of the habitat in which they live.

afforestation Planting trees to establish an area of vegetation in an area where there was no forest.

age/sex pyramid A diagram that uses horizontal bar graphs to show the age–gender characteristics of a population.

age–sex structure The number or proportion of males and females in each age category of a population.

agricultural yield The amount of crop or livestock produced in each year per sq km of a farm.

agriculture The cultivation of the soil for the growing of crops and the rearing of animals.

aid agency An organisation committed to providing emergency support and long-term economic and social development to the world's poorest people.

alluvium The material deposited by a river.

anti-natalist policies Strategies designed to limit a country's population growth by reducing its fertility rate.

aquaculture The rearing of aquatic animals or the cultivation of aquatic plants for food.

aquifer A layer of porous rock that stores underground water.

artesian well A means of extracting groundwater through a pipe drilled down from the Earth's surface to an underground aquifer.

atmosphere The layer of gases commonly known as air that surrounds the Earth and that is held in place by the Earth's gravity.

atoll A ring-shaped reef, island, or chain of islands formed of coral.

bioaccumulation The gradual build-up of substances such as pesticides at increasing quantities in organisms through the food chain and trophic levels.

biocontrol The control of destructive organisms such as aphids by the use of other organisms that are the natural predators of the pest.

biodiversity The range of species within an ecosystem.

biofuels Fuel made from plants.

birth rate The average number of live births in a year per 1000 people.

bycatch The unwanted fish and other marine creatures trapped by commercial fishing nets during fishing for a different species.

capital Money used to invest in industry or business.

carbon capture and storage The process of trapping carbon dioxide produced by burning fossil fuels and storing it so it is unable to enter the atmosphere.

carbon cycle How the element carbon cycles in different forms between living organisms and the environment.

carbon dioxide A colourless, odourless greenhouse gas produced from burning fossil fuels.

carbon fixing Describes the process by which carbon dioxide in the atmosphere is converted to complex carbon compounds such as carbohydrates by producers during photosynthesis.

carbon footprint The amount of carbon dioxide released into the atmosphere as a result of the activities of a particular individual, organisation, or community.

carbon offset Programmes involving the planting of trees by companies and individuals to mitigate or lessen the impact of their own carbon dioxide emitting activities.

carbon store The accumulated carbon dioxide stored in forests as a result of carbon fixation by trees.

Carboniferous period A period of geological time that extends from 358 to 298 million years ago; conditions during this time were ideal for the creation of fossil fuels.

carrying capacity The maximum number of species of living things that the resources of an environment can support.

cash crop A crop grown to sell for profit.

central business district (CBD) The central and most accessible zone within a large settlement, which has many offices, large shops and public buildings.

chlorofluorocarbon (CFC) Gases containing carbon, chlorine, fluorine, and sometimes hydrogen that are used as refrigerants, cleaning solvents, and aerosol gases – CFCs are a major cause of stratospheric ozone depletion.

channel flow The name given to water moving through a defined channel, for example a stream or river.

chlorophyll The green chemical in chloroplasts that captures light energy from photosynthesis.

cholera A disease caused by bacteria in contaminated water resulting in severe diarrhoea and dehydration.

climate Average weather conditions over a period of at least 30 years.

climate change Alteration to global wind, rainfall and temperature patterns as a result of the greenhouse effect.

commercial farming Growing crops or rearing animals for sale at market to achieve a profit.

community All of the organisms that live in the same habitat.

congestion charge A charge made to drive into an area, typically a city centre that suffers heavy traffic.

conservation The protection of species and habitats to prevent their loss or destruction.

consumer Organisms that eat other organisms in order to obtain their energy via respiration.

consumption The action of buying, using (consuming) and disposing of resources.

continental shelf The area of seabed around a large land mass where the sea is relatively shallow compared with the open ocean.

convection current Heat from the Earth's core (which, at 6000 °C, is very hot) is carried up to the mantle through convection currents; the currents move around, destroying the crust in some places and creating new crust in other places.

core The centre of the Earth.

coriolis effect The effect that the rotation of the Earth has on moving objects such as tropical storms.

costs and benefits The process by which the advantages of a proposed development or action are evaluated against the likely disadvantages or problems it could generate.

crust The top layer of the Earth, which can be either continental (with land on top) or oceanic.

cultivation The planting, tending, improving, or harvesting of crops or plants.

death rate The average number of deaths in a year per 1000 people.

decomposer An organism that feeds on dead plants or animals, or animal waste.

deforestation Clear felling of large areas of woodland or forest.

dehydration Loss of too much water.

densely populated This describes an area where a lot of people live, expressed as the average number of people per sq km.

deoxygenated Lacking in oxygen.

dependency ratio The link between the number of adult people in a country who create wealth and the young and elderly population who depends on them for support.

deposition The laying down of material that has been transported (by water, ice, sea, rivers, wind).

desalination Removing dissolved salt from seawater and brackish water.

desertification The degrading of land through soil erosion in dry land areas to such an extent that the environment comes to resemble a desert.

desulfurisation The removal of sulfur or sulfur compounds from coal or flue gas.

diarrhoea An illness that produces large amounts of watery faeces.

drought A prolonged period of very low or no rainfall leading to a shortage of water.

earthquake A sudden violent shaking of the ground as a result of movements within the Earth's crust.

ecological niche The unique way in which an organism is adapted to living in a habitat.

ecology The study of living things and their interaction with the environment.

economic development The process of increasing the wealth of countries and the prosperity and wellbeing of their inhabitants.

economic growth The growth in wealth generated from the increased production of goods and the provision of services in a country.

economic recession A slowdown or decline in business activity leading to a drop in the amount of wealth a country creates.

ecosystem A community of organisms in an area that interact with the living (biotic) and non-living (abiotic) elements of their environment.

ecotourism Tourism that is concerned with conserving natural environments, local economies and the integrity of cultures and communities.

exclusive economic zone (EEZ) A maritime zone, no more than 200 miles off the coast of a country; within the EEZ, the coastal state has sovereign rights for the purpose of exploring, exploiting, conserving, and managing natural resources.

emigrants People leaving a country.

emigration The movement of people away from a population.

emissions The production and discharge of gases.

energy mix The energy consumption of a household, region or country. Energy mix includes both renewable (for example, wind power, wave power, solar power) and non-renewable (for example, oil and natural gas) energy sources.

energy security When a country has enough sources of power to cover most, if not all, of its energy needs.

enhanced greenhouse effect The warming of the Earth's atmosphere caused by an excess of carbon dioxide and other greenhouse gases, which act like a blanket preventing the natural escape of heat into space.

El Niño southern oscillation (ENSO) An irregular variation in winds and sea surface temperatures over the tropical eastern Pacific Ocean.

environment The surroundings in which a person, animal or plant lives and interacts.

environmental impact assessment A survey or evaluation that assists planners in assessing the likely environmental impacts of a proposed development.

epicentre Point on the Earth's surface directly above where an earthquake occurs.

erosion The wearing away of the land by an agent such as water that carries away the rock particles.

eutrophication The pollution of water bodies by nutrients leading to the rapid growth or blooms of algae and deoxygenation.

evaporation The conversion of liquid particles of water to become a gas (water vapour).

evapotranspiration Loss of water into the atmosphere from plants (transpiration) and water surfaces (evaporation).

fish aggregation device (FAD) A man-made object placed in the sea to attract larger pelagic fish such as tuna.

fishing quota A legal limit to the amount, size and species of fish that can be caught in a year.

faeces The undigested material that remains after digestion of food in humans.

famine Starvation of many people in an area as a result of extreme shortage of food.

fault line A line fracture in rock caused by Earth movements.

fertility rate The average number of children women in a country or region have in their lifetime.

fish factory ship Also known as a fish processing vessel. This is a large ocean-going vessel with extensive on-board facilities for processing and freezing caught fish.

flood defence Structures such as dams, artificial channels and levees that are built to protect an area from flooding.

floodplain A naturally occurring area of flat, low-lying ground adjacent to a river, formed mainly of river sediments and subject to flooding.

focus The point within the Earth's crust where an earthquake originates.

food chain The succession of organisms that eat another organism and are, in turn, eaten themselves.

food web Shows how individual food chains within a habitat are linked together and interdependent.

forced migration When people are made to leave a country, for example, because of war or natural disaster.

fossil fuels Non-renewable organic energy resources such as oil, gas and coal that are hydrocarbon based.

fracking The process of drilling down into the Earth before a high-pressure water mixture is directed at the rock to release the gas inside.

fresh water Water upon which human life depends found in different stores such as lakes on the surface of the Earth.

freshwater scarcity The lack of sufficient available water resources to meet water needs within a region.

gene pool The set of all the genes or genetic information of a particular species of organism.

genetic engineering The transfer of a gene from one organism into an organism of a different species in order to develop or enhance particular physical traits.

geothermal power Power from magma, hot rocks and hot water within the Earth.

geographic information system (GIS) A computer system that can store and analyse 'layers' of different types of spatial information.

global warming Warming of the Earth's atmosphere as a result of the release of gases such as methane and carbon dioxide (CO_2) through human activity.

global positioning system (GPS) A high-tech mapping system that uses satellites to locate places on the Earth's surface with great accuracy.

Green Revolution The series of technological and search advances that increased farm yields through the application of chemical fertilisers and pesticides and the creation of new disease-resistant crops.

greenhouse gas A gas such as carbon dioxide that contributes to global warming by absorbing infrared radiation.

groundwater Water in the soil or in the pores of rocks.

groundwater flow The movement of water through rocks.

growth curve of population An ecological theory that describes how the number of living things in an area changes over time.

gyres A circular system of ocean currents rotating clockwise in the northern hemisphere and counter-clockwise in the southern hemisphere.

habitat The location within an ecosystem that meets the living needs of a particular plant or animal species.

hazard risk map A map that highlights areas that are affected by or vulnerable to a particular hazard.

heavy metal Any metal with a specific gravity of 5.0 or more that is potentially toxic to living organisms.

herbicide A synthetic chemical that is used to kill weed plants.

herbivore An animal that eats plants.

hydroelectric power The production of electrical power through the use of the gravitational force of falling or flowing water.

igneous rocks Rocks formed from the cooling and solidification of magma.

immigrants People arriving in a new country from abroad.

immigration The movement of people into a country to live permanently having moved from another country.

impermeable Rock that will not absorb water, nor let it pass through.

improved sanitation A system that effectively separates human waste from drinking water.

indigenous Something originating in or occurring naturally in a particular place.

industrialised country A country that generates most of its wealth from the manufacturing of goods and the provision of a wide range of services.

industry Economic activity concerned with the extraction and processing of raw material into manufactured goods.

infant mortality rate The proportion of children dying at birth or before their first birthday per 1000 live births.

infiltration The downward movement of water through the soil and into the rock layer below.

infrastructure The network of basic physical facilities such as roads, power and water supply required by industry and services to run efficiently.

insecticide A synthetic chemical used to kill insect pests.

interception Water that is caught and stored by vegetation.

irrigation Artificially diverting water to farming areas to grow crops and sustain livestock.

lag time The amount of time between peak rainfall and peak river discharge.

lahar Highly dangerous, fast-flowing mixture of rainwater and ejected volcanic materials.

lava Hot molten or semi-fluid rock erupted from a volcano.

leaching The loss of dissolved mineral nutrients in soil water as it soaks deeper into the ground beyond the reach of plant roots.

less economically developed country (LEDC) One of the poorer, less industrialised countries of the world.

life expectancy The average number of years that a person is expected to live.

liquefaction A process by which water-saturated sediment temporarily loses strength and acts as a fluid. This effect can be caused by earthquake shaking.

lithosphere The hard and rigid outer surface – the crust and top of the mantle – of the solid Earth.

magma Liquid rock found beneath the Earth's crust.

magnitude The strength of an earthquake.

malaria A water-borne disease caused by the parasite Plasmodium transmitted by mosquitoes.

malnutrition Not getting the right amounts and balance of nutrients in the diet.

mantle The part of the Earth between the crust and the core.

manufacturing The process of producing a finished product from processing raw materials.

mechanisation The increasing use of technology and machinery, often at the cost of manual labour.

metamorphic rocks Rocks that have been changed by intense heat or pressure from one form to another such as slate into limestone.

mid ocean ridge A long, seismically active underwater mountain system. These are found at constructive plate boundaries such as the Mid Atlantic Ridge.

migration The movement of people from one place to another.

million tonnes of oil equivalent A unit used to compare energy sources by relating them to the equivalent amount of energy produced from one tonne of oil.

mineral A naturally occurring solid and inorganic chemical substance with a crystalline structure found in rock.

mineral ion Nutrients that plants and animals need in small amounts to be healthy such as nitrates that are required for making amino acids.

monoculture A large area devoted entirely to the cultivation of a single plant crop.

more economically developed country (MEDC) One of the wealthier, more industrialised countries of the world.

Marine Protected Areas (MPA) Protected areas of seas, oceans or large lakes. MPAs restrict human activity for a conservation purpose, typically to protect natural or cultural resources.

mass rapid transit (MRT) An urban public transit system using underground or elevated trains.

multiplier effect The additional economic benefits experienced when money is spread throughout a community.

multipurpose dam A single dam that has a number of purposes such as power generation, irrigation and flood control.

mutation A change to the genetic makeup of an organism that alters its characteristics.

national park Area of outstanding natural value protected by law and established to conserve and enhance the environment and local communities as well as encouraging people to visit and enjoy the countryside.

natural disaster A natural event such as a flood, earthquake, or hurricane that causes great damage or loss of life.

natural hazard All naturally occurring events or phenomena such as earthquakes or cyclones that have the potential to harm humans, their settlements and economic activities.

natural increase /decrease The rise or fall in a population calculated by subtracting the death rate from the birth rate.

natural resources Naturally occurring materials such as minerals that can be exploited for economic gain.

nitrogen fixing bacteria Bacteria found in the root nodules of some plants such as clover that enables them to convert atmospheric nitrogen into nitrate ions in the soil.

non-government organisation (NGO) A not-for-profit organisation that is independent from national governments and international government organisations such as the World Bank.

non-renewable resource A naturally occurring material or source of energy such as copper or coal that can only be used once for economic gain and cannot be used again.

nuclear power Electricity generated by using nuclear reactors in thermal power stations.

nutrient cycle How nutrients move from the physical or abiotic environment into living organisms and then eventually recycle back through decomposition into the physical environment.

ocean current The movement of water in oceans from one location to another. These are driven by tides, wind and thermohaline circulation.

ocean trench Deep-sea trenches that form long narrow depressions in the surface of the seafloor along a tectonic plate boundary; at between 6 000–11 000 m, these are the deepest parts of the ocean.

overcultivation The continuous cropping of farmland to the point where nutrients are exhausted and the soil degraded causing erosion and desertification.

overfishing When more fish are caught, by excessive fishing, than the population can replace, causing the deplete of the stock of fish in a body of water.

overgrazing When land is overused by livestock leading to vegetation damage and the soil becomes liable to erosion.

overpopulation When a country or area of the world does not have the resources to give its entire people an adequate standard of living.

ozone layer A layer in the Earth's stratosphere at an altitude of about 10 km containing a high concentration of ozone, which absorbs most of the ultraviolet radiation reaching the Earth from the sun.

pathogen A disease-causing organism.

peat A highly organic material found in marshy or damp regions, composed of partially decayed plant matter. Peat contains high levels of stored carbon dioxide.

pelagic fish Pelagic fish can be categorised as coastal and oceanic fish, based on the depth of the water they inhabit.

percolation The downward movement of water from the soil into rock.

permeable rock Rock that can be penetrated by water.

pesticide A synthetic chemical used to kill either potentially damaging weeds (herbicide), insects (insecticide) or fungi (fungicide).

photochemical reaction A chemical reaction caused by the interaction between chemicals and sunlight.

photosynthesis The process carried out in plant cells that makes sugars by combining carbon dioxide and water molecules using energy from light.

plate boundary The edges of tectonic plates. These can be constructive, destructive or conservative.

pollution The introduction of potentially harmful or toxic substances that cause damage to the environment, people and other organisms, often as a result of adding chemicals to the air, water or land.

population A group of organisms of the same species living in a particular habitat.

population density The average number of people living in 1 sq km area.

population distribution The way in which a population is spread out over an area.

porous rock Rocks that absorb and store water.

potable water Water that is safe enough for drinking and food preparation; sometimes called improved water.

precipitation Water deposited on the Earth's surface in a range of forms such as rain, hail, snow, sleet and dew.

prevailing wind Winds that blow predominantly from a single general direction over a particular point on the Earth's surface.

pro-natalist policies Strategies designed to stimulate a country's population growth by increasing its fertility rate.

producer An organism that creates its own food such as plants using energy transferred from light in photosynthesis to produce glucose.

purse seine fishing A technique of fishing that utilises a purse seine net to capture large schools of fish, especially tuna.

pyramid of energy A diagram that shows the transfer of declining stores of energy between organisms at different trophic levels.

pyramid of numbers A diagram that shows the number of individual organisms in different trophic levels of a food chain.

pyroclastic flow Flow of materials such as ash ejected during a volcanic eruption.

quality of life The standard of health, comfort and happiness enjoyed by an individual or group.

raw material Any substance such as oil or cocoa beans in its natural state before being processed through manufacturing into a finished product such as aviation fuel or chocolate.

recurrence interval An estimation of the interval between particular levels of flooding and how frequently they will occur.

recycle To make new materials using old ones rather than starting with raw materials.

relief The highest and lowest elevation points in an area.

remediation Making safe by demolishing industrial plant, removing machinery and disposing of toxic waste.

remote sensing The technology of using satellites to obtain images of the Earth's surface.

renewable energy Energy from a source such as wind that is not depleted when it is used.

renewable resource A naturally occurring material or source of energy such as wood or wind that can be exploited continuously for economic gain.

resource management Using all available materials, people, money and information as effectively as possible.

respiration The chemical process in which glucose is broken down inside the mitochondrial cells, releasing energy and producing carbon dioxide and water.

respiratory disease Diseases of the lungs that cause difficulty in breathing.

restoration Returning something to its original condition.

retrofitting The process of strengthening older buildings in order to make them earthquake resistant.

reuse Using something again after it has been used that is economically, environmentally or socially worthwhile.

Richter scale The scale used to measure the magnitude (or intensity) of an earthquake.

rift valley A steep-sided valley formed when a constructive plate boundary is found on land.

rock The dry, solid and naturally occurring material that forms the Earth's crust.

rock cycle The continuous process of formation, breakdown through erosion and weathering and reformation of a rock as a result of sedimentary, igneous and metamorphic processes.

rotation Regularly changing the crop grown or livestock reared on a particular field according to an agreed sequence.

rural population The proportion of a country's population living in the countryside in villages and hamlets.

Saffir-Simpson scale A scale used to measure tropical cyclone intensity.

salinisation The build-up of soluble salts such as magnesium in soil to the extent that soil fertility is severely reduced.

saturated soil When soil has reached its capacity to absorb water.

seamount A mountain rising from the ocean seafloor that does not reach to the water's surface (sea level), and thus is not an island.

sedimentary rocks Rocks formed by the compression and consolidation of layers of mud, sand, silts and living organisms such as chalk, limestone and clay.

sedimentation The settling and build-up of silt and rock particles such as along the bed of a river or against a dam wall.

seed bank A store of the seeds of plants in order to protect biodiversity in case seeds elsewhere in the world are destroyed by natural or human events.

seismometer A machine used to measure the strength of an earthquake.

selective breeding Cross-breeding organisms that have different desirable features to create offspring that combine all of these desirable features in one organism.

sex ratio The proportion of males to females in a population.

shield volcano A low gently-sloping volcano formed from thin, runny lava and frequent gentle eruptions.

shifting cultivation A type of subsistence farming sometimes called slash and burn, in which farmers cultivate one area of land until it is no longer fertile and then move on to a new area of land to begin again.

slash and burn A method of agriculture in which existing vegetation is cut down and burned off before new seeds are sown, typically used as a method for clearing forest land for farming.

soil erosion The washing away of soil as a result of wind and rainfall when there is little vegetation to hold on to the soil.

solar radiation Incoming energy emitted from the sun.

sparsely populated Describes an area where few or any people live expressed as the average number of people per sq km.

species A group of organisms that share many features and can interbreed to produce fertile offspring.

stewardship The responsible and sustainable management of the environment.

storm hydrograph A graph that shows how the discharge of a river can change over time in response to a rainfall event.

storm surge A significant increase in sea level due to sudden, very low air pressure.

storm track The path followed by a tropical cyclone.

stratovolcano Also known as a composite volcano, made up of alternate ash and lava layers and often has very violent eruptions.

stratosphere The layer of the Earth's atmosphere above the troposphere, extending to about 50 km above the Earth's surface.

sub-tropical Relating to the regions just north of the Tropic of Cancer and just south of the Tropic of Capricorn.

subduction Where oceanic crust is forced under continental crust at a plate boundary. These form ocean trenches.

subsidy Compensation payments given to farmers, usually by governments.

subsistence farming Self-sufficiency farming in which farmers grow or rear enough food to feed themselves and their families with little or no surplus.

subsurface mining Extracting minerals and ores through tunnels and shafts.

supply and demand A term that refers to the price of a commodity rising when it is in short supply and falling when there is a glut or oversupply.

surface mining Extracting minerals and ores by removing the soil or rock that overlies them.

surface run-off The movement of water over the ground surface following precipitation – also known as overland flow.

sustainable Something that can be used on a long-term basis with very little adverse effect on the environment.

sustainable development The development of technology and the environment to meet increasing human needs and living standards without impacting negatively on the ecosystems.

systemic pesticide A pesticide such as a weed killer that is absorbed by the leaves or stem of a plant so that pests eating the plant are poisoned.

tar sands Sandy soil containing tar, which can be converted into crude oil through an environmentally destructive process.

tectonic plate The Earth's crust, divided into large pieces called plates.

temperature inversion A reversal of the normal decrease of air temperature with altitude, which leads to fog forming.

thermal power generation When heat energy is converted to electric power in a power station. In most of the world the turbine is steam driven. Water is heated, turns into steam and spins a steam turbine which drives an electrical generator.

thermohaline circulation The oceanic circulation system driven by variation in ocean temperature and salinity.

topography The height and shape of the land.

tourism The industry associated with people going on holiday; can be either national or international.

trade The buying and selling of goods and services between countries.

transpiration Loss of water from the leaves of vegetation into the atmosphere.

treaty A formal agreement between countries.

trickledown An economic theory that describes how the wealth created by the largest industries and services will in turn pass down to smaller companies and eventually to the population as a whole.

trophic level A feeding level in a food chain or food web, for example producer or primary consumer.

tropical A geographical area situated between the Tropic of Cancer and Tropic of Capricorn with a generally hot and wet climate.

tropical cyclone Intense spinning storm with high winds and torrential rain around a calm centre (the eye); at a certain point of intensity it becomes a cyclone or hurricane.

troposphere The lowest and densest region of the Earth's atmosphere.

tsunami Huge sea wave created as a result of a major earthquake or volcanic eruption.

upwelling A process in which deep, cold, nutrient rich water rises towards the surface.

urban population The proportion of people in a country living in towns and cities.

urbanisation An increase in the percentage of people living in urban areas.

vaccination Introducing a small amount of a pathogen into the body to build up resistance and immunity to disease carried by that pathogen in the future.

volcanic explosivity index A scale used to measure the intensity of a volcanic eruption.

vulnerability A measure of the capacity of an individual, community or country to cope with the effects of a natural disaster.

water conservation The preservation, control and development of water resources.

water cycle The process by which water continuously circulates between the Earth's oceans, atmosphere and land.

water-poor regions Areas where the proportion of the world's population living there is larger than the proportion of the world's water reserves stored there.

water-rich regions Areas where the proportion of the world's population living there is lower than the proportion of the world's water reserves stored there.

water table The upper edge of the water-saturated zone in porous rocks.

water transfer The transfer of water from one drainage basin to another to meet demand for water.

water vapour Water held in the atmosphere in the form of a gas.

water-borne disease Diseases caused by pathogenic micro-organisms that most commonly are transmitted in contaminated fresh water.

weathering The breakdown of rocks by physical, chemical and organic processes with little or no transportation of the resulting rock particles.

wildfire A forest fire that rages out of control.

Index

Acknowledgements

The publishers would like to thank the following for permission to reproduce images. Every effort has been made to trace copyright holders and to obtain their permission for the use of copyright materials. The publishers will gladly receive any information enabling them to rectify any error or omission at the first opportunity.

Cover and title page image: Silvia Iordache / Shutterstock

Introduction

1 daseugen / Shutterstock; 2 hramovnick / Shutterstock; Case studies map: Collins

Section 1

Section break: Mariusz Szczygiel / Shutterstock; 1.1 Andrew Longden / Shutterstock; 1.2 Gigi Peis / Shutterstock; 1.3 Megan R. Hoover / Shutterstock; 1.4 MarcISchauer / Shutterstock; 1.5 RGB Ventures / SuperStock / Alamy; 1.6 minik / Shutterstock; 1.7 alexandre zveiger / Shutterstock; 1.8 Collins; 1.9 Bildagentur Zoonar GmbH / Shutterstock; 1.10 NASA / Wikipedia / public domain; 1.11 Ken Tannenbaum / Shutterstock; 1.12 vvoe / Shutterstock; 1.13 Kagai19927 / Shutterstock; 1.14 Alice Nerr / Shutterstock; 1.15 Cultura Creative (RF) / Alamy; 1.16 imageBROKER / Alamy; 1.17 AlanM1 / Wikipedia / CC BY 3.0; 1.18 Greenshoots Communications / Alamy; 1.19 Gunter Marx / Alamy; 1.20 paulo fridman / Alamy; 1.21 Inu / Shutterstock; 1.22 f9photos / Shutterstock; 1.23 NASA / Wikipedia / public domain; 1.24 Zute Lightfoot / Alamy; 1.25 iofoto / Shutterstock; 1.26 David Hughes / Shutterstock; 1.27 kavram / Shutterstock; 1.28 blickwinkel / Alamy; 1.29 Collins; 1.30 Gunter Marx / WC / Alamy; 1.31 © 2016 Google Earth; 1.32 Chris Cheadle / Alamy; 1.33 Wolfi Poelzer / Alamy

Section 2

Section break: Korionov / Shutterstock; 2.1 curraheeshutter / Shutterstock; 2.2 Dmitriy Kuzmichev / Shutterstock; 2.3 Billion Photos / Shutterstock; 2.4 Jouve; 2.5 Jouve and MagentaGreen / Wikipedia / CC BY-SA 3.0; 2.6 dieKleinert / Alamy; 2.7 Collins; 2.8 Tennessee Valley Authority / Wikipedia / public domain; 2.9 XXLPhoto / Shutterstock; 2.10 Collins; 2.11 Collins; 2.12 WorldWide / Shutterstock; 2.13 ESB Professional / Shutterstock; 2.14 timothy auld / Shutterstock; 2.15 miker / Shutterstock; 2.16 cleanfotos / Shutterstock; 2.17 Bikeworldtravel / Shutterstock; 2.18 chris kolaczan / Shutterstock; 2.19 saraporn / Shutterstock; 2.20 Accent Alaska.com / Alamy; 2.21 Jouve; 2.22 Cheryl Casey / Shutterstock; 2.23 kajornyot wildlife photography / Shutterstock; 2.24 Technical Sergeant Adrian Cadiz / Wikipedia / public domain; 2.25 Collins; 2.26 Everett Collection Historical / Alamy

Section 3

Section break: JunPhoto / Shutterstock; 3.1 blickwinkel / Alamy; 3.2 Kate Jewell / Wikipedia / CC BY-SA 2.0; 3.3 michael smith / Alamy; 3.4 Nigel Cattlin / Alamy; 3.5 Greenshoots Communications / Alamy; 3.6 Nigel Cattlin / Alamy; 3.7 Alec Scaresbrook / Alamy; 3.8 Edward Bent / Alamy; 3.9 Ilyshev Dmitry / Shutterstock; 3.10 AfriPics.com / Alamy; 3.11 Wayne HUTCHINSON / Alamy; 3.12 All Canada Photos / Alamy; 3.13 Hans Blossey / Alamy; 3.14 Art Directors & TRIP / Alamy; 3.15 Olaf Speier / Shutterstock; 3.16 BSIP SA / Alamy; 3.17 Aurora Photos / Alamy; 3.18 imageBROKER / Alamy; 3.19 Christine Osborne Pictures / Alamy; 3.20 imageBROKER / Alamy; 3.21 Videowokart / Shutterstock; 3.22 alexmisu / Shutterstock; 3.23 ClassicStock / Alamy; 3.24 Fotokostic / Shutterstock; 3.25 Green Stock Media / Alamy; 3.26 mattckaiser / Shutterstock; 3.27 Everett Collection Historical / Alamy; 3.28 Chris Hill / Shutterstock; 3.29 york010 / Alamy; 3.30 Matjoe / Shutterstock; 3.31 Fred Cardoso / Shutterstock; 3.32 Collins; 3.33 Leonardo Gonzalez / Shutterstock; 3.34 Everett Historical / Shutterstock; 3.35 Dorothea Lange / Wikipedia / public domain; 3.36 Collins; 3.37 frans lemmens / Alamy; 3.38 Matthew J Thomas / Shutterstock; 3.39 Chris Talbot / Wikipedia / CC BY-SA 2.0; 3.40 Thamizhpparithi Maari / Wikipedia / CC BY-SA 3.0; 3.41 Em7 / Shutterstock; 3.42 Collins; 3.43 NASA / Wikipedia / public domain; 3.44 Jeff Schmaltz, MODIS Land Rapid Response Team / NASA / Wikipedia / public domain; 3.45 Steven Frame / Shutterstock; 3.46 Milosz Maslanka / Shutterstock; 3.47 NV77 / Shutterstock

Section 4

Section break: camera obscura USA / Shutterstock; 4.1 Collins; 4.2 shutterlk / Shutterstock; 4.3 Collins; 4.4 vovan / Shutterstock; 4.5 Intrepix / Shutterstock; 4.6 Collins; 4.7 Collins; 4.8 Lakeview Images / Shutterstock; 4.9 FloridaStock / Shutterstock; 4.10 PACIFIC PRESS / Alamy; 4.11 Kunal Mehta / Shutterstock; 4.12 trekandshoot / Shutterstock; 4.13 Andrea Izzotti / Shutterstock; 4.14 africa924 / Shutterstock; 4.15 Eitan Simanor / Alamy; 4.16 Mik Lav / Shutterstock; 4.17 TasfotoNL / Shutterstock; 4.18 Collins; 4.19 YolLusZam1802 / Shutterstock; 4.20 Collins; 4.21 Dereje / Shutterstock; 4.22 Art Directors & TRIP / Alamy; 4.23 Collins; 4.24 Collins; 4.25 Greenshoots Communications / Alamy; 4.26 Andrew McConnell / Alamy; 4.27 Stefano Ember / Shutterstock; 4.28 Hemis / Alamy; 4.29 Avalon/Photoshot License / Alamy; 4.30 NASA/GSFC, Modis Rapid Response / Wikipedia / public domain; 4.31 Designua / Shutterstock; 4.32 Lourens Smak / Alamy; 4.33 lynn hilton / Alamy; 4.34 zakir hossain chowdhury zakir / Alamy ; 4.35 Mike Goldwater / Alamy; 4.36 Alex Tihonovs / Shutterstock; 4.37 Collins; 4.38 Jouve and NIAID / Wikipedia / CC BY 2.0; 4.39 Kletr / Shutterstock; 4.40 punghi / Shutterstock; 4.41 © 2015 World Health Organization ; 4.42 hikrcn / Shutterstock; 4.43 Thomas Barrat / Shutterstock; 4.44 Collins; 4.45 Nature Picture Library / Alamy; 4.46 Collins; 4.47 epa european pressphoto agency b.v. / Alamy; 4.48 dpa picture alliance / Alamy; 4.49 epa european pressphoto agency b.v. / Alamy

Section 5

Section break: superoke / Shutterstock; 5.1 Collins; 5.2 travelpeter / Shutterstock; 5.3 Worraket / Shutterstock; 5.4 Teun van den Dries / Shutterstock; 5.5 B.S. Halpern (T. Hengl; D. Groll) / Wikimedia Commons / CC BY-SA 3.0; 5.6 urbans / Shutterstock; 5.7 shao weiwei / Shutterstock; 5.8 Collins; 5.9 Collins; 5.10 © AquaMaps / www.aquamaps.org; 5.11 US Government / Wikipedia / public domain; 5.12 US Federal Government / NOAA / Wikipedia / public domain; 5.13 Designua / Shutterstock; 5.14 Universal Images Group North America LLC / Alamy; 5.15 C. Ortiz Rojas / NOAA / Wikipedia / public domain; 5.16 © Paul Hilton / Greenpeace; 5.17 © Greenpeace; 5.18 Mark Conlin / Alamy; 5.19 Vladislav Gajic / Shutterstock; 5.20 Tonko Oosterink / Shutterstock; 5.21 Jamesbox / Shutterstock; 5.22 Paul Hilton / Wikipedia / CC BY-SA 3.0; 5.23 Collins; 5.24 S. T. Sundstrom / NOAA Historic Fisheries Collection / Wikipedia / public domain; 5.25 Kerry

Lagueux, New England Aquarium / Wikipedia / CC BY-SA 3.0;
5.26 © Global Fishing Watch; 5.27 © Global Fishing Watch;
5.28 Richard Dorrell / Wikipedia / CC BY-SA 2.0

Section 6

Section break: travelfoto / Shutterstock; 6.1 shooarts /
Shutterstock; 6.2 Collins; 6.3 Collins; 6.4 Universal Images
Group North America LLC / Alamy; 6.5 corbac40 /
Shutterstock; 6.6 Tom Bean / Alamy; 6.7 mapichai /
Shutterstock; 6.8 My Good Images / Shutterstock, 6.9 mTaira
/ Shutterstock; 6.10 Jouve; 6.11 Collins; 6.12 photka /
Shutterstock; 6.13 ODI / Alamy; 6.14 Reynold Sumayku /
Alamy; 6.15 ryan junell / Wikipedia / CC BY-SA 2.0; 6.16
Collins; 6.17 Egg / Wikipedia / public domain; 6.18 Robert A.
Rohde / Global Warming Art / Wikipedia / CC BY-SA 3.0;
6.19 © MODIS Ocean Group / NASA GSFC / University of
Miami; 6.20 Collins; 6.21 Collins; 6.22 NASA / Wikipedia /
public domain ; 6.23 Russell Watkins / Department for
International Development / Wikipedia / CC BY 2.0;
6.24 Neil Cooper / Alamy; 6.25 National Hurricane Center /
NOAA / Wikipedia / public domain. 6.26 Chris Warham /
Shutterstock; 6.27 Collins; 6.28 Collins; 6.29 Brisbane /
Shutterstock; 6.30 David Marsh / Wikipedia / CC BY 2.0;
6.31 Collins; 6.32 Ashley Cooper pics / Alamy; 6.33 Mark
Pearson / Alamy; 6.34 Roy Riley / Alamy; 6.35 Oxfam East
Africa / Wikipedia / CC BY 2.0; 6.36 Tom Grundy /
Shutterstock; 6.37 USDA / Wikipedia / public domain;
6.38 Brad Rippey / NOAA / Wikipedia / public domain;
6.39 Oxfam / Wikipedia / CC BY 2.0; 6.40 Alun McDonald /
Oxfam East Africa / Wikipedia / CC BY 2.0; 6.41 William
Cho / Wikipedia / CC BY-SA 2.0; 6.42 chensiyuan / Wikipedia /
CC BY-SA 4.0; 6.43 kavram / Shutterstock; 6.44 Jacques
Descloitres / MODIS Rapid Response Team / NASA / GSFC
/ Wikipedia / public domain; 6.45 NASA / Wikipedia / public
domain; 6.46 arindambanerjee / Shutterstock; 6.47 Darrenp /
Shutterstock; 6.48 © NOAA; 6.49 Malacanang Photo /
Alamy; 6.50 Niar / Shutterstock

Section 7

Section break: Victor Lauer / Shutterstock; Atmosphere image:
Collins / Designua / Shutterstock; 7.1 Collins; 7.2 Collins;
7.3 Montri Thipsorn / Shutterstock; 7.4 Alex Segre / Alamy;
7.5 Andrew Babble / Shutterstock; 7.6 Collins; 7.7 © Copyright
Worldmapper.org / Sasi Group (University of Sheffield) and
Mark Newman (University of Michigan); 7.8 Ryan McGinnis /
Alamy; 7.9 LEXXIZM / Shutterstock; 7.10 LensTravel /
Shutterstock; 7.11 NASA / Wikipedia / public domain;
7.12 NOAA / Wikipedia / public domain and Collins; 7.13
Environmental Protection Agency; Headquarters: Washington,
D.C., U.S.A. / Wikipedia / public domain; 7.14 Collins and
Jouve; 7.15 Jouve; 7.16 INSAGO / Shutterstock; 7.17 NASA /
Adam Voiland / LANCE MODIS Rapid Response / Jeff
Schmaltz / Wikipedia / public domain ; 7.18 Collins;
7.19 Amirin / Wikipedia / public domain

Section 8

Section break: Alexander Image / Shutterstock; 8.1 Collins;
8.2 Giantrabbit / Shutterstock; 8.3 Collins; 8.4 Collins;
8.5 jiratto / Shutterstock; 8.6 Collins; 8.7 ChiccoDodiFC /
Shutterstock; 8.8 robertharding / Alamy; 8.9 Collins;
8.10 Collins; 8.11 Collins; 8.12 Collins; 8.13 Alan Gignoux /
Alamy; 8.14 Iain Masterton / Alamy; 8.15 E.J. Baumeister Jr.
/ Alamy; 8.16 TonyV3112 / Shutterstock

Section 9

Section break: Dr Morley Read / Shutterstock; 9.1 Juriah
Mosin / Shutterstock; 9.2 mark higgins / Shutterstock;

9.3 NoPainNoGain and Baurz1973 / Shutterstock; 9.4 Collins;
9.5 Collins; 9.6 Collins; 9.7 Collins; 9.8 Ryan M. Bolton /
Shutterstock; 9.9 KPG_Payless / Shutterstock; 9.10 Martin
Mecnarowski / Shutterstock; 9.11 Trong Nguyen /
Shutterstock; 9.12 Frontpage / Shutterstock; 9.13 Sunflowerey
/ Shutterstock; 9.14 Les Gibbon / Alamy; 9.15 Richard A.
McGuirk / Shutterstock; 9.16 Pedarilhos / Shutterstock;
9.17 Alexander Mazurkevich / Shutterstock; 9.18 THPStock /
Shutterstock; 9.19 Ruslan Kalnitsky / Shutterstock;
9.20 Wuttichok Panichiwarapun / Shutterstock; 9.21 Sergey
Uryadnikov / Shutterstock; 9.22 chris kolaczan / Shutterstock;
9.23 Joerg Boethling / Alamy; 9.24 Collins; 9.25 Leo Francini /
Alamy; 9.26 Northwest College Agriculture / Wikipedia / CC
BY 2.0; 9.27 FLPA / Alamy; 9.28 Mnolf / Wikipedia / CC
BY-SA 3.0; 9.29 PhilipYb Studio / Shutterstock; 9.30 Johan
Jooste / Alamy; 9.31 Chris Howey / Shutterstock; 9.32a Daniel
Prudek / Shutterstock; 9.32b Abeselom Zerit / Shutterstock;
9.33 Dave Stevenson / Alamy; 9.34 Collins; 9.35 Rich Carey /
Shutterstock; 9.36 Jacques Descloitres / MODIS Rapid
Response Team / NASA / GSFC / Wikipedia / public domain;
9.37 Steve Taylor ARPS / Alamy; 9.38 SUWIT NGAOKAEW /
Shutterstock; 9.39 surassawadee / Shutterstock; 9.40
blickwinkel / Alamy; 9.41 Daniel Schreiber / Alamy; 9.42 FLPA
/ Alamy; 9.43 Avalon/Photoshot License / Alamy;
9.44 © UNESCO / North Devon Biosphere; 9.45a © Crown
Copyright and database 2016 Ordnance Survey 100019783;
9.45b © Crown Copyright and database 2016 Ordnance
Survey 100019783 / Collins; 9.46 Peter Turner Photography /
Shutterstock; 9.47 Paul White Aerial views / Alamy; 9.48 Ivan
Walters / Alamy; 9.49 Paul Glendell / Alamy; 9.50 Paul
Glendell / Alamy; 9.51 Nicolas Primola / Shutterstock

Questions

Section 1, Q3 Collins; Section 1, Q6 NooScapes / Shutterstock
and DmyTo / Shutterstock; Section 1, Q10 A_Lesik / Shutterstock

Section 2, Q10 Collins; Section 2, Q19 chris kolaczan /
Shutterstock; Section 2, Q24 USCG / Wikipedia / public domain

Section 3, Q4 Matthijs Wetterauw / Shutterstock and Ruud
Morijn Photographer / Shutterstock; Section 3, Q9 Lodimup
/ Shutterstock; Section 3, Q12 ShaunWilkinson /
Shutterstock; Section 3, Q18 DiversityStudio / Shutterstock

Section 4, Q3 Collins; Section 4, Q6 mike amerson / Shutterstock;
Section 4, Q9 ChameleonsEye / Shutterstock and meunierd /
Shutterstock; Section 4, Q10 DMA / Alamy; Section 4,
Q11 MSSA / Shutterstock; Section 4, Q15 PenWin / Shutterstock;
Section 4, Q17 Dutourdumonde Photography / Shutterstock

Section 5, Q8 © AquaMaps / www.aquamaps.org; Section 5,
Q9 Collins; Section 5, Q10 NOAA / Wikipedia / public domain

Section 7, Q3 Collins; Section 7, Q12 © Copyright
Worldmapper.org / Sasi Group (University of Sheffield) and
Mark Newman (University of Michigan) ; Section 7,
Q17 NOAA / Wikipedia / public domain and Collins

Section 8, Q4 Funny Solution Studio / Shutterstock; Section
8, Q5 Collins; Section 8, Q6 Collins; Section 8, Q12 Iakov
Filimonov / Shutterstock; Section 8, Q19 Collins

Section 9, Q8 Pichugin Dmitry / Shutterstock and D'July /
Shutterstock; Section 9, Q9 Joe McDonald / Shutterstock;
Dr Morley Read / Shutterstock; Steve Bower / Shutterstock;
Christian Musat / Shutterstock; Section 9, Q10 Kuttelvaserova
Stuchelova / Shutterstock; Section 9, Q13 Vectomart /
Shutterstock; Section 9, Q16 MaxyM / Shutterstock; Section 9,
Q18 Mikadun / Shutterstock; Section 9, Q23 erwinf. /
Shutterstock

Authors

David Weatherly is currently a School Improvement Adviser working at all stages of learning in the United Kingdom and internationally. He combines his role in education with support work for a range of environmental management and conservation bodies in the UK and abroad. Previously he was Geography Adviser and Lead Curriculum Consultant at a large local authority in the UK, a department, faculty and senior manager in a number of secondary schools and, most importantly, he has been a teacher constantly for almost forty years.

Nicholas Sheehan is the Academic Director of Jerudong International School on Borneo – a large 3–18 British school that offers IGCSE, A-level and the International Baccalaureate. Prior to this current appointment, Nicholas worked as an AST for Devon County Council school improvement team and as a Head of Geography in Devon. He co-authored the Geographical Enquiries series for Key Stage 3.